American Law Enforcement

American Law Enforcement

◆

Does Not Serve or Protect!

Johannes F. Spreen

with Diane Holloway Ph.D.

iUniverse, Inc.
New York Lincoln Shanghai

American Law Enforcement
Does Not Serve or Protect!

iUniverse, Inc.

For information address:
iUniverse, Inc.
2021 Pine Lake Road, Suite 100
Lincoln, NE 68512
www.iuniverse.com

ISBN: 0-595-31780-4

Printed in the United States of America

Contents

Part VII   *Community Policing*

Part VIII   *Mobile Foot Patrols*

Part IX   *Dual Purpose Policing*

Acknowledgements

I thank my wonderful wife, Sallie Ann Spreen, for her love and for much support and encouragement throughout our fifteen years of marriage. Her understanding of my writing, and not begrudging the time necessary, I much appreciate.

I thank my daughter, Betty, for her love and strong belief in me.

So much thanks goes to Dr. Diane Holloway, my collaborator. Without her tremendous help and expertise, this book would never have been.

My special thanks to Bob Cheney for his brilliant work in proofreading and reviewing the book before publication.

Also thanks to all the people and police officers I have met and worked with during my career, both the good and the bad. One can learn from both.

Preface

A friend of mine, a fellow police officer, told me not long ago, "My God, the guys now being allowed to come into the job are the ones we used to lock up! Many are coming in with minor records, even major records, now expunged because of lowered standards and pressure for minority group representation."

It set me to thinking about what has happened to policing and law enforcement in general. I realized that people seem to have lost respect for police officers, sheriff's deputies, and law enforcement officers in general. They could use Rodney Dangerfield's slogan, "I don't get no respect!"

Of course, there are the usual guesses about why that has happened. Ask the old-timers and they'll tell you law enforcement isn't as good as it used to be in the past because of lowered standards for recruits, Affirmative Action, lawsuits against the police, media exploitation of police actions, less respect, more corruption, insensitive actions and shootings, pay scale not commensurate with duties, American Civil Liberties Union, and, of course, it's a damned sight more dangerous now!

I started putting together what I had seen and learned in my 44+ years in law enforcement as a New York City cop, Police Commissioner of Detroit and Michigan sheriff. I re-evaluated some of my long-held beliefs about how police are supposed to prevent crime, not just respond after the fact. I also gathered the latest information and I think I have some answers.

Hold on to your seat belts. It may be a bumpy ride!

Introduction

In my first book, *American Police Dilemma: Enforcers or Protectors?* I explained why the American police face a serious dilemma based on my 25 years in the New York Police Department, my service as Police Commissioner of the Detroit Police Department, and later as elected Sheriff of Oakland County, Michigan. Throughout that book, I interspersed some of my feelings about why policing is in trouble.

With over 44 years in the study and practice of law enforcement or policing, I frankly state that the dilemma is whether American police are "protectors" or "enforcers." The scales for justice are out of balance here. We have tipped too much in favor of enforcement at the expense of protection.

The police cars of America usually carry the words "To Serve and Protect." In essence, in reality, there is very little service and protection rendered by today's law enforcement agencies. Why? Because their main mission is to respond, investigate, apprehend and attempt to convict.

This helps some people, yes, victims of crimes, assaults, thefts, etc. But this does not help other people, good citizens who are rarely in contact with police officers, especially with good helpful police officers.

Law enforcement only "serves and protects" in a very limited way. Webster's Dictionary defines "enforce" and "enforcement" thusly:

1. To give force to

2. To urge with energy

3. To constrain, compel

4. To effect or gain by force

5. To execute vigorously.

Enforcement implies the exercise of executive or police power. Necessary, yes, but not really compatible with "to serve and protect."

We have lost the real concept of "serve and protect" with the type of policing we do today. Now they are very short on protection and very long on law enforcement, whether tickets, citations, arrests or necessary force are used. There is really no specific implementation of the service and protection roles to be provided for a community. It is the *prevention of crime* that really does the most to serve and protect.

In *American Police Dilemma*, I brought out the fact that August Vollmer, former Chief of the Berkeley Police Department, issued his dictum: "With the advent of the automobile patrol, foot patrol is obsolete." Police chiefs all over the United States embraced this.

Yes, the auto, the radio motor patrol car is very important and necessary. But it is not the complete end all, not a complete answer.

In fact, allow me to say, the police in the responding mode, lights flashing, sirens screaming, have caused fright and apprehension in many sectors of American life. That same police, caught up in the dynamics of the situation, have acted or been forced to act unwisely.

It is not unreasonable to say that improper police actions by such responding units have caused community tension, violent reactions, even insurrections and riots in our American cities.

August Vollmer held that motorization by car amplified enormously the *striking power* of the force. Since then police administrators have overemphasized the use of the automobile, in effect putting all their eggs in one basket. Foot patrol gradually disappeared.

We need change badly. We need police officers who have the time, inclination and freedom to really do the "serve and protect" function of policing.

Rapid response is, of course, possible and necessary by auto (unless snagged in the voluminous traffic holdups of today.)

But computerized radio motor patrol cars generally have no time for "service and protection" in a crime preventive way. They are all much too busy in these times—and in a radio police response car it is almost impossible to stop, talk with and get to know good people.

Vollmer and other police authorities have emphasized the advantages of the police car with such phrases as "striking power" and "combat power." Yes, true! And this is the image currently in the minds of young and old alike in minority communities. Police are not considered friends, but rather enemies.

Is this the fault of police officers or of police executives? Yes! No! Our police under present day methods cannot really do their job to "serve and protect."

What is required is a change in law enforcement, a radical change. I favor the term "policing." It is more inclusive. Law enforcement is only one side of the true police role. The other side is that which emphasizes "to serve and protect." Good policing should embrace both.

We need our police to have the opportunity to do the complete policing job: Service and Protection and also to Enforce the laws by quick response.

I now advocate a radical change to Dual Purpose Policing: police officers with different concepts of their function.

To *Serve and Protect* is really good *Community-Oriented Policing*. To *Respond* quickly to crimes or trouble is really good *Law Enforcement*.

Many police departments over the last several decades have gone in for *Community-Oriented Policing* in various modes and concepts. (I started such in Detroit in 1968 and 1969.) But most police executives have almost exclusively used the police car in their planning and operations methods. Many studies and experiments have been made, but always with police cars.

Some have used foot patrols with mixed results. Others have used bicycles to enable police officers to be more visible and approachable.

I now offer a different approach—not entirely new—used before by me but for several reasons not able to be followed up.

I strongly suggest a method of patrol by two-wheeled scooters as Mobile Foot Patrol. I believe that scooter officers in teams assigned to a neighborhood should work in harmony and rapport with the police car personnel. I call it Dual Purpose Policing. I will elaborate more on this concept in ensuing pages. To me it is the only way to go to restore the faith and respect, which the former old time beat (foot) officer had.

PART I
Police

American Law Enforcement Does Not Really Serve and Protect

I have been in American law enforcement for most of my life. When I came into the New York City Police Department there was not much talk about law enforcement. It was not the New York City Law Enforcement Department; it was the New York City Police Department.

Yes, law enforcement, or the term law enforcement, has come a long way. Maybe it has gone too far.

Years back the term law enforcement was not heard—it was policing. I believe the term "law enforcement" came about with the emerging precepts of police administrative science, helped along by a progressive Californian, August Vollmer, who began a career in the small college town of Berkeley. It was a career that made him a most prominent police chief in America. Despite the fact that his education ended in grade school, he became a university professor.

Beginning as an elected town marshal with a six-man force in 1905, with the increase in population, Marshal Vollmer became Berkeley's Chief of Police.

Vollmer was creative, innovative and established a liaison with the University of California at Berkeley; amazing with only a grade school education.

In his excellent book, *The Blue Parade,* Thomas Repetto credits Vollmer with instituting a number of innovations, including distribution of his police force based on better calculations of workload, the use of automobiles, the institution of formal training, and the adoption of scientific detective methods such as the polygraph.

Repetto, with whom I shared an office as fellow professor at John Jay College in New York, further states that Vollmer "was able to devote a good deal of time to systematic study, since unlike big city chiefs, he did not have a heavy workload or intense political pressures to keep him occupied."

Repetto said that Vollmer "saw patrolmen as something more than efficient menials. He saw them as social workers dealing with a range of societal problems which manifested themselves in crime and disorder."

Repetto states that reformers like Arthur Woods, Raymond Fosdick and Bruce Smith "could be seen as proponents of a bureaucratized police with some emphasis on social service while Vollmer favored a socially sensitive police with some emphasis on bureaucratic efficiency."

In effect, a bureaucratic police force would not require college-educated police except at the top. Vollmer's professional force would need them at all levels.

With this, I mostly agree. But I do disagree very much with Vollmer's statement: "With the advent of the radio patrol car, foot patrol is obsolete."

And this became so, and so became an America of increasing crime, handcuffed police, inner city deterioration, racial conflict, youth crime and vandalism, etc., etc., all tearing at the very soul of a city. The police became isolated and alienated from the people they serve.

In my concept of Dual Purpose policing, which I will develop in this book, of course we surely need the fast moving police patrol car responding to whatever. But we also, differing with Vollmer, must bring back the old time foot patrol officer who took care of his beat or particular area. (In New York, we did not use the word beat; it was patrol post.)

I believe that we must put those police that are socially sensitive on two-wheeled motorized scooters and so arrange for a greater area or sector, or "piece of turf" for the police to win friends and influence people by getting to know each other.

Scooter teams should not be in competition with patrol cars but should work in harmony and rapport with them, for the ultimate end of a better police force serving a better community through dual purpose policing.

The *Detroit News* quoted me on 12/29/83 when I was Oakland County Sheriff commenting on the state of law enforcement.

"We've got a lot of officers out there who feel their job is nothing but 'shoot—chase—shoot—chase.' Their job as a social scientist and all the good they can do has somehow eluded them."

Should Policing Prevent Crime?

Police are deployed on the city's streets to reduce crime, accidents and incidents that disturb the peace. The patrol division is the essential element of the police organization. All other functions are supportive in nature. Fundamentally, it is crime prevention as well as detection and punishment that the science of criminology is all about. The total service of prevention combined with response is the reason-for-being of the police patrol force.

There is and always has been controversy over the purpose of patrol. "Prevention is not a measure of the effectiveness of patrol," Arthur Niederhoffer told me in 1972. He wrote several landmark books on policing which will be discussed later.

Prevention has its burden of cost but the cost of crime is difficult or impossible to measure. The cost of crime includes not only tax dollars, but the misery and human suffering of the victims, the physical injury, the loss of peace of mind and the impairment of the quality of life in our communities.

The psychological penalties of crime may be even greater than the measurable economic costs. These economic costs only begin with the value of property and individual resources appropriated from society by the criminal for his own use through crime.

When crime is permitted to increase, the cost of enforcement of our criminal codes quickly outstrips the cost of preventive patrol. There are more prosecutions, and more prosecutors to be educated and placed on the public payroll. As court loads increase, more trials generate the need for more courts and court personnel, including judges. Correction and punishment involve a greater investment in jails and prisons and their supervision. Probation needs escalate. The penalized criminal may have a family whose support then becomes a social welfare burden.

Worst of all, what happens to the image of a community when crime and disorder spreads? How do you measure the cost of the loss to the community of its best and most prosperous citizens, who have the ability and mobility to flee from the danger, discomfort and unpleasantness of community crime, never to return? How do you measure the cost of the flight of business and industry, the shoppers who no longer come to the community to shop, the meetings, conventions and tourists that no longer use its facilities?

When crimes are committed on impulse or opportunistically, as is the case with most crime, the principal way in which police can have a deterrent effect is to prevent the opportunity. Elimination of the sociological and environmental factors that contribute to crime and criminal motivation is the responsibility of the community at large, not of its police. Police action to minimize the opportunities for crime is basically the patrol function.

As moral and social deterrents weaken, and the pressures that engender criminality bear more heavily on those least able to withstand them, the increasing number of potential criminals seeking an opportunity to exploit their fellow citizens decreases the ability of police to anticipate every possibility. Saturation patrol of an entire city is both physically and economically impossible, so patrol has to be metered out on a selective basis, where the probability of crimes is greatest.

Police have to make a choice. Police have to make the most of mobility and surprise, to offset their inability to be everywhere at once by creating an appearance of omnipresence. Police need to cultivate the fullest cooperation of citizens as extra eyes and ears.

When I was police commissioner in Detroit, I had a running gag with the press about the various dimensions of policing. The "first dimension" was conventional surface patrol of the city streets, whether by foot, horse or vehicle. The "second dimension" was airborne. The "third dimension" was waterborne, patrolling the Detroit River, which is an international boundary between Michigan and Ontario.

When we introduced police scuba divers to "patrol" underwater that became the "fourth dimension." Then we used video cameras to survey crowded areas, freeways, and secluded spots such as pedestrian street-crossing tunnels, arcades and lobbies. We called that the "fifth dimension." But most important of all was the "sixth dimension;" public participation, cooperation and support, which as one of my police students pointed out, is the "glue that cements the other five together."

The development and sustained control of an effective patrol force begins with planning, the conceptualization of the mission and the force, and the facilities and requirements to perform the mission.

The structure of a patrol force and the complexity of the planning and organization functions will vary in direct proportion to the size of the problem (the community size and the incidence of crime) and the strength of the police agency.

Perhaps the principal source of difficulty in preserving the preventive function of police service has been our looseness and generalization about "crime" and how to prevent it.

As studies of crime and its causal factors increased in numbers and depth over the years, the first thing that became apparent was the complexity of the situation, and the interrelationship of multiple factors whose precise position in the chain of crime causality was most difficult to determine. Prevailing philosophies of life and the human condition had an impact. To what degree was human conduct the result of freedom of choice, for which the individual was responsible, and to what degree the result of external pressures and forces over which the individual had little or no control?

If lack of personal virtue and self-control led to criminal acts, then the first line of defense was the inculcation of a code of personal conduct as a deterrent to criminal behavior. This was the area of responsibility of church, government, community, school and family. Crime prevention basically began with the moral restraints of society itself and its institutions. The preventive function of police service was secondary, aimed at limiting the opportunity to commit crime for those tempted beyond their capacity to resist.

Patrol and response are interlocked and both have preventive value. Patrol is a kind of "shotgun" approach to denying the criminal opportunity. A second deterrent is the psychological aspect, the fear of being caught, which is heightened if the criminal experience indicates that the chances of getting away with crime are slim.

This assumes the criminal is capable of examining the risks rationally, before committing the crime. Such an assumption is of no validity when the crime is committed out of passion or strong emotion, without premeditation or studied forethought, or by one who is mentally incapacitated, through natural deficiency or artificial befuddlement from the influence of alcohol or other drugs that affect one's judgment and bodily control.

What are the kinds of crime that police can effectively prevent by their presence? How do police prevent crime, if they do, and what kinds of crime can they prevent?

The police can indirectly deter the initial commission of crime by contact, rapport, education, and assistance in removing the incentives to crime. They can prevent the repeated commission by contact in the field, good investigation, analysis of evidence and painstaking patrol, surveillance, leading to the arrest and detainment of an offender so he cannot repeat. They can sometimes prevent crime by their presence as in riots or they can deter purse-snatching in public places such as shopping areas. Neighborhood patrol cars can counteract the car thief. Police presence or the illusion of their presence is a powerful crime deterrent.

The Advantages of Foot Patrol

Foot patrol is the oldest form of sustained mobile vigilance known to man. It provides the closest intimacy with the area and people being protected, has the least relative mobility, and requires the most costly investment of manpower.

Adding mobility to manpower is the basic principle of all other forms of patrol, and the variations have been directly related to man's progress in transportation.

I'm sure the ancients had chariot patrol, camel patrol and even elephant patrol, using every type of animal that could be domesticated for man's use, and every type of vehicle that could be adapted to animal-power.

Horses have been a part of patrol from Hammurabi to J. Edgar Hoover, although many people seem to think the police horse went out when the Tin Lizzie came in, which isn't so.

In the Gay Nineties, when bicycle traffic became an object of police regulation, police were also equipped with bikes. They had to have good wind and powerful legs to catch the cycle speeders of that day, or "scorchers," as they were known in some areas.

The gasoline engine provided the greatest revolution in patrol, but unintentionally, it has served to cripple the patrol function and divert patrolmen to a different type of function. Gasoline-powered patrol mobility has been provided by the motorcycle, the automobile, and more recently the airplane, the helicopter, and the motor scooter. In cities where there is water commerce, police operate in high-powered motorboats, and in a reversal of the trend, have gone back to human leg power with the flipper-equipped underwater recovery teams of scuba divers.

The advantages of the foot patrolman is that he is close to the people, places and things he must protect, observe and check; closer than any other more mobile and therefore more fleeting type of patrol. He has the opportunity for maximum observations, and more thorough coverage of the area he is able to patrol. Because his patrol area is relatively limited, he can do a more effective job in that area.

There is no present alternative to patrol on foot in areas of high population density, and particularly where both business places and residences are in high-rise structures. Off-street security in high-rise structures varies, depending both on the occupants as well as the availability of public or private patrol officers. High-rent apartments in major cities are apt to have their own doorman or other private guard, and video cameras monitoring lobbies, stairways and elevators.

In New York City, there are specialized, publicly employed transit police, for the subways and other mass-transit elements, and housing police for the large residential high-rise complexes that abound in the city. These are separate from the conventionally staffed street forces of the New York City Police Department.

When the housing police agency was begun in New York, I was an instructor at the New York Police Academy and helped to train the first three classes. The housing police concept was nearly aborted when some landlords wanted them to do janitorial and custodial jobs as well. Others and I strongly resisted such a misuse of individuals specifically hired and trained for policing. Housing police today do have peace officer status; they are not part-time janitors.

There is an old anecdote that has been going around for some time in New York police circles about how a jurisdictional "technicality" was resolved between the street patrolmen and the transit police force. A drunk was found in an underground subway platform by a transit police officer that, rather than leave his post to take the drunk in, simply escorted him up the stairs to the street and left him in the jurisdiction of the beat patrolman. When the beat patrolman came around and found the drunk reeling woozily outside the subway exit, rather than leave his post to take the drunk in, escorted the drunk back down the stairs to the subway platform. By the time this little charade had taken place a few more times, the drunk had sobered up enough to take himself home.

Other advantages of the foot patrolman are that he provides an information service for urbanites unfamiliar with the town. He can acquire information more readily from neighborhood residents and can develop informants better than the man riding by in the car. The foot patrolman can deal more readily with downtown traffic congestion than the scout car man, whose vehicle is frequently contributing to the congestion or is trapped by it. He doesn't have a vehicle to worry about or to be responsible for and can approach a ticklish situation quietly and inconspicuously.

The disadvantages of foot patrol are the limited mobility and the inability to cover a larger area. The foot patrolman is no faster than his legs and cannot carry a great deal of equipment. Once he has made an arrest, he has a problem in securing his culprit and getting the individual successfully to the station house.

Before the radio, the foot patrolman was an officer in trouble. In an emergency, he could rap his nightstick on the pavement if another patrolman was within earshot. But he was troublesome to the station house when he could not be located or reached in an emergency.

Street dangers and the police unions have made foot patrol more of a tactical and economic problem. There is considerable pressure to send foot patrolmen out in pairs rather than singly. Paired patrolling is a necessity for the safety of the police officers in certain urban neighborhoods. However, the availability of personal radios offered new flexibility, and even where the paired patrol is desirable, the two men need not walk side by side to provide mutual support. They can operate across the street from each other, checking more stores and keeping an eye on each other at the same time. Too often side by side patrolling turns into a conversational stroll instead of alert police observation.

With the hazards that changing conditions in many cities have brought to policing today, the foot patrolman must have the ability to contact his support elements quickly by radio, either a cruising car or his precinct station.

The foot patrolman has no protection from the elements. After a while, he may decide to linger under an awning. After a couple of years, he's taking shelter inside the store. The criminal can clock and predict foot patrol conducted on a routine basis.

Human nature gets in the way of this kind of patrol because of the lethargy of the individual. The beat patrolman can get too close to some kinds of people, which can lead to petty graft and corruption.

What kind of patrol do we have in American policing today? Most air and water operations are strictly specialized, occasional types of patrol. The standard method of the day is patrol via the automobile, with foot patrol remaining only to a limited degree.

You get an alarm and you go out. Maybe you get the criminal and maybe you don't. But the deed is done. Would foot patrol prevent the deed from occurring? Maybe. Would the car prevent it? Not that much. By day it's too fleeting and by night the police car is just another pair of headlights.

You don't see a foot patrolman often anymore. Scout car patrol is virtually the whole ball of wax today. The advantages of patrol by car are flexibility, wide coverage, carrying capacity for equipment and it gets the policeman where he has to go faster and less expensively than by foot. It's possible for one or two officers in the car to cover as much territory as ten or more foot patrolmen. The obvious question remains. Do the scout car men cover the territory as well?

The car can act as a sort of temporary mobile "prison" for arrested suspects. It can also be a mobile "prison" for the police officer too. The car is comfortable and safe for the officer and even formidable in crowd situations. Its wide-ranging ability and speed in moving from one sector to another rapidly contributes to the feeling that the police must be everywhere. Undeniably the impression of police omnipresence can be an important deterrent to crime.

The officer in the car is protected against bad weather, against traffic, and even to some degree against the dangers of criminal gunfire. The car makes it possible for two officers to travel together, a necessity in certain stress situations. It can carry a dog for those departments that make proper use of the potential of well-trained animals in detection and apprehension.

The advantages of the car are usually contrasted with foot patrol, rather than measured against the possibilities of other types of powered patrol. In spite of the fact that most police departments have gone overwhelmingly to scout car patrol, the picture is not totally in favor of the automobile because of some disadvantages.

The car's mobility can carry it too far and too fast to permit the officers to pay close attention to the details of their territory, a disadvantage in preventive work. The very benefit, which makes the car especially effective in a "response" situation, is to a degree a drawback in a "prevention" situation.

The officer can get too comfortable and secure in his automobile. He can get "car-bound" and not get out of it often enough to find out for himself what's going on. He comes to rely on his radio to tell him what to do, instead of his eyes and ears.

He may feel that he is less subject to the public scrutiny and notice of the people on his beat, and may be inclined to take some liberties with this advantage.

Because of the radio contact, it is often thought that the scout car officer is easier to supervise than the foot patrolman, who before the days of the radio could be out of contact for long intervals between phone calls. But there's the question of whether radio contact in itself is supervision.

The scout car man may be in communication with the dispatcher or his supervisor, but that doesn't mean the supervisor really knows what he is doing. I remember an incident in the East that nobody's forgotten who heard it or heard about it. A police officer of questionable judgment as well as integrity was taking advantage of several of the conveniences of automobiles with a girl friend, and nobody would have been the wiser until the gal in the car accidentally hit the radio switch, and the whole tuned-in police department got an unexpected play-by-play broadcast.

It's not often mentioned, but a car, like any other piece of equipment, can affect morale adversely or beneficially, depending on the condition it's in.

Whatever else may be said about weighing the car's advantages and disadvantages, the fact is that in most departments, that's the only vehicle the police have. It's the accepted principal tool, and few have bothered to take a second look in the past 40 years at whether the changes in policing dictated by almost total dependence on the automobile are all for the best, or whether they may be responsible for some of the difficulties we face in modern policing, particularly in connection with person-to-person contact in the street.

What has happened is that the car, introduced originally for special pursuit missions, has become the most generally used piece of equipment in all operations, including patrol. But is it patrol that the scout car of today truly performs? If not, is a police department that no longer offers preventive patrol providing the service its community needs? Is there any other alternative to the choice between a foot patrol with little response capability, and a response force with serious patrol disadvantages?

As recently as 1998, James R. Miller, a patrol officer of the Detroit Police Department, wrote a stunning research paper on "The Failure of the Detroit Police Department to Provide Adequate Police Services to the Citizens of Detroit." In his summary he wrote,

> I have concluded through interviews, personal experience, and listening to the way things used to be done, that the police precincts in the City of Detroit are in desperate need of an overhaul on how things are done. With additional personnel, the officers would be able to clear up the calls for services and would have time for routine patrol. Routine patrol would include something as simple as just talking to citizens or stopping by a high school football game. This would create a friendlier environment between the public and the police and after a short time, would begin to reduce crime because the community would be working alongside of the police.

Unfortunately, despite being one of their own, I have seen no apparent change in the Detroit Police Department resulting from Miller's work and conclusions about patrol.

The motorcycle is a vehicle that bloomed in popularity with police ahead of the car, but lacked the all-around versatility to ever make it anything but a specialized type of high-speed, maneuverable pursuit or escort vehicle. Two-wheel and three-wheel types are currently in use for specialized functions.

The advantage of the two-wheeled motorcycle is its flexibility in traffic with great speed and maneuverability, which makes it useful for pursuit and traffic enforcement. It is also at an advantage for special escort and parade marshalling duties. In some areas, motorcycle men in their helmets and puttees have been used as "commando-type" shock troops for riots and disturbances. Their psychological impact can be both good and bad.

The disadvantage is that the motorcycle is used most frequently in punitive situations such as chasing traffic offenders and ticketing citizens. Some people like to see the motorcycle officers pursuing a violator but others resent him hiding out of sight looking for a speeder or "victim." The vehicle itself is noisy and relatively costly in terms of its specialized use. It is also relatively hazardous to operate, and involves the department in the expense of hospitalization for officers injured, and a "hazard" salary differential.

Additionally, it is limited by inclement weather. Because it requires constant attention and careful control, it limits the ability of the officer to observe his surroundings.

Three-wheeled motorcycles have been used either with a "sidecar" or a "trunk." They have more operating stability than the two-wheeler, and are somewhat more maneuverable in traffic than a car. Unless equipped with a cab or canopy, they offer no protection against bad weather. They have been used principally for parking enforcement.

Boats are necessary for patrol in harbor cities where large bodies of water are part of the geography. Parks with large lakes often have a police boat patrol. An international boundary city like Detroit, separated from Canada by the Detroit River (actually a "strait") has made good use of patrol boats to prevent smuggling.

Boating has become both a widespread pastime and a status symbol. With such intensive use of rivers, lakes and harbors, you've got to have a cop on the water, too, for safety's sake as much as to prevent criminal action.

Drownings involve special search and recovery procedures involving police. A modern touch in many cities is a scuba diving team for underwater recovery, not only of drowning victims, but also of evidence in connection with crimes.

Waterside business locations, including docks and warehouses, can be patrolled better if water-borne police units are employed as well as land patrol.

Helicopters and airplanes have the advantage of broad control in a large area. The vantage point of an aerial "command post" is unexcelled for the mobilization and maneuvering of manpower and vehicles on the ground.

Traffic deaths continue to soar and police can't do the safety job that is required without advanced equipment and effective aerial observation. The helicopter has the advantage of being able to hover for closer observation than the airplane, which can miss a lot of detail. There are no traffic jams in the air to tie up police vehicles, at least not yet. For open country, roadways or bodies of water, the plane or helicopter has special advantages for search and pursuit of lost persons, escaped felons, zoo animals, fleeing immigrants and those evading arrest.

The chief disadvantage of airborne vehicles is their cost to obtain and operate. It has to be used for the speed, observation and control situations to which it brings unique advantages, and to be used properly if it is to be economically justifiable. But used properly, it can provide services nothing else can do.

The plane or helicopter requires specialized personnel for operation and maintenance, whose aviation skills could not be utilized on other types of police duty. However there are opportunities for exploitation of the special features of airborne equipment that have been barely thought of, much less tried.

Use of helicopters in traffic control need not be limited to daylight hours, although they are tremendous assets for checking traffic flow and monitoring tie-ups on parkways and expressways. They serve the news media during rush hour for the valuable information to drivers about what to avoid. Whenever they see a slowdown or a jam they can move in either by loudspeaker on the spot or direct surface police vehicles to the scene and immediately begin to divert traffic. They can also quickly warn residents of the need to evacuate an area in time of hazard by the use of their loudspeaker. Equipped with special lighting equipment, the night-duty helicopter can floodlight an area as large as a football field to guide officers pursuing a suspect.

Suppose you've got a highway at night with heavy speeding traffic. Suddenly there's a six-car collision with smashed cars sprawled all over the traffic lanes and a couple of dead and injured people. You can take a night-equipped helicopter and illuminate the whole area as if it were day. You can help the surface units get their cars and reports and pick up the injured right away. Depending on the type of helicopter, the aircraft itself could provide the necessary ambulance service for the victims quicker than a road-bound machine. The illumination helps alert oncoming traffic to the danger ahead as well.

Such a piece of equipment could be helpful in night searches, patrolling broad park areas (although some park users wouldn't want to be spotlighted at night), looking for lost children and suspicious prowlers.

A helicopter once helped to make possible the speedy capture of an abortion ring. As soon as the warrants were issued, they and the arresting officers were carried by helicopter to the arrest site before any "tip-offs" could be made.

It may be technically inaccurate to refer to the video camera as a method of patrol, but the facility exists and extends the range of surveillance of the police. Even if it is not a moving, roaming police element, it is certainly an aid to patrol in locations that are either relatively inaccessible or require continuous observation.

The video camera in effect telescopes time and space. You can put it on a roof, in a lobby, a passageway, in a car. You can scan motor and pedestrian traffic and observe streets, playgrounds, park areas and parking lots.

Besides the added observations, it provides a permanent record in the form of videotape as to what was observed. The fact that what is going on is being filmed and cannot be controverted by subsequent false testimony can also act as a deterrent. Banks are using private video systems extensively, and hundreds of bank robberies have already been filmed, assisting significantly in the arrest of the criminals involved. It has helped in the apprehension of car-thieves and car-looters.

The video camera obviously can conserve manpower by scanning widely scattered areas. To be a deterrent, of course, the presence of the camera has to be known to the criminal. It can be an advantage as a deterrent yet it could be a disadvantage if citizens at large felt squeamish and "over-watched" by its use. Too many feel that police are playing a "Big Brother" role but the use of video cameras by stores to deter shoplifters and buildings to deter undesirables have diluted the criticism of police use.

The concern over excessive information gathering about private citizens is real and extensive. All of us already are aware that "they" have got our names in "their" computers. They've got the information that I didn't pay a $5 credit check once. It's locked in the computer. They've got the fact down that I once ran three red lights in Las Vegas and then gave the justice of the peace a hard time. (Not me, of course.)

Can there be a "little bit" of surveillance without the feeling that there is an excessive invasion of privacy? Or is it like pregnancy, all or not at all?

As I see it, it's coming, it's got to be. The only question is, are the users of the all-seeing video camera going to be "good" or "bad" Big Brothers, protecting or snooping? We're all going to be in the computer, and we're all going to have an electronic "eye" on us. Our technical achievements are piling on top of us. Do we cease to avail ourselves of their potential for good, or do we make sure we use them well and control misuse?

Compared to employing the number of police it would take to provide the same degree of consistent or widespread observation, the use of video cameras is relatively economical. It makes possible 24-hour service, 365 days a year. It is impervious to changing weather conditions. It doesn't require a paycheck every pay period. It doesn't require a pension when its years of service have been completed.

The future of successful police administration and efficient patrol lies in the economical use of manpower, and the use of laborsaving devices like the video camera to the fullest extent.

There are still inevitable limitations, of course. The video camera can't see in poor lighting conditions any more than the human eye can. In time there may be special means for continuous lighting or floodlighting on signal, electronic or other. We have special types of low-light films right now, and even infrared "no light" films.

Video cameras are good for prisoner surveillance in jail. Of course, for instant police response, somebody has to be watching the monitor.

You can use the video camera to film the license plates of vehicles at terminals, bridges, housing entry points, and other places. By means of a computer relay and existing information networks, police can identify those cars that need to be stopped.

They are good for large concentrations of people and traffic. A central monitor can use video cameras to control traffic flow into congested freeways, or send police or aid vehicles in a hurry to check a violation or assist at an accident scene.

Video cameras already have been used for parade control in a number of cities. They can help reduce crime in underground garages and other areas out of the range of normal street-level police surveillance.

Because a piece of equipment like a video camera can save as many as five men's time, since it takes five men to handle one assignment 24 hours a day, 365 days a year, assuming a 40-hour week plus vacations, sick and court time for each individual, it's going to have increasing appeal to city governments looking for new ways to save money without reducing essential services.

The principal disadvantage is the potential resentment of citizens who dislike the Orwellian implications of the all-seeing eye. Initial installation costs would undoubtedly be substantial. But this is part of the future and the equipment is already in use.

Aren't Officers Supposed To Be Fast?

The books on patrol that deal with prevailing practice tend to see only two basic alternatives, foot patrol or car patrol, and deal with the rest as limited specialties. It's important not to limit one's thinking only to prevailing practice.

Technology is far ahead of police theory. We took the foot patrolman and made him mobile, and the same can be done with the electronic eye of the video camera. Is it too far-fetched to consider the possibility of remotely controlled or piloted aircraft or hovercraft with video equipment that could patrol aerial "beats" above the city's streets, steering surface response units to trouble spots? After all, that is already being done at international borders to prevent illegal immigration and drug smuggling.

But nobody writes a book about a technological invention or a technological hero. The public is usually more familiar with detectives than any other form of policing or police officer. From Sherlock Holmes to Chief Ironsides, heroes of police tales almost universally have been detectives. This was probably inevitable, due to the dramatic qualities inherent in crime itself, and the mystery and suspense of the detection process.

Good detectives deserve their laurels. However, the glorification of the detective, who is a specialist in only one phase of police work, has tended to obscure the importance of the man in the blue uniform; the man who makes up the bulk of any police department, and must perform the basic functions of prevention and protection.

How many times have we seen the patrolman as the hero of a TV show or movie? Only recently have we had the patrolman hero as in the series called "Adam-12." Before that we had a spate of "private eye" sagas, where the actual official cop, as often as not, was characterized as a "dumkopf." The private eye was slick, smart and daring, and always got the girl, while the professional policeman was a colorless figure wearing a nondescript hat and chewing a cigar.

"Dragnet" came along and eulogized the professional police detective, as did "NYPD-Blue." Rarely did the uniformed man get any serious attempt to portray him in his most important work. And yet the uniformed patrolman is to the police profession what the general practitioner is to the medical profession.

He's the only man in a position to stop the crime "germ" before it strikes, or catch it early enough to keep it from doing more serious harm.

When you have to call in the specialist, in crime or in medicine, the patient is already pretty sick. That's one reason why the patrolman is not recognized as the general practitioner of police work that he ought to be. His original function has been eroded by an increased workload, and new demands. The description "patrolman" hardly fits him any more, and yet all police theorists agree that patrol is the backbone of police work.

Patrol implies a constant police presence in the neighborhood by a man who knows and is known by his people. The sight of his face and uniform is a reassurance to the law-abiding, and a deterrent to the criminal.

Gradually we've tried to give our limited number of patrolmen greater range by equipping them with Detroit's most famous product; the car. In the process, however, we have hidden the man inside a steel and glass vehicle and reduced his neighborhood contact.

Where crime rates are high, the man in the scout car may spend virtually all of his time on duty responding instead of patrolling, dashing from one crime call to another. Admittedly, when police resources are thin and the social and economic environment creates a thicket of motivations and opportunities for crime, police departments are left in an almost impossible dilemma.

With narcotics, burglaries, robberies, muggings, murders, traffic accidents, etc., the police executive begins to feel he is facing a crumbling dike with more leaks than he has fingers to plug them with. How can you husband your resources to deal with each critical area and still be able to shift the emphasis away from sheer response back to crime prevention and protection?

The universal crisis atmosphere is the reason why I have been so high on the development of the scooter-ranger concept to put the patrolman back on patrol. The officer on the scooter is a visible presence again in the neighborhood. He has the contact opportunity of the foot patrolman, and ten times the range. The economy factor is important in this era of tight municipal budgets. The price of one scout car will buy six to eight scooters, an appealing budgetary consideration.

To me, the effective combination of officer, scooter and personal radio transmitter is the best means available for giving neighborhood citizens better protection for their tax dollar. Nowhere has the scooter been fully applied to date. This concept would make the Ranger cop not just another specialist, but the new general practitioner of policing in modern America.

Take the specialist label away from the man on the scooter, and give it to the man who deserves it, the man in the car. The scooter cop would then be considered the generalist and the patrol car officer would be the specialist.

Yes, the detective force is necessary. The response elements in their cars and other supporting police forces are necessary. But first and foremost, and most essential, are the men, women and equipment needed to provide effective deterrent patrol. You cannot measure the worth of a general practitioner in policing by the number of arrests he has made, and the number of tickets he has issued, or the dramatic highlights of the crimes he has solved. His worth is measured by the crimes that *didn't* happen because he was there.

His worth is measured by the peace of mind of the storekeepers who wave as he goes by, by the rapport that exists between the officer in uniform and those who respect and respond to the person inside that uniform, and by the inner satisfaction the man in uniform himself gets from this kind of community acceptance. In turn, acceptance helps him do a better job.

For nearly a decade, I listened to all the arguments pro and con about the scooter. I heard all the disadvantages and I had to come up with answers to all the arguments.

The point is, that with all the technological advances in equipment, the traditional scout car is not and need not be the only ultimate vehicle for police use. Certainly it has demonstrated great versatility and importance.

Speedy response time has always been an important factor to measure in police service. The National Institute of Justice reported that in 2001, the national average police response time in 60% of crimes of violence was within 10 minutes and response time in 80% of property crimes was within one hour. Most police departments strive to maintain an average arrival within 6 to 7 minutes on violent crime scenes. There is no doubt that police cars can respond more quickly than any other vehicle when driving on many streets and highways. The presence of smaller, more mobile vehicles with the smiling face of an ever-present officer is of more value in prevention than in pursuit.

Recently Atlanta, Georgia authorities decided that Hartsfield International Airport would purchase ten Segway human scooters to give police a stronger presence and quicker response time to airport incidents. These are small motorized scooters that quickly transport a standing person without the fatigue factor.

There is more to the question of police response time. Most of our best police officers are good men whose training and experience have made them expert in one thing, responding to emergency runs. There is a certain danger and recklessness that occurs when driving a car that can go more than 100 miles an hour.

Police chases and speed are very exhilarating and the rush of adrenalin can obscure judgment. There are numerous horrific examples of injuries caused by speeding police cars and speeding drivers being pursued by police cars.

In Lubbock, Texas, Jerome Baker was indicted for a 1996 crash that injured three while being pursued by police. Police noticed his state vehicle inspection sticker had expired and after a lengthy chase, he drove his car through a park where several children were playing. Police continued to pursue the driver and Baker ran a stop sign and hit another car hard enough to turn it over. The car's driver, a 19-year-old girl, and another 18-year-old passenger and her one-year-old daughter were injured. In my opinion, the officers as well as the man they were chasing for a minor offense should have been dealt with.

Police pulled over a young lady after her car ran off the road and hit a stop sign in Luthersville, Georgia in January 2003. Radio trouble forced the officer back to his police car and the girl dashed back into her vehicle, speeding away and setting off a chain of events that ultimately killed a man. Police traveling at approximately 94 miles an hour pursued Loraine McCrary when she hit Chuck Vicha. She pleaded guilty to vehicular homicide and was sentenced to 15 years in prison. State Senator Mitch Seabaugh held a hearing on high speed police chases and various law enforcement officials testified that Georgia's police officers do not receive special training on how to safely end police chases.

A 19-year-old man died and his two female passengers were injured in Cincinnati, Ohio in 1997 when a police officer crashed into their car while chasing another motorist. Other officers continued the chase as the speeding suspect struck two vehicles, but no one was injured. The officer involved in the fatal crash was placed on administrative leave.

The Supreme Court heard arguments in 1997 on when police can be held liable for someone's death or injury in high-speed chases. After the death of 16-year-old Philip Lewis by a sheriff's deputy driving 100 mph, his parents brought a lawsuit against the Sacramento County Sheriff's Office. "This is a phenomenal problem that kills hundreds of people every year," said the Lewises' lawyer.

The Association of Trial Lawyers of America spokesman Howard Friedman said that there have been 5,306 deaths during police pursuits from 1980–1996.

The International Association of Chiefs of Police (IACP) has approved guidelines for when officers should break off a pursuit and Congress is considering a national standard for police pursuits. However, many have objected to this, arguing that police activity is essentially a state responsibility.

After swerving on the road, police chased a 35-year-old man who drove past a school bus loading students and continued on to hit nine cars and injure ten people as well as himself in February 2003. Authorities in Stanton, Delaware questioned why the chase continued after officers saw the school bus loading.

A fatal Sacramento police chase resulted in the settlement of $1.75 million for the family of 50-year-old Andy Sorgatz in 1997. Police struck his car while traveling 80 miles an hour while chasing a man driving a stolen vehicle. The officer involved in the collision learned during the chase that the stolen vehicle had been apprehended. It was his responsibility to slow down and deactivate his warning lights. Instead, he turned off the warning lights first and maintained a high rate of speed for several blocks before colliding with Mr. Sorgatz's vehicle. The Sacramento Police Department reportedly changed their police pursuit policies following the accident.

A policeman chasing an SUV for a minor traffic violation in December 2002 killed a 19-year-old Houston man. The Houston Copwatch, a local police oversight group, wrote to their mayor to request that police officers not chase people for minor traffic violations. Their letter said, "The risk to our city's children is far too high to allow the current free-for-all chase approach to continue."

The police responded in writing saying, "You should spend what little resources you have and do public awareness commercials, advising the public to not run from the police under any circumstances. If citizens (who automatically are felons if they evade in a vehicle) don't run and simply pull over, no car chase would occur." Both sides had good points but the fact remains that police chases are dangerous due to the size and speed of cars.

Movies have portrayed police chases in some of the most exciting scenes ever filmed. In *Bullitt*, Steve McQueen played Lieutenant Bullitt who chased criminals on San Francisco streets. Gene Hackman played an undercover narcotics officer who chased cars in *The French Connection* on an elevated subway. Mel Gibson tried to maintain order by chasing futuristic criminals in *The Road Warrior*. *Thelma and Louise*, chased by interstate police across many states, decided to end the chase by driving off a cliff. Police chase criminals through the streets of Paris in *The Bourne Identity*. Even archaeologist Indiana Jones chased Nazi spies in a truck chase in *Raiders of the Lost Ark*.

No glamorous and exciting chases will ever feature a bicycle or motor scooter cop but preserving peace is not always an exhilarating exercise. These are quiet friendly vehicles that prevent crime by their presence and do not endanger the innocent.

Should Officers Protect People or Enforce Laws?

One cannot simultaneously be a strict law enforcer and a promoter of harmonious community relations at the same moment, but the same officer can do both functions at different times. An effective patrol system begins with a sound understanding of human nature and the limitations of man. Then it builds within itself a differentiation of roles for police personnel of differing degrees of capability and experience. It seeks to avoid dumping the most difficult or arduous burdens on the lowest ranks. To expect the beginning officer to be "all things to all people" in the most taxing police assignments is illogical, unsound and ineffective.

The inadequacies of manpower, monetary considerations, the proliferation of the problems of increasingly congested urban life, and the gradual evolution of the patrol function from excessive dependence on shoe-leather to excessive dependence on wheels, have simply created another specialty in policing whether we realize it or not. The computer-equipped automobile, in spite of its versatility and flexibility, has led police departments down the path of quick response but little or no prevention. With rare exceptions, preventive patrol virtually became a thing of the past by the 1960s.

Originally, orders were that 50 per cent of car patrol time should remain uncommitted to allow for general observation and preventive patterns of patrol. Human nature, being what it is, took over. When not rolling on a run, the average officer grabs a bite to eat, talks to his buddies, and takes a brief respite away from prying, inquisitive eyes or raucous voices.

Security companies and volunteer crime watch groups realized the deterrent factor of ever-watchful eyes. They have used labeled vehicles and walkers roaming the streets to deter crime and they have been successful in reducing crime where used. Gradually they have assumed more of the protective role and police have gradually become enforcers of the law.

Now when the "run" comes, the policeman may penetrate into areas where he feels he is not welcome, and with lights blazing and sirens sounding, often invites citizen hostility. Such police officers become hit and run raiders to residents who never see them except for stress situations. Such a response is abrasive to communities because it is the only time the police appear and they may neither catch nor deter criminals from future depredations.

There is little concern with preventive patrol in American policing today. The police know it, the criminal knows it, and if the American people don't know it, many of them at least feel it. Police primarily *react* to crime in most districts today. This is despite good information that criminals decide to commit crimes based on whether they will be apprehended through people protecting suitable targets.

A new concept, a new differentiation, must be included to round out our patrol system, and make it do again what it was originally constituted to do. We need to include a new type of motorized foot patrol officer, whose ability, training, motivation and dedication are at least as important, if not more so, than the means of mobility with which he is equipped. We must create the "generalist" of American policing, a man who more than any other type of police officer can handle the broadest range of contemporary problems from community tensions to serious crime. We need to provide for the exigencies of response without sacrificing the officer's special territorial responsibility, a responsibility which involves a personal commitment on a day-in, day-out total familiarity basis. The patrol officer with the territorial commitment is the key man in policing and he should be so regarded.

He must have the opportunity, encouragement and means to advance in professional status and acceptability. He must be provided with an opportunity for progression up the professional ladder without having to move out of the vital area of preventive patrol. It is up to administrators to provide a professional escalation ladder that involves training, education, experience and evolving responsibility.

Let us consider whether the appearance of a police officer is a deterrent. We will re-examine uniforms and review an interesting uniform experiment.

Despite the efforts of those who organized the English police department, there is no doubt that uniforms, badges, ranks, and a paramilitary tradition permeate the police profession. The uniform itself is endowed with considerable force.

In 1976, Arthur Niederhoffer described the policeman "as a Rorschach in uniform...clothed in a mantle of symbolism that stimulates fantasy and projection."

The nature of the projection can take on a heavy moral significance as evidenced by the following advice provided to new recruits at the New York State

Police training program. "The first thing the recruit is taught at the State Police Academy is that the very color of the uniform-gray-has meaning. There's black thread for bad next to white thread for good and together they make gray."

The uniform not only creates "esprit de corps" between wearers but also affects compliance or aggression against the wearer. Furthermore, psychologist Philip Zimbardo suggests that a process of "de-individualization" takes place wherein the uniform may create a more aggressive interpretation of one's role. Conflict resolution can become more difficult and attitudes towards the non-uniformed wrongdoer can harden.

Perhaps the most striking illustration of the influence of uniforms to affect or alter roles is reported in the Uniform Experiment of J. Tenzel and V. Cizanchas in 1973. To improve community relations, the Chief of Police in Menlo Park, California, shifted police attire from the typical blue military style to a civilian green blazer. The results were dramatic. It was found that assaults on Menlo Park police officers decreased by 30%, citizen injuries resulting from arrest decreased by 50%, morale rose, and the staff turnover rate dropped from 25.5% in the year prior to the uniform shift to 2% three full years into the program. Finally, the community approval of the blazer experiment rose from 69% following their introduction to 80% by 1975.

A more recent experiment with opposite results took place in the mid-1980s in a town in New Jersey. They decided to de-militarize the police force. Uniforms were exchanged for blue dress blazers and gray trousers for male and female officers. Police ranks were shown on uniforms and officers were given extra training in courtesy and customer relations. After six months, public reactions were requested to assess the experiment. The reaction was almost completely negative except they appreciated the extra courtesy. People didn't want a non-police looking responder in an emergency, and felt that a uniformed officer made them feel more secure. Additionally, officers disliked performing police-like tasks while appearing to be civilians. The program was eliminated and they returned to what the police and public were accustomed to expect.

Clothing experiments in psychiatric hospitals have led to the almost total removal of nurse and physician uniforms in favor of ordinary clothes to improve relations with psychiatric patients. However, the abandonment of traditional paramilitary uniforms, rank badges, and guns is not likely to be widespread.

What relevance do these studies have with respect to patrol? The uniform can express and communicate a prevailing correctional philosophy and can influence the manner in which the wearer executes his or her authority and the manner in which those confronted by the uniform respond to that authority. In fact, some argue that the abandonment of uniform attire and/or dress code standards may precipitate an erosion of the respect for authority that is necessary in a law enforcement setting. Nevertheless, it becomes more important for the patrol officer to realize the impact of his attire on others as well as himself and to counteract excessive authoritarianism.

Is Patrol Work Professional?

When all police administrators provide incentives to achieve in the patrol field as the pinnacle of police professionalism, departments will no longer see their best men taking advantage of every opportunity to avoid remaining on patrol.

Just after I was Police Commissioner of Detroit at the end of 1970, there was a police force of almost 5,000 officers of all ranks and about 100 policewomen. Of the 5,000 men, about 450 were detectives, or less than one in ten. Of the remainder, about 4,000 were ranked as patrolmen, about 400 were sergeants, and 200 were lieutenants and higher. Of these 4,000 patrolmen, 2,200 served in the precincts and more than 90% were on street duty. About 400 men were assigned to foot beats and 1,600 to radio scout cars, including 1,200 to two-man cars and 400 to special details. About 200 had inside assignments.

Augmenting the patrol force were more than 100 officers assigned to motor scooters as the "community-oriented patrol" (COP), about 60 men in cars were the precinct support unit, and about 140 men were in the Tactical Mobile Units, a sort of strategic reserve. Also on patrol duty were most of the 400 patrolmen assigned to the Traffic Division, including foot, motorcycle and scout car men, mounted horsemen, and waterborne members of the Harbormaster unit covering the Detroit River. The over 1,100 patrolmen were involved in various administrative, technical and special service units, including special investigations, communications, identification, scientific laboratory, records, police academy, recruiting, intelligence, citizens' complaints and court details.

So about 4,000 men or 80% of the sworn personnel were limited to the single rank of patrolmen with five pay steps based on longevity. At the beginning of the officer's fifth year of service, he got his fifth and final step up in that rank. Salary incentives for the patrol officer virtually ended, therefore, after four years. After he had finally learned the patrol job, he had no place to go except up in rank, for which there was only one opening for every seven men, or into the detective division, in which the opportunity ratio was slightly less.

The department's actual strength was about 10% under authorized strength, so the force had room for about 500 additional police. Of the 5,100 officers on the job, about 12% were black. The black population of Detroit then was more

27

than 40% of the total population. To reach a comparable level in the police department would have required the addition of about 1,400 more black officers.

Recruiting levels had been running about 20% black or some 100 out of a total of about 500 a year. Applicants had been appearing at the rate of 5,000 to 6,000 a year since the Detroit riot of 1967, stimulated by citywide action to improve police recruiting. Black applicants accounted for 40 to 50% of the total, or in proportion to the black share of the total population. About 13 to 16% of white applicants were successful, but only 3 to 4% of black applicants were successful.

Analysis showed that the written examination, year in and year out, was the biggest single factor in the disproportionate elimination of black applicants. Within a percentage point or two, some 60% of both black and white applicants were screened out for failure to meet a variety of preliminary standards. These included age, education, medical background, previous police record, and traffic record, in which there was no significant difference in the number of blacks and whites rejected. Many more whites than blacks were screened out for failure to meet height, vision and weight standards.

However three times as many blacks as whites, proportionately, were eliminated for failing the written examination. About 60% of the blacks taking the examination were screened out by it, compared with about 20% of the whites. In all other screening areas, differences were negligible.

A number of possibilities stemmed from these statistics:

- Blacks in general were intellectually inferior to whites. This, of course, is untrue, genetically or hereditarily, and even if it were true, it would be unacceptable.

- The caliber of black applicants attracted to police work was intellectually of lower quality than the caliber of white applicants. The success of blacks in many fields, while it was not distributed as widely as whites, made this conclusion unacceptably abrasive.

- A cultural gap exists between young blacks and whites, which was highlighted by conventional written examinations. School surveys lent some credence to such a conclusion, since they revealed that teenage blacks came from public schools with lower educational attainment levels than teenage whites, who attended public schools on the periphery of the "inner city."

If certain young people, from whom future police prospects were to be drawn, were receiving an inferior education, it was inevitable that due to no fault of their own, they should do poorly on tests reflecting the results of schooling.

The police department could not wait for changes in the educational system to turn out a larger number of better-educated young people. Different types of tests were sought that would eliminate such cultural bias, if such were the fundamental reason for the problem.

New testing methods were tried in 1969, 1970 and 1971. Uncertainty as to their validity remained. An undercurrent of dissatisfaction was discerned about officers who felt that special examinations, although applied to all applicants, represented a lower standard than previous examinations. The touchy point was, "I want my fellow police officers to be just as good as I am, to back me up in an emergency. Will these tests bring in individuals I can trust in a pinch, individuals who are just as capable as I am?"

This dissatisfaction was multiplied in the 1980s when racial quotas were used by police departments to fill openings. Thus the highest scoring black or Hispanic might be named to fill a position even though his or her score was lower than the highest scoring white.

Currently, the city of Detroit has lost population and is now under one million, which reduced the size of the police force. In 2002, the Detroit Police Department had 4,235 sworn police officers, of which 120 were community policing officers, a slight increase from my time.

In 1997, a consultant was hired to review the Detroit Police Department. Merrick Bobb's report stated that the department's recruiting minimums (18 year olds with a high school diploma or GED) were too low. He suggested age 22 with two years of college. Police Chief Benny Napoleon said state law prevented him from raising the hiring age and increasing educational standards would severely shrink the hiring pool.

Earlier I referred to Detroit officer Miller's document, *The Failure of the Detroit Police Department to Provide Adequate Police Services to the Citizens of Detroit.* Some more of its highlights confirm that little has changed since my tenure as police commissioner there. (The city no longer has a single police commissioner but a board of five police commissioners, all appointed by the mayor.) Miller wrote:

> Basically upper management of the Detroit Police Department looked down on the uniformed patrol officers…. While the mere presence of police may not be sufficient to deter crime, the manner in which they approach their task

may make a difference…. Not only more officers on patrol but better equipped and trained officers would make for a much better police department to serve the community. Not only would you significantly reduce response times for calls for service, but you would also see a greater cooperation between the public and the police department. The officers would have much more time for community policing and would be able to "clean up" their scout car area. I feel that proactive problem-oriented policing would work extremely well in the City of Detroit. If officers had to stay in their assigned scout car areas for eight hours not only would the calls for service be handled but the officers would also handle all the non-emergency complaints within that scout car area as well. Like I stated before, officers just simply talking with neighborhood people on a nice sunny day sure would go a long way toward bridging the gap between the public and the police…In addition I feel that the department should also give officers business cards so that they could pass them out to citizens. If the officer wished, he could even give a citizen his pager number or his cell phone number."

This entire recruiting problem is essential to improving the patrol function. It involves creating new ranks in the patrol force along with a varied range of responsibilities keyed to the education, experience and potential performance of the individual officers involved.

It is irrelevant to continue to debate whether police departments should stress law enforcement over protection or vice versa. Police are subject to the general public expectation that citizens can and must be able to turn to their police for a variety of services in time of need. However, it can be argued that a single-minded emphasis on *law enforcement* has been responsible in part for the alienation that has occurred between people and police in recent years.

How a Patrol Officer Works

It seems amusing now because so many things have changed over my lifetime in law enforcement, but this will show you how much is expected from patrol officers. As mentioned earlier, patrol is the police department's basic method of observing the community it must protect. Observation provides the data for analysis of conditions that contribute to the likelihood of crime. The main duties of the patrol force are the prevention of crime, the quieting of disturbances, the apprehension of criminals, and providing aid and information when needed or requested by citizens.

Public disturbances are always ticklish affairs. This can range from neighbors complaining about a noisy party or family quarrel to rowdy crowds and civil disorder. The officer should employ great restraint and tact in dealing with such volatile situations.

On arriving at a crime scene, the first officers have the burden of tracing down the crook while the trail is still hot. This can be tricky because no matter how docile he may appear, the threat of losing his freedom can push a man into foolish behavior.

In addition to steering people in the right direction, the patrol force can be a valuable aid to city government by reporting obvious civil violations to the various city bureaus. For example, the officer should report fire hazards to the fire department, any backed up sewers causing flooding to the water commission and pavement in disrepair or suggestions for more efficient traffic flow to the highway department.

Foot Patrol:

The foot patrol officer has the greatest opportunity to become acquainted with the people in his zone. This personal contact should create a better public impression of the police service, provided the officer measures up to the best professional standards. This can pay dividends later when the officer needs public cooperation in his investigation of a crime or search for a lawbreaker.

Increased police-citizen contact can also be the root of a dangerous problem facing many departments, when the officer is not guided by the highest professional principles. Citizen respect and cooperation can be alienated by rude, discriminatory or unlawful conduct. Showing favoritism to certain businesses in return for free food or favors is only different in degrees from accepting cash bribes for ignoring illegal activities.

In any event, most departments in downtown areas or where there are many pedestrians or in high crime areas use foot patrol. The foot patrolman should, of course, take care not to repeat his normal patrol route every shift and should vary his routine.

The plain-clothes officer can operate more effectively than the uniformed officer because he can observe situations without detection.

Observation:

Since one of the primary functions of all types of patrol is to be the eyes and ears of the department, the effectiveness of a patrolman depends largely on his powers of observation. Each individual will highlight certain parts of a scene in his later recounting of an event. The good officer learns the effect of his own subconscious on what he sees. Experience is probably the only factor that will sharpen the officer's observation. The most important aspect of observation for the patrolman to remember is to be aware of anything out of the ordinary.

There is no special stereotype of the prime suspect for a crime. Excessive hurrying or nervousness can indicate that a person is trying to hide something but of course it could only indicate that he has many other pressing things on his mind. A furtive look and darting eyes can be taken as outward signs of inner feelings of guilt. But is this guilt criminal in nature? One can feel guilty over forgetting a spouse's birthday. Generally it is wise to observe closely parked cars with people in them and the motor running, especially in high crime areas or at odd hours of the night.

Cars breaking the speed limit should be approached cautiously as there exists obviously the possibility that they are escaping from the scene of a crime. And by the same token, persons running could be trying to escape the scene of a crime. While much of the patrolman's investigations are due to complaints, some of it is nevertheless due to his own on the spot observations of the area. He should try to gather evidence on suspicious activity and perhaps later this can be pieced together with other information.

Interrogation:

If his suspicious are aroused enough, the officer should not hesitate to investigate at once and perhaps stop someone just for a few questions. It must always be remembered that this should be done with utmost tact and courtesy to the point of bending over backwards. Usually nothing will come of these questions. But it is up to the patrolman to be the gathering agent of raw material.

Records and Reports:

The officer's observations should be immediately recorded for presentation in his report. The true recounting of a scene based on an officer's observation is difficult enough without allowing memory to fog the events. Having a detailed report would be particularly helpful to the patrolman if he is called on to testify in court. Most juries tend to give the policeman's testimony heavier weight than other witnesses because he has been trained in this function. Therefore it is the cop's duty to do all that he can to present his case as fully, truthfully and fairly as possible.

Responding to a Crime Scene:

When an officer receives a call he should proceed to the scene quickly, quietly and safely. On his approach he should take note of the people in the area and especially those who arouse his suspicions. The first patrolman at the scene should search or guard the most likely route or hiding place of a criminal. He should wait for other officers to arrive before using his flashlight.

Upon approaching the location, the motor and headlights should be doused to camouflage their approach and they should coast up to within a few doors of the building. If addresses must be checked to find the scene, the spotlight should never be shone on the side of the street where the location is, but on the other side until a close enough number is found. After the place is surrounded, flashlights can be used but should be held away from the body so as not to serve as a bulls-eye for a gunman.

Protecting Evidence:

Signs of breaking and entering should be looked for and those exits carefully guarded. Great care should be taken to protect any evidence, such as fingerprints or footprints in the area, not only from themselves but from the public and other officers as well.

Searching a Building:

In advancing into a building, doors should be swung open quickly and the officer should stand aside and listen for a few moments before proceeding through to search the premises.

Reporting from the Scene:

A brief description of the scene and any clues uncovered initially should be radioed into headquarters so that it can be put over the air to all units so they will know what they should be looking for.

Helping the Injured:

Anyone who was injured at the scene should be taken care of. Perhaps it might be a good idea to send somebody along with them to the hospital to get their story along the way.

Witnesses:

One of the most important functions of the police patrol on the scene is to keep the public back and thus protect the evidence. The officer should get the addresses and identities of witnesses and people in the area and question them all. He should remember, however, that these people, like him, all color what they have seen with their own attitudes, prejudices and emotions. This should be taken into consideration when evaluating conflicting reports. Someone could be trying to avoid involvement; hide his or her own complicity in the crime, or protect himself from being caught in an embarrassing yet unrelated activity.

In searching the area, the policeman should leave no spot unchecked and no person unquestioned. Innocent citizens will usually cooperate if approached courteously. Many people during questioning will reveal important pieces of information, which they did not think were very meaningful. Questioning will alert citizens in the area of the crime and get them on the lookout for suspects.

Handling Fugitives:

Every fugitive should be regarded as dangerous and treated with utmost caution because no matter how trivial the offense, the threat of incarceration can ignite irrational behavior. If he is caught, he should be kept off balance and searched immediately. He should be spread-eagled against a wall or car with his feet as far from the support as possible to keep him at a maximum imbalance. The officer should stay out of reach until help arrives to cover him while he searches the suspect. He should never pass between the line of fire of the covering officer and the suspect. He should limit his conversation to crisp orders.

Sometimes he will have to ignore much verbal abuse and restrain himself from getting into a shouting match that can cloud his reasoning and slow his reactions. He should be especially cautious of the suspect's head and eye movements as these may indicate a plan for escape. As long as he is kept off balance, the officer has the upper hand. He should never turn his back on the criminal or search him from the front.

He should be careful not to use any more force than is necessary in subduing the suspect and keeping him at bay. An overzealous officer can result in a case being thrown out of court because of maltreatment.

In removing weapons and any other piece of evidence, stolen goods perhaps, from the suspect's body, they should be clearly marked, carefully handled and sent to the police laboratory as quickly as possible for analysis.

The suspect should be handcuffed and if there is more than one suspect, they should be properly handcuffed together. This is a dangerous period because many times the officer will let down his guard, forgetting that suspects are not immobilized, only restricted. Suspects can use their manacled arms or legs to inflict serious injury and perhaps escape.

Interrogating Suspects:

The officer should try to get a statement from the suspect only after telling him his rights. While the suspect will be at his most dangerous now because of the threat of jail, he is probably very depressed at the imminence of confinement and being caught in the act, so he may be in a position to admit his illegal acts. Later on when he has the opportunity to sort out his thoughts and discuss the situation with his defense attorney, he may change his story and claim innocence.

Although it can be very important to get a suspect's confession at the time of the crime, in recent years confessions have not proven to be totally conclusive in court. It must be remembered that the suspect's view or recollection of the events are just as clouded by his subconscious, as are the policemen and the witnesses. For this reason, too much reliance should not be placed on the procuring of a confession at the expense of ignoring the physical evidence.

The gathering and protection of evidence for special investigators arriving later is one of the most important functions of the cop at the scene of a crime. Unlike witnesses, criminals or policemen may change stories slightly over the course of time. However, evidence painstakingly uncovered and accurately analyzed will not change. As criminologists become more aware of the deficiencies of human memory and extenuating circumstances which a suspect may later claim, convictions will increasingly depend upon the evidence that has been gathered.

Once a confession has been procured, the police will sometimes relax and neglect a thorough investigation. Sometimes a criminal is set free because a confession is thrown out of court and there is a lack of supporting incriminating evidence.

Truly professional police forces will rely more heavily on the discovery and analysis of fingerprints, weapons, footprints, hair or blood samples, DNA, etc. Those are irrefutable pieces of evidence that cannot change their stories.

The police will also be charged with the duties of speaking with the victim and witnesses in more detail, getting a much fuller statement from them and consolidating this with the earlier reports.

Follow-up:

Part of the investigation, of course, includes a comparative analysis of similar unsolved crimes in the area. If it involves a case of stolen property, known "fences" should be watched closely for the type of goods missing. Second-hand stores should be checked to see if any of the missing merchandise has shown up. At the least this will alert the reputable shop-holders to be on the lookout for certain stolen goods.

Hunting for the Suspect:

If a suspect is in mind because of the evidence found or because of similarities with past crimes, the police will interview the suspect's acquaintances, keep an eye on his home, his known hangouts, and perhaps search his home and his belongings for clues to his intentions or whereabouts.

Depending on whether the police unit has detectives, apprehended suspects will be interrogated in preparation for a courtroom appearance. The police will also interview the victim and witnesses and organize evidence for presentation at the trial.

Unfortunately, many police in their zeal to solve a case will try to pin the crime on the first suspect, despite what could be construed as reliable evidence to the contrary. This not only violates his rights and scars him with the ordeal of a trial; it also lets the true guilty party go free. It is worthwhile to remember that the clearing of the innocent is as important as the conviction of the guilty.

Types of Calls:

In the course of carrying out his duties the patrol officer will have to respond to a variety of calls. Most of the calls will be routine and may become somewhat monotonous. But each of these calls is not routine for whoever called and the caller will be very sensitive to any indifference on the part of the responding officer.

There are always polite ways to end a conversation or put it along more constructive lines. Most people have very little contact with police and most contact is usually negative in the form of traffic tickets. For these reasons, the officer must go out of his way to leave a good impression.

It is a common function of police to give information to a lost person or inquiring child. He will be familiar with the streets after being in the area for a while but it would also be a good idea to keep a street map of the city and a calendar of upcoming events so he can direct any citizen who needs his help.

One of the more unpleasant duties of the patrolman is to deliver the word on the death of a relative. However uncomfortable he may be, it must be remembered that the person receiving the message feels a thousand times worse. He should keep this in mind and stay around long enough to give any assistance he can, such as calling a priest or relatives or neighbors so they can come over and offer their comfort.

Especially when answering a burglary call, the officer should proceed quietly and quickly to the scene. There is a good chance that the criminal may still be on the premises or at least in the area. On approaching the location he must look for suspicious characters and while there is no stereotype of a burglar, suspicious behavior can sometimes give a fugitive away.

The arriving officers should immediately try to surround the area and make sure there are no avenues of escape left open. People in the area should all be questioned and investigated as to the possibility of their complicity with the crime. The owner should be notified and brought to the scene and initial evaluation should be radioed to headquarters. Signs of forcible entry should be noted and guarded. Then the building should be carefully searched.

Answering a prowler call a patrolman would approach the scene in much the same manner. He should approach quietly, stop a few houses away, get out and walk around the area, staying out of the light. He should look for jimmy marks, broken windows, crates piled next to windows where someone could climb up and get in or peer in. The officer should try not to alarm people in the neighborhood but he should make it clear that police are keeping a close watch on things.

Only after the initial search should the patrolman then go to the complainant's address and record his statement, including descriptions, his story of the disturbance and anything else he wishes to offer.

After this, he should take a second look around. If nothing is found, there is little to do but reassure the people and the neighbors that they will keep an eye on the area.

When people are afraid to walk on the streets because of crime, this reflects the prevalence of robberies, drug dealings and muggings where the criminal uses bodily force or confronts the victim with a weapon. It is rare that a patrolman will stumble upon a robbery in progress because the crook usually chooses the time and a remote location.

The presence of patrol vehicles can help deter robberies. Besides making themselves seen, the officers should actively look for signs of robbers and conditions where it might happen. While on patrol, cars should double back occasionally, circle around and otherwise stagger the route of the patrol, never setting any patterns.

In the event of a robbery in a store or gas station, the victim can be very helpful in discovering fingerprints by pointing out what was touched by the crook. The victim can many times give a passable description of the robber. However, even if the criminal is caught red-handed and admits to the crime, physical evidence should not be ignored. The scene should be scrupulously searched and all evidence collected, marked and recorded for later presentation in court. It should not be forgotten that sometimes the caller is the crook.

Family Trouble:

One of the more common calls is when an officer is sent to calm down or mediate a family argument. Walking into a highly volatile situation exposes the officer to great danger and he should not take such a situation lightly.

Upon arrival, he should try to separate the quarreling parties and hear their stories. The astute officer, while keeping his emotions in check, can offer some observations or advice but he should not try to be a psychologist or a marriage counselor. He should not take sides in the dispute and he should not try to belittle one of the members in front of his family. Such an action could precipitate undue belligerency by one of the parties aimed at re-establishing a familial position of authority.

If a neighbor called in a complaint, they would not normally be brought into the conversation so as to avoid later neighborhood disagreements. However, the complainant should be advised that the matter has been attended to. The greatest harm that can happen is if the policeman appears apathetic or uncaring in this type of highly emotional situation.

Officers should try to avoid acting punitive but instead offer tact and understanding. Above all, he must avoid a hot and heavy verbal exchange with any of the parties. If resistance or excessive abuse is directed toward the officer, he has the power and the right to handcuff and take down to the station anyone who puts up such a fuss. This should be his only answer to violent tirades of abuse.

If he is requested to go to the scene of a fight or congregation of people, he should approach with siren blaring. Hopefully this will scare people into leaving the area. When he arrives, he should approach those who are still there with friendliness. Most people will respond to reason, especially if their raucous activity is not criminal in nature but merely disturbing the neighbors.

It is the officer's duty to protect peaceful, legal civil demonstrations, despite his personal feelings on the matter. He is able to take much more flak than others, and a few shouted taunts may just be overzealous adherence to the purpose of the demonstration.

The officer should ignore verbal abuse and shun physical confrontations. Singling out one individual or group can incite the rest of the crowd into graver acts of lawlessness. If a riot is touched off, headquarters should be notified immediately. Excessive force should not be rushed into view of a hostile but law-abiding crowd. This could instigate an added degree of rebelliousness. The policeman should serve as an agent for dispelling wild rumors and should deal with problems openly.

Depending on the situation, dispersal or containment are better tactics than violence when dealing with an unruly mob. A mob bent on destruction should be kept from spreading throughout the area. If the crowd is verbal and drawing strength from the impersonality of the group, they should be scattered.

If the riot is racial, members of the same minority group should be brought to the scene and made visible as soon as possible. Also responsible leaders of the community should be enlisted to talk to the crowd and try to quiet them down.

Vandalism:

It is safe to assume that most vandalism calls involve mischievous kids. The area should be combed for witnesses. Schools should be approached to question children about kids bragging of lawless escapades.

Drunks:

Drunks are the butt of humor in the press, TV and music. In real life, alcoholism is not funny. The chronic drunk should be treated as a sick person. If a drunk is difficult to handle, flattery and sympathy may bring them under control. Sometimes people who look drunk are medically ill and should be given medical assistance and evaluation.

Traffic Control:

Most departments have a specialized section to handle traffic control. Despite this, it is part of the patrolman's function to supervise traffic regulations. Road patrol duties can be summed up in three words: investigation, direction and enforcement. The officer must investigate accidents, be able to direct traffic and inquiring citizens, and exhibit a just but firm attitude to driving offenders.

At the scene of an accident, the officer's first task is to aid the injured and do what is necessary if further medical help is required. Next, he must control the gawkers who create congestion. Oncoming traffic should be routed safely around the accident.

After the injured receive help, the officer can investigate the accident. Witnesses and participants should be interviewed. The cause of the accident and the question of fault are to be determined. The vehicles involved and the roadway should be examined and the scene sketched out for inclusion in the accident report.

The officer should answer drivers' questions and be adept at manipulating traffic flow at rush hour or around roadway obstacles. The public must be convinced that laws are justly enforced and that breaking rules will result in a fine. The strength of deterrence rests on the credibility of lawful retribution.

Unfortunately, since contact between citizens and police is usually restricted to traffic tickets, this is the source of much antagonism between a community and its police force. Therefore, the officer should be courteous and not overly reproachful after stopping a minor traffic offender. However, the officer should not be submissive in pointing out the violation and giving instructions on the correct method. Courtesy does not mean a lessening of firmness. The proper demeanor is a clear and objective statement of the offense and a calm explanation to the offending citizen.

Educator

The police have a duty to prevent crime by advising people about how to avoid becoming a victim. Police may instruct individuals, block watch groups, school students, associations or any number of assemblages. This was the kind of thing I used to tell people about shoplifters and purse-snatchers who take advantage of women.

Always be alert. Half the battle is realizing that many criminals are just looking for you to give them an easy opportunity. Success for the criminal comes when he can cause you to become distracted in some manner. So be on guard. Take these precautions:

- When shopping, don't put your purse on the counter. Keep a hand over the opening of your purse while walking, standing or looking around.

- Be wary of strangers trying to engross you in conversation and distract you.

- Be careful not to display money in public places and don't give away which pocket your money and credit cards are in.

- Never put your purse on another seat in a restaurant. Keep it in your lap.

- Never put your purse on another seat in a theater. Some thieves specialize in seat tipping to cause your bag to slip into their hands.

- Take your purse into the dressing room if you try on clothes.

- If your purse is taken, it will probably be found near where it was taken. The thief will remove the valuable contents and get rid of it as quickly as possible so he won't get caught with "evidence."

- Know the contents of your purse. Keep a list at home of what you normally carry including credit card numbers and checkbook numbers, and the numbers to call to report them missing.

Enforcer of Minor Crimes

The patrol officer, influenced by the "broken windows" policy, reduces crime by citing, arresting, and reminding others of minor violations to maintain community peace and pride. "Broken windows" means that criminals regard an area with broken windows and damage as a target because people and authorities don't seem to care about their property. It signals that nobody is minding the store, so to speak.

George Kelling and William Sousa wrote an important report called "Do Police Matter: An Analysis of the Impact of New York City's Police Reforms" in December 2001. Their study showed that the sharp decline in crime in New York City during the 1990s resulted from police interventions and particularly the enforcement of laws against minor crimes, known as "broken windows" policing.

Additionally, case studies conducted in six New York City police precincts in 2000 showed that precinct commanders used computer technology to identify when specific crimes become serious and designed tactics to combat those problems. Overall, some 60,000 violent crimes were prevented from 1989 to 1998 because of the "broken windows" policing.

Are Police Safer in Cars or On Foot?

Patrol is the most basic yet the most abused operation in policing. Many police officers dislike it. It is not glamorous. It is held to be less rewarding than the criminal investigation work in which detectives specialize. Yet it is the most important of all the police functions.

It needs good men and women, good methods and good tactics to produce the results that can make both police and citizens aware and proud of the worth of this service and the men and women who perform it.

It can be monotonous, but it can also be very interesting and rewarding, depending on the caliber and motivation of the officer who is patrolling, and how he is patrolling, no matter where or when he is patrolling. It is most important for the officer himself to know *why* he is patrolling. Sometimes even his superiors and top administrators also need a reminder as to why he is on patrol!

The patrol officer is the first line of defense against crime. But he must also remember that a defender can frequently defend better by taking the initiative. On patrol he is in a position to take positive preventive steps, to take the offensive against crime by actively enlisting the help of good citizens, who thereby are helping themselves.

His role is not to be a passive observer, waiting for the sound of breaking glass or a blood-curdling scream. He is the direct bridge between the police department and the people. He can patrol actively instead of passively by constant daily contact with those citizens he is pledged to protect. But he needs to have the desire, as well as the opportunity. He has the opportunity to become the most knowledgeable public official about life in the neighborhood, and about the people themselves who live and work in the territory he patrols. He is in a position to render the greatest variety of continuous public service to the individuals and families that are in the area of his concern, his beat or his post.

If he lives up to the opportunities to which he is exposed, to become the most familiar and most respected of all public servants, he becomes an essential institution, the indispensable protector of life, property and personal freedom for the members of the community. The officer on patrol is an extension of the people themselves, accepting as his special vocation a job that all citizens were required to do in earlier, less complex societies.

All of this is what the police officer on patrol could and should be, but is not doing today! Why? One reason has to do with why people enter police work. One police recruit may focus on the victim and his career goal is to keep society's "dangerous classes" in check. They dislike diluting their crime fighting with minor social service and non-enforcement duties.

Another recruit might consider himself or herself like a troubleshooter or social agent who solves problems and may be well suited for a community-policing unit.

Another recruit sees his duty as enforcing laws and plays it "by the book." His goal may be to ascend to command rank rather than be a social worker or a vengeance-seeking vigilante.

Finally, another type may see himself as a watchman to maintain order. He may be more passive when it comes to juvenile misbehavior or traffic violations unless infractions lead to public disorder.

Today, at least in our major cities, police officers suffer verbal "slings and arrows" as well as the physical violence of missiles, knives and bullets as they seek to patrol neighborhoods and protect people they never get a chance to know, and can hardly be expected to understand or relate to. Human relations courses to correct this deficiency, and courses on customs and cultures of so-called minority groups, are only window-dressing at best. At worst such courses are a sham or an affront to the police officer who is sent out to apply these classroom principles without being given the kind of jurisdictional responsibility in which he has the time, public exposure and contacts to apply them.

Police patrol has come a long way in the 63 years that have passed since I was first sworn in as a New York City patrolman. Patrol today really doesn't serve, it doesn't prevent crime, and it is nothing but "fire-brigade" policing, trying to contain problems after they burst out and flare up. Patrol today is anything but the "unsystematic system" that used to create the impression that police were just around the corner ready to stop the criminal and deter him from crime.

Many officers on patrol today are often young inexperienced rookies or unpromotable oldsters serving out their time or being punished with that service for disciplinary problems. The kind of patrol provided by such personnel, often directed by uninspired leaders with an eye on retirement and the clock, all too often has been haphazard, particularly in the high crime areas of major cities, which demand the utmost in professional skill, alertness and judgment. The stress situations of modern urban life especially requires well-manned, well-led police patrol services and positive teamwork between citizens and officers to deter and reduce crime.

Crime in the United States generally has tended to rise with population growth and urban congestion. The keeping of national crime records didn't even begin until the 1930s. Methods of reporting have been tightened, which has had the tendency to discover previously unreported crimes, and perhaps to some degree exaggerate the steepness of the rising crime trend. But whatever sophisticated statistics may indicate about the reliability of past reports, crime in the 1960s and the 1970s continued to burgeon, with crime in the suburbs seemingly trying to catch up with the record of crime in the city.

The people of the United States have been falling behind in the battle against crime. We, the people and the police, have been losing the war. When patrol fails, the entire police department fails, and when this happens, cities are no longer cities, but unlivable jungles.

There are many possible answers to the current dilemma. One is certainly the cultivation of teamwork between police and citizens. Police need superior training, good equipment and more education. To encourage good men and women to stay on patrol where they are most needed, police departments everywhere must provide a "professional escalation ladder," which provides pay incentives and increased status and responsibility for the patrol officer, not just for the specialists and administrators.

Above all, police departments need more effective patrolling, and a better patrol system; one that turns on the police, one that rewards an officer for good preventive work rather than for punitive arrest and summons statistics. A good patrol system will keep the best people where they are needed most in providing preventive protection in the streets.

Today we live in an impersonal world, with a constantly shifting population and specialized and alienated policing. Police officers don't really know the people in their areas. In our cities today, as a general rule, we don't assign our officers to an area small enough to be conducive to the kind of familiarity that was one of the trademarks of the old-time beat cop. He was known, usually respected, invited to christenings, bar mitzvahs and weddings. He was looked up to, and looked for automatically when there was trouble.

Today our police are paired off and sealed off in a cocoon of glass and steel, constantly multiplying a self-feeding cynicism. They are given a territory that they really cannot be held accountable for. They wait for the crackling sharpness of the dispatcher's direction to another run, responding to a small percentage of the inhabitants of the territory; the troublemakers, the losers, the brawlers, the victims; and speeding ceaselessly by the great majority of the general population. Some have even come to fear patrol.

Sequestered in patrol cars, responding to coded radio calls, officers know little about the social norms or the occupants of any given community. Reciprocally, citizens become passive in relation to policing. They do not act as buffers between the police and potentially hostile environments. As a consequence, officers not only perceive the environment to be dangerous but they also begin to describe the inhabitants of the community they serve as hostile. Expecting to be hurt, they play it safe and display suspiciousness, aloofness, caution and authoritarianism in their interactions with those they are to protect.

This problem of fear became so strong in Boston that Police Commissioner Edmund MacNamara ordered them to wear nametags to personalize community relations. The Patrolmen's Association balked at wearing name tags, saying that "the tags would expose the men to easier identification and their families to possible harassment." They also reacted negatively to the redeployment of officers from two person cars to single officer foot beats stating that safety was their main concern.

The Flint Police Department carried out an experiment in 1979 to remove this kind of fear. They operated solely with motorized patrols until January 1979 when they created an experimental community policing patrol. It attempted to handle three problems: the absence of neighborhood services, the lack of citizen involvement in crime prevention and the depersonalization of interactions between officers and residents.

The program began with 22 foot patrol officers assigned to 14 experimental areas which included about 20% of the city's population. The foot patrol officers attempted to serve as catalysts in the formation of neighborhood associations, which articulated community expectations of the police and tried to bring problems to a resolution. The reduction of fear among police officers and the improvement of relationships were found.

The experiment was repeated in 1984 with 64 foot officers. The results again showed that foot patrol officers felt significantly safer than motorized officers. The foot officers felt more confident than motorized officers that citizens would be active in helping them if they were in trouble. Of course, those on foot knew their own community better. Therefore, they conducted far fewer pat-downs than motorized officers whereas motorized officers tended to pat-down individuals who were alien to them. Here are some of the actual results:

Officers Answering Complaints in Own Area
Perceptions of Safety

	Not safe	Somewhat safe	Very safe
Foot officer	1.6%	45.3%	53.1%
Motor officer	6%	74%	20%

Officers Helping Victims in Own Area
Perceptions of Safety

	Not safe	Somewhat safe	Very safe
Foot officer	0%	48.4%	51.6%
Motor officer	8%	68%	24%

Officers Walking Off Duty in Own Area
Perceptions of Safety

	Not safe	Somewhat safe	Very safe
Foot officer	1.6%	46.9%	51.6%
Motor officer	26%	56%	18%

Officers Perceptions of Residents Actively Willing to Aid Them
Perceptions of Residents Helping Officers in Trouble

	Not active	Somewhat active	Very active
Foot officer	9.4%	62.5%	28.1%
Motor officer	40%	60%	0%

The mass of citizens who never become involved in crime or its effects simply do not know our strange, reserved, distrusting, cynical police officer of today. General public protector he is not. Team-partner of an aroused and concerned neighborhood citizenry he is not. It is no wonder that so many of our citizens see him as a cold, unfeeling, uncaring symbol of remote government. He is seen as "The Man" instead of as "a man."

Arthur Niederhoffer studied police cynicism and described it in his book, *Behind the Shield: The Police in Urban Society.* He found that first a police officer develops "pseudo-cynicism" at the training school-recruit level which "barely conceals the idealism and commitment beneath the surface." Next comes "romantic cynicism" during the first five years of an officer's career. Third comes aggressive cynicism, notable at the ten-year mark where "resentment and hostility become obvious." By the end of a career, an officer accepts the flaws of the system with "resigned cynicism."

We must restore the good attributes of "old-time policing" without giving up the undeniable advantages that modern equipment has provided. The police officer needs to have the ability and the opportunity to know the people he is supposed to be serving. Yet even the knowledgeable and well-known police officer of the past had his limitations. To be a genuine public guardian of the future, the police officer must exceed the performance of the foot cop of old in achieving total rapport with citizens.

While not confined inside a car like today's motorized police, the cop of old was still more or less confined to protecting and patrolling the business streets of his "beat," the "glass posts." His "beat" technically might have called for a wider range beyond the thoroughfares and shopping streets, but under the lackluster unrealistic supervision to which he was subjected, it behooved him to remain pretty much in evidence on the main streets. So the residents on the side streets did not really get the total patrol service that the nominal beat schedules supposedly set forth.

Today we must bring to the job of police officer the opportunity, the territory and the trust deserving of a professional, so that he will be capable of rendering a new and different style of police protection. Police need to offer a new style of protection that is enhanced by the active concern and cooperation of the neighborhood residents, a style that allows for mutual involvement of the people and their police.

This new officer will need sophistication and professional know-how, fundamental techniques of patrol, and a general understanding of sociological and psychological principles.

There is a parallel between the military and police purposes of patrol in at least a partial sense. The patrol unit is intended to generate early warning of enemy (criminal) intentions, to deter the enemy (criminal) activity in a position to interfere with the successful pursuit of activity, or able to summon intercepting forces strong enough to bring it to an end.

Patrol for the purpose of obtaining information about hostile (criminal) activity is as old as mankind. It is limited by the ability of the patrol unit to discover and promptly report developments so that a timely response is generated. Technological development in communications and transportation has provided patrol units with superior capabilities.

The capacity of the patrol force of observation, communication, mobility and speedy response, all affect patrol strategy and effectiveness. In this day of electronics, it is more economical to "bug" the designated patrol area with equipment than to "man" it with roving patrols. A monitor from a fixed location, using visual and audible "bugs" could cover a patrol area and dispatch mobile police units to any crime scene in a matter of seconds.

The telephone already gave the entire community the opportunity to act as eyes and ears of the police. The cell phone has added that dimension to people driving down the street or in any location. Each has the opportunity to raise the "hue and cry" in the ancient way. However, except when community citizen patrols have been formally organized with 24-hour patrol, observing and reporting responsibilities have not been revived.

The weakness in the application of electronic patrol in place of professional patrol is the lack of human contact and personal involvement. The citizen is screened from contact with the crime victim or criminal and needs to do nothing to preserve his "non-involvement" in the misfortune of another. The professional police officer is screened by his electronic equipment and response-type patrol from human contact with his constituents.

The importance of community support for successful police performance, recognized over 175 years ago has never waned. It is an essential ingredient of successful policing and acts as a counterweight to patrol strategies keyed solely to efficiency that neglect contact between the police and the public.

The idea of personal service provides a further dimension to the patrol mission, which requires the presence of a visible patrol officer to deter criminals and aid citizens in appropriate ways.

Should Cops "Rat" on Other Cops?

The failure of police to become professional became apparent, wrote Sgt. Jeffrey Patterson of the Clearwater, Florida Police Department, in the 1970s. In a document written in the 1990s, entitled "Community Policing: Learning the Lessons of History," Patterson described the problems that have plagued community policing efforts.

A good example was urban riots such as the one in Detroit, which led to my appointment as Police Commissioner. Police, politicians, press and people complained about how the police were no longer close to those they were to serve and protect. They had lost the respect of everyone. They weren't seen as professional but they were seen as tough!

Arthur Niederhoffer co-edited a book called *The Ambivalent Force* in 1976 which included an article by Jerome Skolnick entitled "The Police and the Urban Ghetto." Skolnick told of a 1962 effort by a special unit of the San Francisco Police Department to "reduce crime by reducing despair, by acting as a social service agency to ameliorate some of the difficulties encountered by minority group persons." But the unit members weren't sure what methods to use and didn't know how to maintain a police identity while also winning the confidence of the minority group population. The unit became alienated from the police department and complaints of misconduct by brother officers caused the program to die.

The Police Chief of March 2003, journal of the International Association of Chiefs of Police, spotlighted specialized patrol vehicles, which gave "opportunities for positive interaction between the public and the police." They described electric bikes, scooters, multi-terrain vehicles, and mobile substations. I continue to believe that crime would be reduced by more contact between police and citizens.

Remember the local policeman, assigned to patrol traffic and to see that each child safely crossed to the other side of the street? We recall how he wore a smile, had pockets full of bubble gum, asked the children how they were doing and listened to those who reached out to him. Parents didn't worry about their children on those daily walks home. They rested assured that the community caretaker for the children at the school was on duty and was a family friend.

Those days are long gone. For the most part, city children no longer attend community schools; they are bussed outside their neighborhoods. Policemen like Jimmy have been replaced by crossing guards with little or no authority to intervene on a child's behalf should trouble arise. The following case, State v. Kinzy (Washington, 2000) is illustrative of just how much times have changed.

On a school night in March 1998, Seattle Police Officers Jennings and Kim were working as uniformed bicycle patrol officers in a high narcotics area. At 10 p.m., they saw the defendant, Loreal Kinzy, standing on a street corner. She appeared to be no more than 13 years old. Loreal was with two other girls and an older male. The officer recognized the male because of prior narcotics contacts which they had had with the individual.

They hailed the young girl but she put her head down and began walking away. She was then restrained by the officers and asked her name and age. When she told them she was 16, they did not believe her. She appeared nervous and kept sliding her hands into her coat. Ultimately she was patted down for weapons. Officer Jennings saw white flecks on her coat, which he suspected to be rock cocaine. She tested positive and she then admitted that she had more cocaine in her bra. She was charged with possession of cocaine.

In the past, parents might have been grateful to the officer for intervening on behalf of their child and removing her from a cocaine source. But when Loreal's parents sued the police department, Officer Jennings defended himself using the care-taking function and concern for her safety. The state argued that maintaining the safety of children did not outweigh the child's interest in freedom of association, expression and movement. Judge Talmadge wrote a dissenting opinion when the State won the case but generally the courts have been reluctant to give the community care-taking function a broad scope. This has not helped the police officer that tries to be helpful to errant youngsters.

The family of Loreal Kinzy tried to label Officer Jennings a bad cop but he wasn't. A distinction must be made between officers like Jennings and those who really are bad cops, and they are numerous.

On February 14, 1999, four white New York City policemen fired 41 shots at 22-year-old West Africa Guinean immigrant, Amadou Diallo, 19 of which killed him. Police officer Richard Murphy testified, "When I looked into the vestibule there was no doubt in my mind that he had a gun." Diallo had no gun. His wallet and beeper lay next to him. Diallo had no criminal record, was committing no crime, and had come home from his job selling hats, gloves and videotapes at a nearby market.

Three of the officers had been involved in shootings before, one of which was fatal. The four officers, members of the elite Street Crime Unit, were searching for a rape suspect when they encountered Diallo and approached him, in plain-clothes, with guns drawn. Autopsy reports showed that several of the bullets hit Mr. Diallo while he was on the ground.

All four officers said that it was dark; that Mr. Diallo ignored orders to halt for questioning and that he remained on his feet throughout the gunfire. They were tried, pleaded not guilty to charges of second degree murder and reckless endan-germent and were acquitted on all charges after their attorney told the court, "The officers acted properly."

When the acquittal was announced in May, 2000, it galvanized blacks and Latinos already frustrated by what they called overly aggressive and discrimina-tory police tactics, Mayor Rudolph Giuliani's lack of ties to minority leaders and his indifference to another unarmed black man (Patrick Dorismond) gunned down a month later by plainclothes officers. Giuliani refused to extend condo-lences to the deceased's family and illegally disclosed Dorismond's sealed juvenile records.

As disturbing as the Diallo and Dorismond cases are, an equally serious exam-ple of police brutality has received less publicity despite its possibly greater politi-cal significance. In 1999, an 18-year-old black man in Louisville, Kentucky was confronted by two white police officers, Horn and Kinkade. They said he was reportedly stealing a sport-utility vehicle and fired 22 times, piercing his body with ten bullets, six in his head. A criminal investigation cleared the policemen but there were nearly 60 misconduct claims filed against Louisville's police department between 1986 and 1999, amounting to $3.3 million in total dam-ages.

When Louisville Mayor Dave Armstrong was informed that officers Horn and Kinkade were to be given honors for valor at an annual police award banquet, he demanded answers from Police Chief Eugene Sherrard. Armstrong subsequently fired Sherrard, announcing publicly that a "culture" inside the department urgently needed to be changed. Hundreds of policemen dropped everything and drove to Jefferson Square to demand that the mayor resign instead. He did not.

In another case, a U.S. federal appeals court overturned the convictions of three white police officers in the Abner Louima torture case, finding insufficient evidence that they obstructed justice when they lied during an investigation of police brutality. Louima, a Haitian black man, was arrested outside a Brooklyn nightclub in 1997. He was handcuffed and taken to the station house. Officer Justin Volpe with a broken broomstick shoved into his rectum and mouth while his hands were handcuffed behind his back sodomized him. Louima suffered a torn bladder and intestine and required several surgeries to repair the damage. Volpe pleaded guilty and is serving 30 years. A jury found another officer guilty of pinning Louima down during the assault and four others were convicted of lying to authorities. A federal grand jury indictment handed up a 12-count indictment against five New York police officers and an $8.75 million settlement over police brutality was reached.

It is bad enough when police officers take advantage of their power over others to brutalize them. It is worse when they are encouraged or rewarded within their system. The code of silence (lying to protect fellow officers) occasionally becomes blatant. The code of silence was displayed in the movie about Frank Serpico, with the premise "a good cop never rats on another cop." When an officer breaks "the code" and gives incriminating evidence against another officer, he alienates himself from the "brotherhood." Other officers may not view his coming forward as a sign of integrity. While law enforcement is not the only profession with a powerful code of silence, it is probably the most prominent one.

Joseph D. McNamara wrote an article for the *Sunday Oakland Press* in Pontiac, Michigan on October 1, 1995, called "Code of silence must come to an end." He reported that the number of bad cops is rising. He detailed cases such as the following:

Some Los Angeles County Deputy Sheriffs got caught robbing and extorting money from drug dealers. A New Orleans policewoman murdered her partner and shop owners during a robbery she committed while she was on patrol. While performing drug stings in Atlanta and Washington, D.C., police were found to be stealing and taking bribes. Two white police officers framed a black man for murdering a white woman in Boston. New York State troopers falsified evidence that sent people to prison. Counterfeit evidence and evidence tampering forced a number of cases to be reopened in San Francisco and Philadelphia. A former police chief of Detroit, William Hart, was sent to prison for stealing drug-buy money. A Drug Enforcement agent was sent to jail for stealing laundered drug money.

He argued that the "essential task is to create within police agencies an incentive to break the code of silence among the rank and file and encourage cops to police themselves." He believes that mayors and police chiefs should not use the "few bad apples" defense to cover the fact that the code of silence is allowing bad cops to operate, and tell good cops they will be rewarded instead of punished if they expose bad cops.

When police misconduct surfaces, many administrators attempt to remove the department from public scorn by blaming the incident on "rogue cops." Their position is that "certain rotten apples" acted on their own and will be dealt with to the fullest extent of the law. This position denies the existence of a code of silence. The "rotten apple" strategy allows the agency to distance itself from the incident and the public is satisfied that the guilty officer is being prosecuted. But it behooves us to investigate how things came to be this way and why officers seem willing to endure personal loyalty that forces them into an unnatural relationship which the organization neither requires nor needs.

Police commanders can clean up their departments and cut down on the code of silence by developing career development programs, providing ethics training for all officers, encouraging officers to participate in community functions, ensuring that officers know lying will not be tolerated by administration, training in the importance of truthfulness, ensuring that management rights are not negotiated away, and holding supervisors accountable for the acts of their subordinates.

Television police dramas such as *NYPD Blue* depicts the code of silence and other police problems more realistically than earlier police series. The show's main figure is Detective Andy Sipowicz, a recovering alcoholic, who continually has to confront his racist attitudes. His broken marriage, loss of self-respect, and job-related stress are dealt with frequently. But unlike real life, the police solve most of their cases, can concentrate on a single case for days, and get the bad guys to talk.

Good police officers and administrators abound thankfully and many examples of their good works can be given but none can wipe out bad actions by others.

Why Are Cops So Macho?

Everyone has stress. What's new about that? Is police stress really any greater than the stress of other occupations? Is stress on police officers or on law enforcement agencies great enough that it could have contributed to the decline of policing? Let us examine the various types of stress.

The field of law enforcement used to have a great deal of job security. But many departments have recently downsized because of budget cuts. The move toward community policing has "flattened" some law enforcement agencies. More officers are losing their jobs, not being promoted, or living under the strain of fiscal uncertainty.

There is less socializing among officers and their spouses than in the past. This reduces "bonding" that used to be one of the strongest features of police service. Fixed shifts that allow officers to enjoy social life with their family have decreased socializing with their buddies.

There is more worry about contracting diseases such as AIDS, hepatitis B, tuberculosis, and various other diseases transmitted by contact with body fluids. Perhaps some fears are reduced with accurate information but close contact with diseased individuals is as great for police as for the medical profession but without the preparation of gloves, masks, and antiseptics.

There are stresses similar to other professions such as poor supervisors, lack of career opportunities, inadequate rewards, offensive policies, excessive paperwork, poor equipment, role conflict (especially for community-oriented police officers), a sense of uselessness, and irregular work schedules. But there are some stresses unlike other professions such as fear and danger, human suffering, the need for quick response, the seriousness and consequences of actions, distorted press accounts, unfavorable minority and majority attitudes, and the ineffectiveness of courts and corrections systems.

What are the effects of stress upon police officers? They become tough, cynical, suspicious, emotionally detached, suffer from health problems (heart attacks, ulcers, weight gain, alcoholism, etc.), have reduced morale and work efficiency, are absent more, show excessive aggressiveness, have marital and family problems (infidelity, divorce or domestic violence), and seek early retirement.

The effects of stress on an officer's family have been recognized for years. Arthur and Elaine Niederhoffer wrote about the many difficulties faced by spouses and children of police officers in *The Police Family: From Station House to Ranch House* in 1978.

In one study of 479 spouses of police officers, 77% reported experiencing unusually high amounts of stress from the officers' jobs. They cited the following: unsteady schedules disrupt family life, officer's need to feel in control at home and are unable or unwilling to express their feelings, spouses fear that the officer will be hurt or killed, officers' unduly high expectations of their children, the presence of a gun in the home, friends' discomfort because of the officer's weapon and 24-hour role as law enforcer, too much or too little discussion about work, the officer's paranoia or excessive vigilance and critical incidents including injury or death.

Police officers resent the implication that they have reactions to stress. Their philosophy of self-control and toughness makes it difficult for them to admit that they are stressed. It is even harder for those at the top do so.

Police administrators have stress from similar and additional sources. They suffer from distorted and negative media, adverse local government decisions, budgetary restrictions, jurisdictional isolation, lack of cooperation between agencies, perceived lack of respect, negativism and power plays by politicians, adversarial police unions, pressure groups, and people.

The cumulative effect of stress has changed policing in both good and bad ways that will be discussed. But the important thing is that those at the top must admit and recognize stress and its effects on the organization and the employees.

I thought it was interesting that when I took on the position of Detroit Police Commissioner, the press made such a point about my emphasis on rapport and love. Here is an example of one editorial in the *Detroit Free Press* called "Rapport Is the Key" shortly after I arrived.

> Johannes Spreen is an exceedingly vulnerable guy. Anyone in his position who talks about things like "rapport" and "love" as the key to police work in Detroit puts his neck on the block.
>
> It is so easy to characterize him as offering simplistic answers to complicated problems. But we really are talking about something just that basic.
>
> The black man who complains that the cops are giving him a hard time doesn't want some high-powered formula for having X number of policemen at such-and-such a spot at certain times. What he wants is for the policeman to look at him without curling a lip and to give him a citation or make an arrest without insulting his manhood.

Or to turn it around, the policeman who wants "community support" really wants to be able to make an arrest without having his every move questioned.

In a word, rapport.

What makes this "simplistic" under some circumstances is that this is easy for the commissioner to say, either in his office or on the green pea circuit, but his word is not the law. He has trouble getting the command down to the line officer. The boys on the beat find it a terrible temptation just to laugh when the "old man" starts talking about love again.

The test of Commissioner Spreen's stewardship will not be his goals—they are good, and he is painfully earnest about pursuing them—but whether he can make them the goals of men on the line.

Commissioner Spreen's scooter patrol has enormous potential for breaking down the hostility that exists. An arch-critic of the Police Department confessed to us a few days ago that the scooter patrol is working, that even his own attitudes are being softened up.

But the officer out on the street still holds the key. He has encountered hostility so long that he expects it, and he is not likely to make the first gesture. Yes, if he can, in small ways, begin to break through the wall of prejudice, then he can build the rapport the commissioner is talking about.

And the trouble—the reason so many police officers don't cooperate—is that it is so easy to mistake being considerate for being soft. We can't afford softness on the part of our police, but neither can we afford the kind of blind faith in overwhelming force that the Detroit Police Officers Association (union) so often seems to manifest.

Somewhere in between there is a better way. Commissioner Spreen calls it rapport, and that's as good a word as any.

My Problems With Detroit Cops

There is nothing like personal experience to show how complex the relationship is between law enforcement executives and officers. When I became the Detroit Police Commissioner, I walked into a hornet's nest from every direction, including the police force. The press had many articles about my handling of the force I inherited and I'll quote from some of them.

William Serrin, *Detroit Free Press* reporter, wrote an article called "Spreen: Six Months of Crises."

> When Detroit Police Commissioner Johannes F. Spreen took office in July, the 6-foot-5, 235-pounder was wished good luck. In his six months, Spreen has seen his 4,706-man department hit with three incidents in which police were accused of excess force against citizens. And at least 125 allegations of police misconduct, some of them substantiated, some not, lie on Spreen's desk from his Citizens Complaint Bureau, the quasi police review board.
>
> Police morale sags badly and some say the frustrated and embittered policemen are nearing open revolt. This is probably overstating the case, but many are convinced that an ill-timed clash of antagonisms on the part of both Negroes and police could bring an eruption of major violence at any time.
>
> Whatever action Negroes take is almost certain to bring repressive police response. And that response is certain to bring strident demands from Detroit's Negro leaders. The lines of combat are drawn.
>
> The man in the middle is Spreen who inherited the job only after Mayor Cavanagh had tried to recruit more than half a dozen other men.
>
> Heading a department that needs at least 1,000 more men, and which is noted for a weak top-level command structure, Spreen has hundreds of problems and little money.
>
> Spreen clearly is on the hot seat. Liberals, Negro politicians—some sincere, some intent on grabbing headlines—say he doesn't go far enough to curb the racism that, in some degree, certainly exists in the Detroit department.
>
> Police are angry with him for the 12 officers he has suspended so far. Even Spreen admits: "I've got a lot of policemen mad at me."
>
> The problems have dogged Spreen from the day he took office—July 22, 1968. The next day was the first anniversary of the beginning of the Detroit riot, and for the next five days, Spreen didn't even go home. He camped on a

cot in a conference room next to his third-floor office. During his first week in office, a Detroit policeman was shot and killed while answering a disturbance call. The man charged with the killing was a Negro.

In the following weeks, four other policemen were wounded in gun battles. Then came the incident when dissidents threw a lye-like material in the face of one policeman, marched against a political crowd and injured a dozen or so persons. Next was November 3 when off-duty policemen beat up on a group of Negro youths. State Sen. Coleman Young transformed the incident into a cause celebre.

According to Mayor Cavanagh, a "blue curtain" of police secrecy (Cavanagh meant the police union) hampered the investigation.

But some two weeks later, Spreen announced he was suspending nine policemen.

Last week, a Negro youth charged that a Detroit policeman in a bus incident clubbed him. In an almost united front, Detroit's Negro politicians demanded that Cavanagh personally condemn the police department for racism. They further demanded that the department give psychiatric tests to find racists on the force and called for a federal investigation, if necessary, into the youth's charges.

Next day a policeman was suspended and charged with the beating—the 13th suspension in Spreen's six months in office.

Spreen says unexpected incidents between police and Negroes have kept him from establishing the rapport he'd like to have with his men.

Negro councilman Robert Tindal said warily: "So far, I'll give Spreen 'A' for effort." Yet Tindal and others question why Spreen did not replace aides left over from the former commissioner's days.

Says Marks, "Those are the first guys he should have gotten rid of. He could have done it graciously. He simply should have put in his own people. Everybody would have understood."

A number of people are concerned, too, about Spreen's apparent inability or unwillingness to assert civilian control over the old-line inspectors.

Says one top observer: "There's always been a saying among cops in Detroit. 'We don't give a damn who's commissioner: We'll make him do things our way or we'll break him.'"

Tom Johnson, an official of the Civil Rights Commission who is knowledgeable concerning police, says: "When it gets down to actually who runs the Detroit Police Department, I'm afraid you have to say the D.P.O.A. (union) runs it…the decisions the commissioner and superintendent make are influenced by what the D.P.O.A. will do."

The police reforms that are needed in Detroit are obvious. First most observers say, "Detroit must increase the number of Negro officers and insure that the old-line commanders do not thwart this goal."

Another article in the *Detroit Free Press* during the same week expanded on that last statement.

The experts add that Spreen must take strong command action to insure that the director of police personnel goes along with Mayor Cavanagh's order that police hire a 4:1 ratio of Negroes over whites, until the number of black policemen approaches 40 percent (the same percent of the city's total population.)

Many, like Tindal, are convinced privately that Quaid is blocking extensive Negro recruiting. Says Marks: "Even the white bigots want black officers on the police force. The only people who don't are the white cops themselves."

PART II
Politicians

Too Many Law Enforcement Services

A basic flaw in most local police agencies is that we have too many of them with too few personnel to permit an effective and coordinated approach. Looking at the 18,000 state and local law enforcement agencies in the United States in 2000, they employed 1,019,496 full-time personnel according to the U.S. Department of Justice, Bureau of Justice Statistics.

As of June 2000, local police departments had 565,915 full-time employees including about 441,000 sworn personnel and sheriffs' offices had 293,823 full-time employees, including about 165,000 sworn personnel. These numbers do not include federal law enforcement agencies and personnel.

The average number of full-time sworn local police officers in cities of less than 2,500 was 3, in cities of less than 25,000 was 31, and cities of less than 100,000 was 126. This is an average of about one full-time sworn police officer for every 800 people. Local police departments cost about $80,600 per sworn officer and $179 per resident to operate for a year. Sheriff's offices cost about $107,900 per officer and $65 per resident for the year.

Edward J. Tully, Executive Director of the Major Cities Chiefs Association, wrote in January 2002,

> The consolidation of the more than 17,000 police agencies throughout the United States into a far fewer number of regional forces has been briefly discussed dating back to the 1950s.... Las Vegas and Jacksonville have successfully merged police and the office of sheriff into a metropolitan police force.... The United Kingdom began to consolidate its constabularies in the 1940s and have reduced the number to just 43 organizations. It is the reason that Canadians have instituted the concept of regional forces in several of the provinces.... It could be argued that in both Canada and the United Kingdom regionalization has achieved a higher degree of professionalism among police officers and better police services for the communities they serve. *National Executive Institute Associates Leadership Bulletin.*

Tully believes that the advantages to be gained by consolidation of services outweigh the fear of giving up local control, the uncertainty regarding employment status, and the cost of maintaining numerous small departments. The advantages he cites are that merging police and sheriffs offices limit costs and liabilities and police-related technology is so expensive that those unwilling to share lose that capability.

In this age of litigation, he points out that the actions of one poorly trained officer can result in liability to the governing body and consolidation would spread liability over a larger tax base. And finally he believes that consolidation would lead to better training, better service, and would raise the standards for law enforcement and thereby reduce crime. These ideas were similar to my own ideas in 1973, long before Tully wrote this.

In an article in May 2002 called "Terrorism: The Role of Local and State Police Agencies," he chided the Department of Transportation for having taken over airport security when it could have been turned over to local police agencies with appropriate funding. He described how several of the 9/11 terrorists had been stopped by police officers for minor traffic violations. If they had been properly trained in terrorism and had access to a comprehensive national data bank, the tragedy might not have occurred. He noted,

> The major flaw of some federal law enforcement agencies lies with their arrogance towards other federal, state, and local agencies. Unfortunately there is little justification for the attitude. One of the most serious ramifications of this mind-set is the failure of the federal law enforcement agent to treat the capabilities of other agencies with respect.

Similarly, federal agencies such as the F.B.I. often treat their own agents without enough respect. Perhaps the tragedy of 9/11 would have been prevented if F.B.I. headquarters had heeded a memo two months earlier from a Phoenix agent. He had been investigating a Lebanese student attending Embry-Riddle Aeronautical University in Prescott as well as other Middle Eastern men who were students there and at other Arizona flight schools at the time.

Special Agent Kenneth Williams wrote on July 10, 2001:

> The purpose of this communication is to advise the bureau headquarters and New York of the possibility of a coordinated effort by Osama bin Laden to send students to the United States to attend civil aviation universities and colleges...The individuals will be in a position in the future to conduct terror activity against civil aviation targets...

> Phoenix believes that the FBI should accumulate a listing of civil aviation universities/colleges around the country. FBI field offices with these types of schools in their area should establish appropriate liaison…. FBI Headquarters should discuss this matter with other elements of the U.S. intelligence community for any information that supports Phoenix's suspicions…

Just as the John F. Kennedy assassination revealed, the F.B.I. and C.I.A. failed to share intelligence that could have averted a tragedy. The C.I.A. knew about the terrorist connections of two men, Khalid al-Midhar and Nawaq Alhamzi, who in 2000 moved to San Diego, frequenting Muslim circles that had been infiltrated by the F.B.I.

Some said that if the C.I.A. had shared its information and if the F.B.I. had used its informers more aggressively, the presence of Midhar and Alhamzi in San Diego offered the best chance to unravel the September 11 plot. Alas, the two Saudis boarded American Airlines Flight 77, which crashed into the Pentagon.

Inadequate communication between agencies may have allowed the 9/11 tragedies to occur. The 850+ page congressional report released on July 24, 2003, showed the depth of the communication gap.

> The Joint Inquiry was told repeatedly that host agencies restrict access to information and limit databases detailees can query on security and policy grounds. Access to databases is also impaired…The Joint Inquiry was told repeatedly that a phenomenon known as the "Wall" significantly hampered the free flow of information between the intelligence and law-enforcement entities. The "Wall" is a series of restrictions between and within agencies constructed over sixty years that separate foreign from domestic activities, foreign intelligence from law enforcement operations, the F.B.I. from the C.I.A., communications intelligence from other types of intelligence, the Intelligence Community from other federal agencies, and national security information from other forms of evidence.

Former D.I.A. (Defense Intelligence Agency) Director Admiral Thomas Wilson explained that, "agencies must shed the belief that they own information which belongs to the government." The report made the point that there should be an "Intelligence Czar" to investigate connections between the F.B.I., C.I.A., D.I.A., I.N.S., F.A.A., N.S.A., D.O.J., State Department and probably other agencies.

Baltimore Police Commissioner Edward Norris made a compelling statement about how federal agencies should be communicating with local law enforcement agencies. He told the Joint Inquiry:

> I would like to know exactly what everyone else knows in my city. Whatever Federal agencies are working on in my city...I should know exactly what's happening. We know for a fact that terrorists are living in our cities. We all know they're here; we just don't know who they are, we being the urban police departments in this country.

The International Association of Chiefs of Police completed an 18-month study of sharing criminal justice information in a statewide system and issued their report in April 2000.

They reported that no statewide fully integrated information system exists. Information collection may start with an automated incident report from a field report. That information should be integrated into a Criminal Justice Information System where it can be accessed for arrest and booking, and could be linked to a digital mug shot and automatic fingerprint. It should allow the state to instantly send incident and fingerprint information to the F.B.I.'s UCR, NIBRS and AFIS systems. Subsequent information and activity would be entered and accessed by participating agencies such as the District Attorney, Courts, Corrections, Parole and Probation as an offender goes through the system.

Additionally, other regional state and federal systems, such as Department of Motor Vehicles, social services, intelligence systems or Homeland Security Departments should be integrated where appropriate. Different forms of wireless communication should be interoperable and allow the user to send and receive voice and digital information.

The I.A.C.P. visited five states and reported that while statewide information sharing can be started at the state, county or municipal level, the process and leadership vary widely. Often those who attempt it lack a clear planning process. The I.A.C.P. suggested a model: bring key stakeholders together, develop a governance structure, develop a decision-making process and goals, complete a needs assessment and an information system, assess costs and secure funding, then implement and maintain the system while educating the community about it. I had suggested this when I was sheriff of Oakland County.

I am happy to report that the President of I.A.C.P., Michael Robinson, Director of our Michigan State Police, provided strong leadership on justice system information integration in his state and the nation, and personally sought support for this daunting project from the U.S. Department of Justice. The president of I.A.C.P. in 2003, Joseph Samuels Jr., continued this theme in a March 2003 article in *The Police Chief.* His message was on "Radio Spectrum and Communications Interoperability" in which he discussed the need for instantaneous flow of information with communications systems common to all agencies.

Some of the problems with interoperability are clear when we see that in some places, police officers cannot speak directly to firefighters within their own municipality. Some departments use 500 MHz systems and others use 800 MHz systems and the F.C.C. uses 700 MHz. It costs millions to make major communications changes but Homeland Security Director Tom Ridge believes that the one thing we must resolve to handle rapid communication in the event of terrorist attacks is interoperability of communication between public safety agencies across the country.

I have long thought that merging county police departments would help to solve many problems including information sharing. Paul Gainor for the *Detroit News* wrote about my ideas on October 22, 1970. I quote from his article:

> Consolidation of Oakland County police departments has been urged by former Detroit Police Commissioner Johannes F. Spreen.
>
> Spreen, a consultant to the Oakland County prosecutor's office for six months this year, said the county's present law enforcement structure is not adequate to meet increasing demands.
>
> 'What we have today is not the answer,' Spreen said.
>
> 'Many young people are dissatisfied with things the way they are, and young policemen are dissatisfied and have a tremendous yearning for professionalism.'
>
> He said his suggestions are contained in a report he has given Prosecutor Thomas G. Plunkett.
>
> He called for a 'task force' of federal, state and local police to deal with rising crime rates and street confrontations.
>
> 'What we need is coordination, consolidation of efforts and a working toward eventual consolidation of police departments because no department can do it alone,' Spreen said.
>
> Also, Spreen said, a law enforcement and justice implementation team should be formed by police, the courts, prosecutors, youth and adults to 'get out there with the community and turn it on' to law enforcement. He said: 'What I propose doesn't take much money. We've got a start with very capable people who are now available.'

The great dollar impact of crime as well as the psychic impact creates a serious economic drain on all of us. It is my firm opinion, after years of study and practice of law enforcement that more effective crime control can and should be in the hands of the county sheriff. The future of law enforcement should be directed by a modern Shire-reeve, a tribune of the people, a sheriff who will champion people's rights with proper liaison between local agencies of county, state and national law enforcement agencies, touching all the bases: law enforcement, court service and corrections, and having the power of posse comitatus!

A modern sheriff is a people's representative, the only elected peace office in criminal justice. The modern sheriff can be the key and the hope for better law enforcement in the United States because he is a seasoned veteran who represents the people.

We have many federal law enforcement agencies, state police or state highway patrols, county police, sheriffs and their deputies, local police, and constables. Administratively this kind of setup is chaos, especially when there is no cohesive cooperation among these agencies.

What is the answer? I keep asking myself that question. In 1973, the National Advisory Commission on Goals and Standards recommended the elimination of very small police departments. In an issue of *Law Enforcement News,* Robert DeGrazia faulted the International Association of Chiefs of Police for being a social club that perpetuated the status quo in law enforcement. He further accused the I.A.C.P. of fearing consolidation.

My view is that the police system is archaic, fragmented, overlapping, confused and subject to bickering and jealousy over jurisdictional power. Big cities have the bigness problem, requiring a top-notch law enforcement administrator who can blend education, training, experience and managerial expertise. Long tenure is a problem because some administrators resist leaving. Short tenure is a problem because turnover at the top level cannot provide the sustained direction for programs and progress. Smallness isn't always good either because there is fragmentation of effort and jurisdictional difficulty.

State police are too distant and the "big brother" approach should not displace local police authorities. A national police is even more distant and abhorrent but could serve to support local police agencies. But investigative coordination at the countywide level through the sheriff's department may be a better alternative.

I was asked to give a talk to the first joint meeting between Michigan police chiefs and Michigan sheriffs on June 30, 1981. I told them that it was time for police and sheriffs to unite under the common task of meeting the challenge. I described how there are 103 police departments that encircle Detroit in the counties of Wayne, Oakland and Macomb. This immense fragmentation is a delight to the criminal mind and a frustration to the sincere police officer and police executive.

Most concerned police executives voluntarily cooperate in spite of the fragmentation. But there are islands of isolation where there should be bridges of understanding. This was a group all bound to the same common public trust of protection for the citizenry but divided by our lack of trust in each other. This lack of trust is a natural defense that we have developed in a time of change and financial cutbacks. We become jealous of our positions and we see other chiefs and sheriffs as possible threats. We covet information, rather than share information. But citizens see the police as one body of people, whether the uniform be brown or blue, cooperating to fight crime and prevent accidents. The public does not understand overlapping and fragmented policing service.

I do not believe in one large county police department. As one county executive said, "Is there a way that we can get three, four or five of our cities together and decide that maybe they don't need individual police and fire departments?" If we do not work together to free ourselves of the jurisdictional constraints that impede solving crimes, then do we not invite consolidation by another hand? We must not allow the erosion of trust between agencies to continue. We must share information and make the best use of our scarce manpower. We must complement each other's efforts.

Rather than a county police department, a shared-power concept is needed. We want our police to be close to the people they serve. Rapport between the police officer and the citizen is one of our chief defenses in curbing and preventing crime. But local police cannot do the whole ball game in today's sophisticated crime, brutal crime and terrorist crime.

I asked the Michigan Sheriff's Association to pursue the possibility of non-partisan elections for sheriffs in order to have a better chance to remove politics, factionalism and favoritism that could hinder professional ethics. I strongly feel that a sheriff's role is that of specialized, scientific assistance to the community, usurping no department's authority, and threatening no department's sovereignty. A sheriff's role is to provide policing where there is no policing, and to provide supportive assistance to each department within the county.

Toward this end, we instituted some programs that dealt specifically with cooperation between local police departments and the sheriff's department. We called one program S.H.A.R.E. (Scientific Homicide, Arson and Rape Effort.) I had the pleasure of deputizing a number of local police officers that completed 40 hours of training in homicide investigation, and we then had a team prepared to investigate any major homicide in a participating jurisdiction in Oakland County.

Through the Oakland Community College Police Academy, there is a program whereby data is compiled comprehensively on all arsons that occur in the county. Members of the Sheriff's Department Arson Unit, members of the

Southfield and Troy Police Departments and other agencies work together on major investigations and data sharing.

In the City of Southfield, the city and county have a contract whereby the city pays the salary of a staff of sheriff's detention officers, and the county pays the salaries of five sergeants for professional correction services provided to the city jail. We also provided prisoner transport for all departments within Oakland County to and from the county jail. This takes the burden off the police departments, freeing manpower for protective patrol in their own communities. Oakland County has shared resources for years in our N.E.T. (Narcotics Enforcement Team.)

These types of sharing concepts are only the beginning. Other services of a sheriff's department could and should provide local jurisdictions with specialized traffic programs, accident reconstruction, police driver training and other activities. Other supportive services could include crime lab services, a comprehensive juvenile delinquency prevention program, marine program, canine, and various types of specialized training and aviation services.

We must realize our common dilemma is one that requires immediate action to succeed. Pull together for progress or continue on our divisive paths and fall victim to the consolidation efforts of the efficiency experts as they attempt to force us to do that which we should do on our own: cooperate.

It's Hard to Be a Role Model

I was the Oakland County Sheriff, top cop in the state's second most populous county for 12 years. I was arrested and jailed for refusing to obey a court order to reinstate a sheriff's deputy whom I had fired the year before. You see, on March 11, 1976, I fired Detective Sergeant Keith Lester, 33, after he was charged with larceny by conversion for failing to turn over $200 a court gave him to pay a crime victim. He had pocketed $200 of a $750 restitution payment made by three youths in a larceny case in which they stole a trailer. The restitution was to be collected by Lester and given to the victims.

The charge against Lester was dismissed in February, however, and he sued for reinstatement of his job and back pay of $20,000. Judge Thorburn had dismissed the case because he said Lester should have been charged with embezzlement, not with larceny by conversion. Judge Beer granted the request to dismiss the case.

My view was that the charge against Lester had been improperly dismissed and that Lester was guilty. If I reinstated Lester, it would have lowered morale in the department. Besides that, Lester should have followed normal channels of appeal through the county employee appeal process to regain his job before he went to court.

The Oakland County Circuit Judge William Beer ordered me to be jailed indefinitely on contempt charges. He said I would stay in jail until I changed my mind and intended to lodge me in my own county in a local jail. Sheriff John O'Brien of Genesee County heard the news and sent his administrative assistant to suggest to Judge Beer that I be taken to the Genesee County jail in Flint, Michigan. I was grateful.

The judge's order came late after a day of legal haggling. I had appeared at a press conference with a toothbrush in my pocket, saying that I was ready to be locked up for my principles. I told the reporters, "I never thought I would see such a day when I myself would be charged with a crime. But I'd rather be right than free."

Judge Beer, 67, who had been a judge for 20 years, said that I had violated the separation of powers doctrine by refusing to obey his order. The judge told reporters, "Judges' orders, even if distasteful, must be obeyed."

I slept from about 1 a.m. to 4 a.m. and then decided that was no good way to spend time. So I got up and made some notes. I thought a lot about freedom while I was deprived of it. I'd never been in jail before where I couldn't get out. It kind of gives you a feeling of standing in the other guy's shoes. Being behind bars yourself, you maybe develop a little bit of understanding, a little bit of empathy. Here's what I wrote at 4:00 a.m. on May 7th, 1977.

> You do a lot of thinking in jail. You think about how long you may be in, how long you will stay behind bars. You realize the importance of freedom. You think of your loved ones, particularly when they are dependent upon you and you cannot be there to help.
>
> In my case, you think of why you are here. How can you as a sworn servant of the law possibly be in jail for violating that law? You wonder at the strange turn of events, this strange paradox that has led me down this particular road ending up behind bars. Have I really flouted the law of my country? I guess I have but that was never my intention. And I would not say I flouted, I respectfully differed.

My thoughts were on the protection and service of the people, under the law of our land as the chief peace officer of the county. Yet this had led me into a collision course where principle met principle head on, where I as an officer of the court had to object to its ministrations. I felt for the public good and the people I serve.

Supporters and well wishers sent some 30 telegrams and made 74 calls on my behalf while I was in jail. One telegram from my own department read, "We are proud of you. Hang in there. The department stands taller because of your action."

Another telegram sent by the administrator of the Criminal Justice Institute in Detroit said, "All professional law enforcement personnel salute you as an administrator and as a man." That was very gratifying. I put myself out there on a limb, and it could have been cut off.

Through the night, a 30-page appeal was delivered to a court clerk Saturday morning. By early afternoon, a three-judge panel of the state Court of Appeals freed me on personal bond. They met Saturday and granted my motion to postpone the Circuit Court order pending appeal after I served 23 ½ hours. The judges set no date for the appeal hearing.

I was 57 at the time but I did what I felt was important and necessary. I believed I had an obligation to law enforcement to try to upgrade the profession.

I felt that Keith Lester had violated a trust and to restore him would be wrong. We would have no confidence in him. The public would have no trust in him.

Part of my fervor against rehiring Lester came from previous orders from the appeals board and the courts forcing me to rehire four other deputies. I couldn't have that because after awhile, half the department would be less than satisfactory.

That was not the only time I felt the eye of the public upon me. I knew I must be a role model when I became the Detroit Police Commissioner. I had barely arrived at my new position when I had to quell a riot. Here is an extract from the newspaper article about it on August 3, 1968.

> Caught in the delicate balance between sufficient force and restraint, Police Commissioner Johannes Spreen gave a commendable performance of agility last Thursday morning during the 12th Street incident. Beginning about 12 p.m. with a group of youths breaking windows and setting two cars on fire, the activity slowly mushroomed until a tactical alert was ordered at 2:30 a.m.
>
> Commissioner Spreen, Superintendent John Nichols, Dept. Superintendent Charles Gentry and Sgt. Harold Liggett, aide to the commissioner, arrived on the scene at 2:45 a.m. By then there were seven fires—two suspected arsons and three started by Molotov cocktails.
>
> Bullhorn in hand, Spreen walked the uneasy streets urging residents to return to their homes. He remained upon the scene until the tactical alert ended at 6:43 a.m.
>
> In all, there were 16 arrests, mostly for breaking and entering and one for assault on a Tactical Mobile Unit officer. The officer, uninjured, managed to seize his assailant inflicting only a minor abrasion on his forehead.
>
> Peace returned with the dawn and the weary commissioner departed 12th Street where the riot seeds were planted last July. Spreen has probably not seen the last of 12th Street, a place where scattered minor incidents mark a return to normalcy. Let's hope that when necessary he can match the way he gently nipped last week's riot.

I had arrived in Detroit with no illusions about my position as a commissioner with a probable time limit of 17 months to get things turned around. The tension between the police and the black community was more serious than crime itself. Many things played a part in the problems of Detroit, but I recognized the need to develop a new role model for the police.

I decided on a "wild idea" which was principally to get the cop out of the car and back face to face with the public. I couldn't leave him on foot so I put him on a scooter.

My first crisis during the 100-day "honeymoon" came from a "cop watcher." He complained after disturbances at a George Wallace political rally. The police were caught in the middle. Within four days, the police were accused of terrifying and beating black teens as off-duty police and their wives and the teenagers held simultaneous dances in the same downtown building at Veteran's Hall. A Common Councilman's son was involved. The police command was chagrined when early reports of the trouble were stifled in the precinct. We had to sift statements for the truth. Police morale dipped to a new low when nine officers were suspended and crime figures started to rise after a brief lull.

Then there was a "Poor People's March" held the month before I came to town. The march was a strange case of provocative militancy, which was eventually "rewarded" by national publicity. Police patience wore thin after hours of commendable restraint. I was to resolve it. I struggled to demonstrate fair play and community concern by holding a recruiting drive aimed especially at blacks. It paid good dividends but just as I was about to announce a new budget, black politicos escalated a minor flap over a black teenager resisting arrest into a charge of "police brutality." This was coupled with a police officer murdered trying to stop a robbery.

I tried to decide what to do. I issued a document unique in police annals, an almost poetic dissertation on "love and crime." It called for a 100 day "love in" to unite the community and establish a moratorium on criticism of police until reforms could take effect.

Bob Talbert of the *Detroit Free Press* wrote on February 21, 1969, "Spreen's Love-In: Here's Why We Can't Afford Not to Join."

> Spreen's intention is to humanize the cop. He's taken some imaginative steps in this direction by demilitarizing the prowl car with his scooter-patrol Rangers, men with first names and faces that smile, who laugh with the man and woman on the street.
>
> "I was almost 49 years old and eligible to retire. I had a whole new life planned with my family. Is that bad? But policing was in trouble. My entire career I've had ideas about how it should be, how it could be. Detroit was the place to make policing a profession once again. To give it respect."
>
> On July 22 Spreen took office, inheriting a department's troubled past, and an immediate riot anniversary confrontation the next day. He slept at headquarters the first four days he was in office and found "you make friends quick in the fox holes."
>
> Right away the word got around that here was a positive man who had told the power structure, "if you want a negative commissioner you'd better hire someone else." Respect was the first thing people said about Spreen.

Along with the riot anniversary trouble on 12ᵗʰ Street, Spreen found he had verbal snipers and uncompromising critics who wanted action yesterday, not today or tomorrow.

The critics, the would-be cronies, the crowds, the public and the criminals haven't let up. In six months he's had 366 requests to speak or appear somewhere every meal and evening.

So Big John Spreen has now asked us for love.

He deserves this much at the very least. The man has some dramatic, innovative things to show us about what can happen when policing really works. But he didn't have them yesterday because he wasn't here yesterday. If we give him the time today to show us, he will give us a tomorrow that works.

During this "Love-In" period the best thing we can do is get to know our policemen. Invite them into your homes, your offices. Get to know them socially as people with first names and faces.

So what is this love that Johannes Spreen is talking about? He says:

"It's caring about your neighbor so you report an assault you witness upon him or his home. It's caring about your city so that you don't want to see it suffer. It's doing your thing well within the law and within the bounds of propriety. It's putting your personal desires and politics second to your concern for your city.

"It's helping to professionalize your police rather than policing your police. It's your never getting tired of asking what can we do to help. It's wanting to change things with calm, cool reason and considered judgments, not with destructive 'to hell with it' attitudes. It's having faith in people and police officers and the hope we can all live together in a better Detroit. It's making the policeman 'my man' not 'the man.'

"It's believing that a miracle can work in this city. The miracle of those silent, uncommitted citizens of our city speaking out and committing themselves. That's what love is. That's what it can be. That's what it must be."

Spreen has laid it on the line. You and I can't afford not to join his "Love-In."

The media helped get the idea out to Detroit that love could be the new basic ingredient of peace and could counteract violence. I was showing Detroit a role model of a man who talked about love and care. I thought that was important then but I really know it's important now.

Police and Politicians in Emergencies

As the September 11, 2001, attacks showed, the local police and local fire fighters will often be the first responders to any and all incidents. Many police and fire leaders were killed in the first hours of the attack and the emerging role model for the country came in the surprising form of outgoing New York City Mayor Rudolph Giuliani. His care and love for his city and its people became obvious to all, and his optimism displayed reassurance to all Americans.

The primary goal during a major terrorism event is public safety. The perception of danger can send a community into chaos. Local police leadership must act to allay fear and emotions. The confidence a chief exudes in responding to and controlling situations will affect how safe citizens feel and how they react.

I wrote in my first book about the police administration "POD" which includes:

- Planning

- Organizing

- Directing

The International Association of Chiefs of Police used this model to develop recommendations for law enforcement leaders to manage emergency and terrorist events. Their recommendations include the following.

Planning before an incident occurs is one of the main responsibilities of public safety leaders. This includes developing policies and procedures, training personnel, rehearsing possible events, acquiring equipment and communications, and establishing mutual aid agreements and multi-jurisdictional teams.

Police chiefs must plan how to gather and process intelligence with state and federal agencies as well as with local agencies. Chiefs should establish local meetings to build these relationships and network with local chiefs to share information. They can exchange home phone numbers, cell phone numbers, and 24-hour contact numbers. If they develop trust and open communication during quiet times, immediate contact with their counterparts will ensure that all agencies are on the same page during emergencies.

Chiefs must assign an officer or a unit to identify potential targets and to beef up security at those targets. A list of sites where large crowds assemble, transportation facilities, tourist spots, water sources, utilities and communication centers and municipal buildings must be checked and regularly updated. Public utilities such as electric, water, gas, waste treatment systems must be tested and alternative sources considered as contingencies. Fire departments must have contingency plans and back-up generator systems. Groceries, banks, and hospitals must have contingency plans and be helped to prepare for emergencies.

Law enforcement executives must release accurate and immediate information to the public through the media. An established route for releasing information will help the community respond correctly and alleviate panic. A strong, open media liaison should be established before an emergency occurs.

The public looks to law enforcement to respond and deal with emergencies. First responders play an important role in reducing further damage and injury. Chiefs must take the lead in identifying where and how to access food, shelter, aid, transportation, and civilian assistance. The chief must not become too directly involved in any one function but must establish an incident command system in which each person knows his role.

A visible police presence at vulnerable areas must be quickly established. Chiefs should make public statements about the readiness of the community to handle an incident while reminding the public that order and respect for others must prevail. Training and rehearsal reduce confusion in establishing communications between fire, police, EMS and other service providers. Recovery will depend upon economic and governmental resources and politicians must be encouraged to summon these.

It will be important to establish a command structure in which responders are controlled and achieve stabilization. Resources must be mobilized, communications must be effective and stress must be expected and minimized. The chance to save lives is highest during the first hour of an emergency, so first responders must coordinate their actions. Using the idea of unity of command, personnel must share objectives under the supervision of only one person.

Law enforcement personnel are highly visible during crises and must use correct procedures. A single spokesperson should be designated to deal with the media in order to correct rumors and give important information to the public. The agency head, however, must speak if the community is to be reassured. They should be candid and emphasize prior training and preparation, while also describing the agency responses. Chiefs should be available to the media to minimize paranoia and backlashes against people who are of the same race as the perpetrators. A chief's promise to investigate and prosecute acts of hate provides some reassurance and deters violence. The chief's presence and his manner are critical factors in community healing.

Chiefs must reduce workloads for exhausted personnel, recognize heroic actions by those at the scene, avoid turf issues, and act as role models in critical incident stress management. Key civic leaders (elected leaders, civic association heads, physicians and religious leaders) can help control rumors and be additional good role models. Strong relationships over a long period of time will pay off when they provide help during crises.

Finally, lessons learned in previous crises are the following: Agencies should avoid unnecessary delays in sensitively delivering death notifications and the release of victim remains to families. Mental health services should be made available for victims and responders. Agencies should establish a task force to be sure the victim needs are identified and addressed. Agencies should develop special screening and training for volunteers who work with terrorism victims and their families.

It is important for police administrators to discuss emergencies and plans for emergencies with political leaders before incidents occur. Regular meetings updating community leaders on the needs and vulnerabilities to disaster are highly recommended. This will ensure a more effective resolution of crises and will help politicians speak more carefully to media. There is nothing worse than a conflict of information and aims between police and politicos during a crisis.

The New York Miracle

Sometimes politicians can make a big difference in crime and I want to describe one such instance.

The New York Miracle was the remarkable drop (over 60%) in that city's crime during the 1990s during the term of Mayor Rudolf Giuliani.

Giuliani championed the "broken windows" theory of crime after he learned about it from William Bratton. Bratton, the first Police Commissioner appointed by Giuliani, used "broken windows" as the key to changes in the police department. He expanded that individuals who are prepared to commit serious crimes will also disregard laws regulating everyday interactions. For example, those prepared to commit serious crimes won't bother to pay their subway fare. Arrests for any little thing, including subway fare dodging, is sometimes called the "zero-tolerance" theory, clamping down on all crimes.

Here is a brief review of the different types of policing that Giuliani and Bratton considered. "Broken Windows" is policing of the "little things" and often includes intelligence-led policing. "Intelligence-led policing" is using technology and intelligence to target hotspots and likely offenders. "Zero-tolerance" is a total clampdown on all crime without individual police decisions or targeted arrests. Community policing is community and police partnerships to identify and solve problems. Problem-oriented policing includes intelligence-led and community policing to tackle specific problems.

Other things played a part in the New York Miracle. Prior to the implementation of "broken windows," New York's police force was increased by 10,000 officers (a 25% increase). (If I had been given another 1,000 officers, perhaps Detroit could have been saved.)

Another factor was a change in the drug market. Still another was a decline in the number of young males in New York City, the most crime-prone group. Bratton had already learned, as head of the New York City Transit Police, that fare dodgers often had outstanding warrants, and their arrests cut subway crime significantly.

Giuliani's "Quality of Life Initiatives" included arresting jaywalkers and speeding cab drivers, and rezoning sex shops. Additionally, statistics were used to note the highest level of disorder and crime called "hotspots." More crimes were committed in small areas, which could be reduced by police making random stops of around 15 minutes in these locations. The structure of the NYPD was decentralized to give precinct commanders flexibility to deploy officers to hotspots and relentlessly follow them as they shifted about.

The concentration on places ("hotspots") reduces crime and so does the concentration on certain individuals. It has been shown that a large proportion of crimes are committed by a small number of offenders. So police can aim to reduce the crime rate by getting repeat offenders off the streets.

A study in the United Kingdom aimed at known, suspected, and potential burglars found that by targeting these individuals for arrest, burglary rates fell by 62% in the target neighborhood. We had such a program in Oakland County, called SCAT (Sheriff's Criminal Annoyance Team) to get criminal repeaters.

In New York, they netted repeat offenders by policing softer crimes. But New York is different from many cities. There was a highly criminal population with many outstanding warrants on the streets and these people were caught when the police toughened up on minor offenses. Other cities do not have this same problem and the same strategy may not be as effective elsewhere.

What can other communities learn from the New York Miracle?

1. If criminals believe there is more likelihood of getting caught because of police presence, they are not as likely to engage in criminal activity.

2. If police patrol high crime hotspots, stopping randomly for around 15 minutes, their possible presence deters crime.

3. If a district has fewer troops and cannot arrest everyone for every crime, targeted arrests of repeat offenders will get many criminals out of circulation.

4. If communities do not expect that arrests will uncover offenders with outstanding warrants, targeted arrests of repeat offenders may be more beneficial than arresting new offenders for petty crimes.

5. If a district has a smaller police force, statistics can help target the areas of greatest criminal activity and these can be patrolled more frequently.

While Mayor Rudy Giuliani may not deserve all of the credit for the New York Miracle, it was his efforts to support and publicize it that brought down crime and made other cities pay attention. Political support and close relationships between politicians and police executives can help accomplish peace and order within communities.

Politicians, Jails and the
Mentally Ill

The actions of politicians have changed how we deal with the mentally ill. That has turned out to impact the correction system of criminal justice negatively. Following President Kennedy's signing of the 1963 Community Mental Health Centers Act, state hospitals discharged patients with major psychiatric illnesses into our communities.

Mental health centers were under-funded from the outset. Inadequate funding has caused existing centers to restrict their care to only the most seriously mentally ill. As the mentally ill flooded the streets, unwelcome by treatment centers and families, they swelled the number of homeless people and began to be arrested for disturbing the peace in one way or another.

The number of mentally ill people in U.S. jails and prisons grew to 283,000 in 1999 as the number of patients in state and county mental hospitals declined from 600,000 in 1950 to 72,000 in 1994. The movement toward community placement and the lack of success in self-medication and self-maintenance resulted in more police burden with the jailing of those who belonged in state hospitals.

The jail is operated by a unit of local government for the detention of unsentenced persons, no matter what the charge, and for sentenced misdemeanors where the punishment is one year or less. Most jails are county jails and are managed and operated by sheriffs in most of our 3,000 counties in the United States. Prisons are operated by the state for sentenced prisoners, generally for felonies punishable by over a year.

When English colonists came to the new world, "gaols, lockups and stockades" which doubled as warehouses, were used as places of confinement for those who broke the law. These structures also housed the insane, the poor, vagrants, orphans and sometimes the ill.

The jails in the United States eventually gave birth to the American innovation of the penitentiary at the state level. However, the local jails at the county level continue to pose major problems for the sheriff and administrators throughout the country. These problems encompass escapes, riots, dangerous contraband material being introduced into secured areas of the jail, physical and sexual assaults upon inmates by other inmates, suicides and even murders. In addition, many facilities are badly overcrowded and undermanned, which adds to the tension of the inmate population.

Most jails in the country are dangerously overcrowded these days. Jails are the intake point for the entire criminal justice system. Jails are the catchall for social and law enforcement problems. The jails feel the effect of community, police and court problems, but can do very little to control the population confined therein.

Jails contain a population more varied than any other type of correctional institution. Large numbers of people come into contact with detention facilities and can be greatly affected by the confinement experience. The basic goals of the jail are:

1.   the safekeeping and welfare of the prisoners,

2.   the protection of society,

3.   and the safety of jail personnel.

The goals must be achieved under the pressure of a diverse prisoner population including drunks, aggressive homosexuals, fearful first offenders, sophisticated criminals and increasing numbers of the mentally ill. The first offenders as well as the mentally ill are profoundly affected by their first experience in a jail and are often used and abused by other inmates.

When arrested, police may try to take a mentally ill patient to a hospital where he may or may not be admitted. But often he is taken to jail where he will be accepted, usually on a disorderly person charge. The impact of housing the mentally ill in a jail has been taxing to the sheriff and his jail officers, creating even more problems for the jails.

While many sheriffs' departments have adequate medical care, few jails are able to provide full-time professional care for mentally disturbed inmates. The courts haven't devised any system to speed up the process as it relates to the mentally ill; consequently those charged with felonies usually wait nine months to a year before they are processed through the court.

In 1980 in Oakland County, we saw a 46% increase in the persons requiring mental health intervention when compared against 1979. Over my 12 years as sheriff, I made numerous requests to the Oakland County Board of Commissioners to no avail. However relief came for staffing due to a class action suit commenced in 1978 and we were finally to get some new staff positions plus additional medical, psychological and psychiatric help.

The Los Angeles County jail, often referred to as the largest mental hospital in the United States, spends more than $16 million a year, including $5 million on psychotropic drugs alone, to treat 2,300 inmates with psychiatric illnesses, said Daniel Borenstein, M.D. in 2002. When released from jail, many psychiatric patients are dropped off at a bus stop with nothing more than a bus card or bus fare. In contrast to psychiatric facilities, jails are not required to have a discharge plan.

According to a U.S. Department of Justice July 1999 report, 16% of those in local jails reported either a mental condition or had stayed in a mental hospital. The U.S. Department of Health and Human Services reported in 1992 that at least one-third of the 600,000 homeless people in America are mentally ill. Twenty percent of inmates with psychiatric illness were homeless during the year before their incarceration.

Jails and prisons have become the mental health system of our day. Mentally ill inmates require far more jail and prison resources due to treatment and crisis intervention. Taxpayer dollars are paying for police officers to repeatedly arrest, transport and process mentally ill defendants.

As Ohio Supreme Court Justice Evelyn Stratton pointed out in a speech January 30, 2002, "In the 1800s, the greatest challenge to the mental health and criminal justice systems was to get the mentally ill out of jails and prisons and into appropriate treatment. Still today, we face the same problem."

President Kennedy's decision to reduce the cost of mental health centers was political. He intended to cut the welfare budget to benefit taxpayers and hoped to receive credit for lowering taxes which would turn into votes and re-election. He did not foresee that additional taxes would be needed by the criminal justice system to deal with the mentally ill. Nor did President Ronald Reagan who similarly axed welfare programs and left the police to deal with many more sick and homeless people, young and old.

It would behoove politicians to seek the advice of police executives when planning programs which will affect the peace and order of communities. However, this is unlikely to happen. Rather, it would behoove police executives to seek private meetings with politicians to suggest legislative remedies for issues which affect peace and order and the criminal justice system.

City Council Members Crave Publicity

When I was the Detroit Police Commissioner, it was very frustrating to deal with City Council members in Detroit. David Cooper, a reporter for the *Detroit Free Press* captured some of the problems in a 1969 article entitled "When the Council Turns on the Heat."

Appearing before Detroit's Common Council is one thing. Making a presentation to the council without being interrupted by some councilman is another. And getting most councilmen to listen and understand—well, that's sometimes as difficult as trying to squeeze ice cream.

Last Friday, for example, Police Commissioner Johannes Spreen, somewhat new to the city and the bumptiousness of its councilmen, took the witness stand in the council chambers on the 13th floor of the City-County Building to make a major pitch for increases and improvements to the city's Police Department.

Spreen had a prepared text. He said at the outset he hoped to get through it and then would be glad to answer any questions. He had barely begun, however, before he was interrupted by Councilman Billy Rogell. Soon, other councilmen were jumping into the middle of Spreen's careful presentation.

At one point during a later discussion, Rogell told the commissioner, "Don't give me that stuff!"

Rogell's comment sounded more like something the former Tiger player might have shouted at an umpire whose call he did not like than what a councilman would say to a commissioner.

At one point, Spreen sat silently for 10 minutes, a slightly puzzled look on his face, as councilmen began a discussion of their own not directly related to Spreen's presentation.

Councilman Mary Beck was chairing the meeting, and kept relatively quiet until a TV cameraman placed a microphone by her side. After that, she was off and running.

Earlier last week, police department officials went before councilmen on a minor request. They wanted authority to spend $900 for a consultant who would aid in the computer program portion of a study of police procedures being made by Wayne State University.

The proposal was comparatively simple, but most councilmen did not seem to understand it. One of their problems may have been that various councilmen kept interrupting police officials during the explanations. Councilmen held up the proposal for several days, approving it last Friday, unanimously.

Sometimes councilmen have valid reasons for their distress with city officials. When councilmen asked an official of the DSR, the city-owned bus line, why Mayor Cavanagh's picture is plastered on city buses in an election year, the straight-faced reply came back that it was just "promotion of the friendly DSR bus drivers."

Of the city's nine present councilmen, only three, Mel Ravitz, Nicholas Hood and Louis Miriani, seem to try most of the time to listen courteously to city officials and to try to understand what they are saying. Two others, Tony Wierzbicki and President Ed Carey, listen sometimes, but occasionally join their other colleagues in badgering and harassing officials before they can complete an explanation.

At times, one of the city's new councilmen, Robert Tindal, speaks so often and interrupts so frequently that he seems to be trying to become the council's male Mary Beck.

Last week Tindal led the council in passing a resolution that is designed to require all city departments to inform councilmen of plans, projects, or perhaps even thoughts, before they discuss them anyplace else in public. The thrust of the resolution was that councilmen want to hear it themselves before they read it in the papers. Even Congress does not set itself on such a lofty throne.

In an off-hand comment during one discussion last week, Miss Beck said, "We have to be both legislative and executive." When the Common Council learns to listen it may begin to fulfill its constitutional duty as a legislative body.

After Cooper's article, another reporter, Mark Beltaire, wrote an article called "Our Secret Council."

If Detroit's Common Council feels itself misunderstood, it can thank its own methods of operation for leading to that condition.

All the hastily assembled press conferences in the world cannot make up for the fact that the council operates in secret. The real budget decisions were not made as David Cooper of our city-county bureau has noted, in those 22 votes of 9-to-0 to override the mayor's veto.

They were made by the council in informal sessions, away from the glare of public attention. Surely, in those sessions, there were shadings of opinion that the people ought to know about. Some individual differences were brushed aside in the drive for a show of unity.

What do the council members think the people of Detroit hired them for? Are some of them being made pawns by the candidates for mayor among them?

Maybe Mayor Cavanagh's budget was, as some of the councilmen have suggested, merely an empty public relations show. But such a show, at least, is preferable to a council that refused to acknowledge that it should have some sort of relations with the public.

Still a third article on this subject was by John Griffith, for the *Detroit Free Press*. He quoted me saying, "We must solve the crime and community tensions now—today. And there is only one way, the right way. The choice is there: The tax collector or the mugger, the burglar, the robber or worse. If the police are shortchanged, so is every Detroiter."

I had outside advisors studying the department and they had concluded that we were short of at least 1,000 men. I was so upset about this that I nearly quit, but instead decided to stay on. Another newspaper story by the editor of the *Free Press* was called "Spreen's Decision to Stay Offers Council Reprieve." Here are a few of the comments in this article:

Louis Miriani was also conciliatory, though on Saturday he produced the inane quote of the week when he said, "I thought we had a pretty good Police Department for many, many years. I don't know what he has done with the Police Department since he's been here."

The answer is obvious if Miriani or the other council members would look. During his first months on the job Spreen conducted the most effective recruiting program in the department's history. He introduced the scooter patrol, despite a great deal of ridicule, and the scooters have proved popular and effective. He's gotten more men on the streets, is currently having an efficiency study made of the entire department, from his office on down.

And he's been on the chicken and peas circuit, drumming up popular support for a dispirited department, meanwhile fending off the long knives wielded by Common Council and trying to make do with one of the most undermanned forces in the country on a per capita basis.

I also had problems with micromanagement by City Councilmen. An example was in still another *Detroit Free Press* article around the same time entitled "Council Interferes with Spreen."

In a week marked by more than its quota of silliness, one of the silliest statements was Councilman Philip Van Antwerp's hint that if Police Commissioner Spreen doesn't promote more detectives Common Council may charge him with "malfeasance or misfeasance" in office.

What utter nonsense. It is precisely because of this sort of interference and restriction that the job of police commissioner in Detroit is so difficult. How does the council know that 70 percent of the detectives deserve promotion to sergeant?

The police commissioner ought to have some latitude over promotions, and he ought not to be given a quota by the Common Council or by the detectives association. To impose this kind of restriction on him is to undermine his ability to do his job.

If there is misfeasance in office, it may instead be in the council, which bartered away the commissioner's power to decide how many detectives deserve promotions.

Will Muller wrote an article for the *Detroit News* called "Jeers Switch to Cheers for the Scooter."

Of late, there have been indications that the former New Yorker's dogged persistence in the face of recurring crises and city hall back-stabbing is getting through, at least to the people, with his message: To win the fight against crime we must have the support of the community.

There is, of course, the recent *Detroit News* Poll which showed 55 percent of all Detroiters crediting Spreen's department with fair enforcement. That figure contrasted with the 15 percent who thought the City Council, the Pandora's box of Spreen's sufferings, was doing a good job…

Last week, six women, led by an officer of the National Association for the Advancement of Colored People, went to the department and offered their best help.

From the tenor of comment around the town's ordinary people, the same question is rising generally among those concerned with living and working and feeling secure in Detroit. In the absence of leadership elsewhere, many people are looking to Spreen.

Every count was against Johannes Spreen when he took the job. He was an outsider police officer, a former operations director in the New York department, certain to be resented within the Detroit department.

He came at the call of a mayor in deep political trouble who had been hunting for months for a police commissioner to take over a city deep in racial trouble. Detroit, like every other major city, has a long reputation for pillorying its police commissioners in every real or fancied crisis.

Spreen has been here less than one year. It's something for Detroiters to say in a public opinion poll, in street discussions and by their actions that they have more empathy for him than for their own councilmen.

This city is about to undergo the trial of an election. Who is police commissioner next year hangs on who is elected mayor, and none can predict the outcome. One thing is obvious. Only a foolish candidate will make Spreen the target of his campaign.

After the election and my departure, 600,000 people moved out of Detroit.

PART III
Pressure Groups

Unions Are Good and Bad!

Law enforcement in the big cities is not working well for many reasons. One reason is that the commissioner or chief at the top doesn't last long enough, even if we assume he is selected professionally. In the City of New York since 1898, commissioners have lasted on an average of just over two years, hardly time for proper planning, implementation and continuity of programs. In Detroit, from 1968 to 1978, there have been six chief executives averaging a little more than a year each.

Now I know that there can be a transitional chief. This was endorsed in an International Association of Chiefs of Police 1999 conference called "Police Leadership in the 21st Century." Conference participants recognized the acceptability of a transition chief or "short-tenure" executive to transform organizations. This transitional chief may become more prevalent, they said, and has a contribution to make. But I won't discuss transitional chiefs since I want to focus on a major reason for short tenures among top cops.

Today's chief must be all things to all people. A chief must be a leader, decision maker, confidante, politician, disciplinarian, therapist, mentor, administrator, taskmaster, spokesperson, community leader, educator, change agent, facilitator, partner, negotiator, role model, steward, student, parent figure, visionary, manager, minister and leadership developer? Of course chiefs can't be all these things and sometimes unions don't want him to be all these things.

Police unions have become very sophisticated. They have realized that they can influence politicians by using the no-confidence vote. It is now one of their most powerful tools and they use it to influence wage negotiations, decision-making, and removal of the police chief. However, unions and police benevolent associations have a few ideas that may help a chief to survive a dreaded no confidence vote.

Unions may threaten or actually take votes of no confidence against the police chief hoping that the negative publicity will embarrass local officials who appointed the chief, thus serving as leverage for higher wages. They use it to gain the attention of top management, to force the chief to listen, and to indicate their frustration. The no confidence vote is used after other attempts have failed or when the union believes the chief to be incompetent, disinterested or uncaring. It is used to request that the chief be removed from office. When a no-confidence vote occurs, the chief should determine immediately why it was taken.

In 1991, the F.B.I. National Executive Institute Associates issued the results of a five-year study of 35 such votes and reported that over half of the chiefs involved were removed from office. Thus such a vote is disruptive and demoralizing to a chief.

The usual reasons for such a vote is lack of leadership or lack of communication or lack of support for employees. There may be union doubts about the chief's integrity or his interest in supporting the needs of his employees. The union may want input into the decision-making process. They may perceive the chief as being aloof, dictatorial, unfair in promotions and discipline, and they may get back at the chief through the vote of no confidence.

What can a chief do to avoid the end of his tenure if such a vote occurs? The Southern States Police Benevolent Association published an opinion in "The Front Line" in their January-March 2003 web site about this. They said that how the chief reacts might determine whether he stays or leaves!

A chief must determine how many employees (union members) voted and how many were eligible to vote and how many expressed no confidence. Next he must determine if employees have been treated unfairly. He must examine whether he has been open to communication and whether he has shown support for his people. And he must learn the answers to these questions quickly. Then he must acknowledge and correct mistakes, promise to solve the problems cited, and take other appropriate action as needed. To deny mistakes or refuse to recognize problems will probably doom his administration.

If there is no validity for the vote of no confidence, the chief must clarify this immediately and set the record straight by actively defending his or her character. Although the tendency is for the chief to lash out at his accusers, he must react professionally and not take it personally or show emotions. Those chiefs who withdraw usually lose their jobs. Those who remain as visible as possible and walk through the department and the ranks show care for employees.

Of course, an inept union leader may take reckless steps for his/her own advancement and cannot control the militancy of a few members. The chief who speaks out on behalf of employees and cares what they want and how they feel may be able to overcome this. A chief must show good character through fairness, respect, dignity and compassion. He must consider what is right rather than who is right.

A chief must ensure that union leaders do not have to go through a complicated chain of command to communicate with him. There must be many avenues for communication with the union such as informal contacts, periodic scheduled meetings, and participation of the union in staff conferences. There can be labor-management retreats, committees, advisory groups, newsletters, suggestion programs, surveys, etc.

The chief must demonstrate trust and fairness. A chief must avoid playing favorites, give credit to others, treat employees with respect, give them the freedom they need to do their job, listen to different opinions, treat others as they want to be treated, value individual diversity, support and encourage people, and give fair performance feedback.

The chief should also develop good relations with community leaders, the mayor, the city manager, city council members, and others. These will be valuable if a no-confidence vote occurs. Chiefs should also treat employees like community-oriented police treat citizens, as customers who need respectful service.

Finally, to maintain a chief's tenure, he/she must show the employees that they care about them. This will avoid no confidence votes.

Can management and police organizations travel the same track in the interest of law enforcement services and protection? Frankly, I am pessimistic. Why? Because of the narrow viewpoints and positions of our many organizations representing law enforcement personnel.

However, let us remember some of the benefits of unions to their members. They protect employee's job security and guard against unfair labor practices. They obtain higher wages, fringe benefits and safer equipment. They enable employees to collectively exercise political strength through the bargaining process and endorse prospective elected officials. They provide legal assistance to members. Lastly, unions have the force to change the status quo and to redefine the police role.

Some police unions are simply resistant to departmental changes in procedures and policies. Sometimes they lack consideration of the ability to pay their higher wage demands. Sometimes they challenge administration through strikes and work slow-downs, which weaken the overall mission of peace and order in a community. Sometimes their political involvement unduly polarizes a community. And sometimes unions are the refuge and protection of lazy employees and those unwilling to upgrade themselves, insisting upon senior rather than the most qualified personnel for job assignments, and offering protection or legal assistance for those that are below professional standards.

At the bargaining table today are three interests: the union, with their various economic and non-economic demands; the political subdivision such as the city or county; and the law enforcement chief executive such as the chief or sheriff. As Police Commissioner in Detroit, I watched and felt the rise in power and influence of the unions.

The crippling malady afflicting police management today is that management cannot effectively achieve its legitimate goals. In some departments, management has allowed employees to virtually determine their own working conditions and the level of services to be delivered to the public. Other agencies have failed to understand the nature of collective bargaining and surrendered basic management rights. And then there are those departments that have attempted to fend off some of labor's illegitimate demands only to find themselves manacled and shackled by either the courts or labor arbitrators.

May I suggest some reasons why law enforcement administration simply does not work in its present form? You are not alone. You are not alone sitting in your seat of department leadership. The police unions are trying to sit there too. The important question is who really controls law enforcement today? Is it law enforcement management? I don't think so. Money talks. We in management don't have dues paying members but unions do.

Management must somehow strive to attain at least equal rights and be a proper balance wheel for working constructively with police unions for a better law enforcement function for all of us.

Obviously, police unions are only one of many union pressure groups. Others are groups that represent a section of the public on some particular issue that may become popular when people feel that the government doesn't listen to them. Prominent public pressure groups include trade unions such as the AFL-CIO. In 1984, the AFL-CIO had about 18 million members, about 20% of the workforce. But is has been weakened by allegations of racketeering, corruption and infiltration by organized crime. The weakness is also due to the fact that individual trade unions within the AFL-CIO have their own autonomy.

Professional organizations like the American Medical Association and the American Bar Association have always been involved in politics. The A.M.A. was unable to prevent Medicare but it has stopped a major expansion of it and the health reform program under Clinton was dropped. Potential election candidates who want major health reforms would not receive backing by the A.M.A. The A.B.A. has played an important role in the selection and nomination of judges and is a major interpreter of the law for politicians.

Pressure groups also include private corporations (General Motors, Microsoft, etc.) and other groups like the Ralph Nader Organization, Common Cause, and the National Rifle Association. The N.R.A. pushes presidential candidates to declare themselves on the individual's right to bear arms. In view of the Columbine massacre, the public would have been more receptive to gun control. However, the diluted approach to gun ownership and gun control by Al Gore and President George Bush suggests the potential clout of the N.R.A.

At state and federal government levels, such groups often hire lobbyists. At the local level, they use their presence, demonstrations, picketers, rallies, marches, flyers, and the media. They also use privileges and money and try to oblige law enforcement groups to favor them because they offer donations.

Some pressure groups are very professional and play by the rules. Some are grass roots groups and don't know the rules but try to learn the proper way to have their points heard once they have been given the correct information. Others use a variety of unsavory tactics to gain attention for their cause.

Overall, unions and pressure groups can be good and/or bad. A worthy law enforcement executive will search for the most valuable core of their accusations and pleas to improve himself and his department.

Chiefs and Unions

After I was released from jail, I gave an address to the National Sheriff's Convention on June 20, 1977. What I told them then is just as true now. I began my address rather humorously.

> I don't know if I should speak to you today as Sheriff of Oakland County, Michigan, or as Prisoner #7702276, Genesee County Jail. This has much to do with labor unions and I will tell you about that. But first let me say that law enforcement does not work in these United States. It probably never has and it probably never will. The big cities and their police chief executives are embattled just as are the suburbs and their myriad of small independent departments.
>
> As Police Commissioner in Detroit, I watched and felt the rise in power and influence of the unions as they grew smarter, more powerful, more militant and encroached upon some of the territorial imperatives of management. I was also saddened by the political polarization between the mayor and the unions, as gleefully reported in the Detroit press.
>
> Strikes in public employment are illegal, of course, but what does that really mean? Making a strike illegal doesn't mean that employees won't strike. So what happens if a law enforcement employer seeks to obtain an injunction against an admittedly unlawful strike? The Supreme Court has ruled that a *public* employer cannot obtain an injunction unless he proves exactly the same things needed to end a *private* employment strike; namely violence and irreparable harm. The result is that no one is able to get an injunction.
>
> What if a public employer really does decide to discharge his employees for striking? In one Michigan county, a sheriff has been restrained from disciplining anyone involved in a strike until it could be determined whether he had the lawful right to just *say* what action he intended to take.
>
> Judicial interference in labor matters has not been limited to strikes. Circuit courts in Michigan issued injunctions against two law enforcement agencies when one required a union steward to wear a police uniform while on duty and the other prevented a department from rotating the shifts of its sergeants to break up a "buddy" system that had resulted in sloppy supervision and bribe-taking.
>
> When arbitrators are used, very few issues, large or small, escape their keen eye for detail. I was amused when a union asked an arbitrator to rule on

whether washrooms in a county jail should be equipped with roll or napkin-type toilet paper. The arbitrator agreed with the sheriff that he should be allowed to determine which type of paper would be furnished. Once he made this decision, the arbitrator directed that the sheriff had a *contractual obligation to ensure* that the paper containers were *kept well filled*. Of course, the arbitrator's decision was based upon the labor contract's language governing "employee safety procedures."

Headlines in the press vividly display conflicts between the leaders of police unions and city mayors and councils. Who really controls law enforcement today? Is it law enforcement management? It's those who have money. We in management ain't got much and the union has! We in management don't have dues paying members but unions do. Members and money mean clout!

Speaking of union power brings me to my own incarceration. Let me tell you about the "Lester case" in Oakland County and how I became a number in the system. I went to jail to uphold the standards of the law enforcement profession. I have now spent 36 years in law enforcement. I have had an unblemished record, and yet I wound up in jail with a number, was searched, my property was removed, and I was incarcerated like a common criminal. Why? Because I refused to return a man to duty as a sergeant, a man whom we had dismissed on charges of thievery. A sergeant should guide, supervise, instruct and set an example for those under his charge.

The prosecutor appealed the dismissal of criminal charges. I did not return the man to duty. I was released within 24 hours on $50 personal bond by the Court of Appeals of the State of Michigan. I felt I had to go to jail in order to uphold the standards, ethics and honor of law enforcement.

In addition to the emotional trauma of going to jail, there was some family trauma. My wife was ill and confined to a wheelchair yet the judge denied my request to make arrangements for her care before commencing to serve my jail sentence and sent me directly to jail. Yet, I would do the same thing again. If I had to choose one or the other, I would rather be right than free.

I had inadequate representation on my behalf from the county attorneys. The Civil Counsel of the County admitted that they were not on a par with the experience and expertise of the sharp lawyer for the union who specializes in such matters. The union has almost unlimited funding to hire attorneys. We played with cap guns while the union was manning heavy artillery.

There is no doubt that we at the top must become better managers and be fair and square. Some cooperation between unions and management is most essential. We should be working together for each other in the people's interests.

But management needs rights too, and management needs professional help to allow us to respond to the unions on more equal terms. When I was the Sheriff of Oakland County, Michigan, in our department of 400 employees, only the sheriff, the under sheriff and the secretary were not union members! But when I needed union support for a crime and prevention patrol after the murder of seven kids, where was the union as we lost funds on a close vote by the city council?

To cure these problems, we must re-examine our roles as police administrators. We must believe in and retain our right to manage while recognizing our fundamental accountability to the public we serve. Let us be the managers of our enterprise and be the main man in that seat with our hands firmly on the throttle. We can certainly ride together with unions on the same track that leads to professional status of law enforcement, but we must control the train. That is what we were hired to do!

PART IV
Press

The Media Controls Public Opinion

Public opinion does not exist in America today. The media's opinion has shaped public opinion for the last several decades. Research by the Statistics Department in Washington, D.C. showed that at the end of the 1990s, the average American annually watches about 1,000 hours of network television, 400 hours of cable television, reads the newspaper for 150 hours and spends about 100 hours reading magazines.

The press is out to make a profit. Since the goal of the press is to sell their work, they often select news to entertain or titillate the senses rather than providing objective information to readers. Many media executives believe that conflict sells. If there is no conflict, there is no news. Often they attempt to create conflict where there is none. To do this, they may ask provocative questions to stir up emotions and make a more interesting story.

On a daily basis, reporters need material for stories and all they have to offer in return is media exposure and sometimes flattery. Those who seek attention may be happy with exposure and flattering or even non-flattering coverage, as long as they get the coverage and attention.

The cynical handling of some issues by the media and their preference to depict conflict make society's problems harder to solve than they would otherwise be. Often, the press gets in the way of society solving its own problems. In fact, their sensationalism often incorrectly exaggerates menaces, making citizens more fearful than they need to be.

Reporters often irresponsibly convince the public by their slanted articles that public officers cannot be trusted. They do this by claiming to look into issues and calling it "investigative reporting." These "investigative reports" often yield alarming results that must be disclosed by reporters because they are being hidden from the public. The media then proceeds to bring out the worst in every person in public life, driving serious candidates away and rewarding gutter-fights. Our "news" is the result of hundreds of judgment calls made by reporters and publishers instead of objective news reporting.

The November 2000 election was the first national election in which the Internet had a real impact. Overall, little research has been done on whether the Internet influences votes or whether political parties use it effectively. A recent presidential candidate appeared to use the Internet effectively at the outset but other parts of his campaign fell short.

It is clear, however, that campaign media consultants can make or break presidential candidates. It has been ascertained that television's interpretation of primary election results can influence voters as well as candidates.

Speeches are composed for the media and not for the audience. Short speeches attacking opponents have presented reporters with more sensational material. There is no doubt that the trend of attacking the opponent and negative campaigning suits the media and their wish to sell stories.

The press claims to have the license to criticize and defame but they shun the license to be responsible in serving the public. Rather than serving only the selfish side of the human spirit, they should serve the striving, inquiring side. They should help voters and readers sift through facts, information, and propaganda, equipping them to evaluate issues intelligently. The press could ask the readers what issues they want candidates to discuss instead of putting their own questions to candidates. When they plan to interview public officers, they could ask readers to submit questions for the interview instead of reporters creating questions themselves.

It is true that speeches, wars and violence must be reported but how it is presented determines whether the reader feels happy, angry, powerless, betrayed or involved with their institutions and political system. The focus of television is image, 30 second sound bite phrases, and only incidentally upon the definition of real issues.

Investigation, explanation and fair-mindedness should be the tools of reporters. If they are not, the media gets in the way of society solving its own problems. Irresponsible reporters contribute to the public's anger and distrust of their own public officials. The media's real goal should be to make what is important also interesting enough to learn about, understand, and use to improve life.

Sometimes members of the press recognize and write about these problems. I was delighted to read an article by Kathleen Park of *Tribune Media Services* in September, 2003. I will quote some of her salient points.

> It is indeed too soon to pass judgment on Iraq, but bad news is what compels and sells. Journalism's once heroic goal of seeking truth has been subjugated,

it seems, to the more commercially expedient mandate of "sexing up" the news.

With notable exceptions, the media increasingly are perceived as the world's pimp, selling cheap stories for slicker suits and flashier careers. In the absence of salable truths about lying politicians—the Woodward and Bernstein template that introduced careerism to newsrooms—reporters are increasingly willing to fictionalize.

Not all, of course. And honest mistakes admitted and corrected are something else. But too many of today's mistakes are of a different order. Too many reporters maliciously alter truth, from fabricating stories and sources (Jayson Blair) to selectively using partial quotes to purposely distort meaning.

Just last week, the *Washington Post* ran a correction on a story that took one of Vice President Dick Cheney's quotes so out of context that the impression presented was exactly the opposite of what Cheney obviously meant.

We so want bad news, apparently, that we'll avert our eyes from the good. But do we so want bad news that we'd rather fail in Iraq? That we're willing to compromise American lives? Not consciously, perhaps. Not the way France wants us to fail, as *New York Times* columnist Thomas Friedman described in that same paper. (Friedman's column was entitled, "French appear bent on becoming enemy.")

But our obsession with the downside, ignoring the progress that is being made in Iraq (too extensive to list here) in favor of items that suggest failure and quagmire borders on the pathological. Has our self-loathing come to this?

It is refreshing that a prominent reporter like Kathleen Parker would point out the problems of her own profession. Beneath her picture with this article was a quotation by her, "Apparently we take such glee in bad news that, lacking any, we'll make some up."

Detroit Riots Were Televised

One fateful night, July 23rd, 1967, baseball fans turned on their television to see the Detroit Tigers play the New York Yankees. As people tuned in, little did they know that three miles away from the Tiger Stadium, there was much unrest.

Willie Horton and Earl Wilson were black Detroit Tiger players, but generally black baseball players were not altogether welcome. There was a 30% unemployment rate for blacks in Detroit and it was not Lyndon Johnson's "Great Society."

As the game progressed, black clouds of smoke and fire appeared on the horizon. Buildings and homes began burning that night over a 25 square mile area. Baseball concession stands closed early. Airlines cancelled flights. The Mayor issued a curfew. Governor George Romney sent in federal troops and President Johnson sent in 5,000 troops. Riots raged on and on creating the largest negative image for a city ever televised.

For baseball fans, Detroit was winning but there was still the final game to be won. There were 15,000 empty seats because fans were afraid to come out. The home team lost in over time. So 1968 was going to be the chance for the Detroit Tigers to break back. Martin Luther King, Jr. and Robert Kennedy were assassinated in the spring of 1968, and many thought there would be fights again.

But it was the year of the Tigers. We set a home attendance record and Detroit was called Tigertown, U.S.A. It was between the St. Louis Cardinals and the Detroit Tigers. The Cardinals had led the series until the final game, which was played in St. Louis. The "City on Fire" shut down to watch the game. The stadium was filled to capacity. The Tigers finally won their first pennant since 1945. Mayor Cavanagh, using the V for Victory, said the win saved the city. When the Tigers won it, black and white fans gathered at the airport to greet the winners. It seemed like life was back to normal again. I knew better.

To this day, Detroit has never really recovered its image. Straight from the shoulder, the police can often be a major problem. Police officers that do not measure up to professionalism are police that are biased, bigoted or brutal, including police who do the wrong thing or do improper things. Yes, a few bad apples will infect the whole box, the media will see to that. And that hurts all other police officers nationwide.

Police officers today must combat the feelings or attitudes of cynicism. That's somewhat difficult because their duties expose them to the many bad experiences of conflict and hostility with people. Police feel a constant frustration with human imperfection. Police work mostly at night so who do they see? Who do they have to handle? Of course, it's the bums, the pimps, the prostitutes, the criminals, and the parasitic scum that abounds. Police must have more opportunities to meet and interact with some of the decent, caring people they protect.

The news media tend to cater and pay more curious attention to the abnormal than the normal. Just as curiosity killed the cat, such media philosophy helps to kill a city. Extremists get a disproportionate amount of attention in our media, and therefore create a false sense of alienation between those in the mainstream of life. The media often give people a chance to vent their spleen. Good news gets the back page because controversy is what sells.

Advertisements cater to basic appetites, as do news stories. Sexual material sells well and stories about sex sell well also. Big disturbances and loud noises catch the headlines, the camera and the microphones. People who are quiet, reflective, and weigh all the issues acting with moderation are toast in the papers.

The press should be fair, even-handed, giving equal space to all sides of issues. Consumers of media, you and I, have a special impact on a city's image and therefore a special responsibility. They and we should balance negatives with positives to keep a city's image in balance. I've often said, why can't the newspapers have one page, at least, called the "Good News Page." It may not sell papers but it can sell the city's favorable image. Improper or erroneous reporting can wreck a police department and it can wreck a city.

The Image of Law Enforcement

When I gave an address on Unions to the National Sheriffs Convention on June 20, 1972, another speaker to the group was Acting Director of the Federal Bureau Investigation, L. Patrick Gray. Gray, an ex-submarine commander during WWII, had been appointed the Acting Director on May 4, after J. Edgar Hoover's death on May 2, 1972. It was a great surprise because most people assumed that an F.B.I. insider would be chosen. However, President Richard Nixon apparently wanted one of his loyalists to assume command.

It later, of course, became known after the Watergate Affair that Nixon used the F.B.I. to reward his friends and punish his enemies. Gray had a law degree and was Assistant Attorney General at the time, and was quite surprised with his appointment to the F.B.I.

At that time, there were two requirements to enter the F.B.I. as a special agent. One had to have a law degree or an accounting degree. The other unwritten requirement was that only males needed to apply. Gray would change that by appointing the first two female special agents but that was later during the only year that he was with the F.B.I.

Unknown to me on June 17, only three days earlier, was that there had been a break-in at the office of the Democratic Headquarters in the Watergate building complex in Washington, D.C. When four men were detected and arrested in the break-in, the police had found much cash on their persons, papers suggesting that one worked for the C.I.A. and information showing that Howard Hunt was a C.R.E.E.P. insider. That was the Committee to Re-elect the President. The police were astonished when a lawyer appeared to defend the men, none of whom had called for a lawyer. The F.B.I. was immediately involved in the investigation, which would ultimately lead to the resignation of President Richard Nixon.

Before Gray withdrew from consideration as the permanent F.B.I. director, he testified about John Dean's visits as a White House representative to ask him to squelch the investigation. The idealistic Gray opened the door for Senator Sam Ervin to interrogate Dean and discover the great cover-up. In fact, a C.B.S. report in 1972, an *Atlantic Monthly* article in 1998 and a CNN report in 2001 have pointed the finger at L. Patrick Gray as the "Deep Throat" source to *Wash-*

ington Post reporter Robert Woodward who printed information from an unknown source that led to Richard Nixon.

But all I knew on the day that Gray gave his address to the same group of sheriffs I addressed was that he was a fresh face in the F.B.I. They had, in 1972, 59 F.B.I. field offices and offered their services to state, county and local law enforcement agencies. Their Washington, D.C. headquarters offered a laboratory, identification and computerized information. Their facility at Quantico offered training of police officers, which I had already sampled and found extremely valuable.

Gray had held this office for less than six weeks. Knowing law enforcement agencies, I knew that as an outsider, he would have a tough row to hoe. When law enforcement agencies got outsiders such as myself, a New York cop being appointed a Police Commissioner to Detroit, one doesn't get much help from the agency officials who feel overlooked. I listened carefully to Gray's seven-minute talk and I was extremely impressed at his grasp of law enforcement, considering that he had never been part of it.

He began by offering F.B.I. help to the 3,100 sheriffs offices in the United States. He was opposed to a national police force and described the local peace officer as the nation's principal defense against crime. He described the importance of the image and the performance of municipal, county and state law enforcement "peace officers."

He described all those who demean and attack the police, from the media to libertarians to legal advocates and judges to prosecutors. He maintained that laws rather than men rule us. However, the image of law is inseparable from the image of the men charged with its enforcement.

He said that disrespect for law and order begins with the denigration of the policeman. To the young impressionable males, law is not a document or a dusty volume in a legal library. Law is the man in the blue uniform. A youngster's respect for the law centers on his admiration for that man. He charged the audience with ensuring that their employees maintain a record of solid performance, giving citizens full respect for civil liberties, strict conformity with due process, maintaining standards of integrity and service, and being impervious to scandal, corruption, and privilege.

He added that it was not enough to be right but we must look right as well. He reminded us that local deputies and policemen are in a fishbowl. Everyone watches everyone. He urged sheriffs and deputies to conduct tours and talks especially with kids, to work with the community and civic organizations, and take part in social and cultural affairs. He explained that this could forge bonds of understanding and open communication. He believed that this would motivate people to turn to rather than against law enforcement officers in times of trouble and crises.

He described the many instances of citizens turning their backs on officers, due to lethargy, indifference, callous refusal to aid and other reasons. He impressed the audience by saying that in this republic, every citizen has an obligation to not only uphold the law himself but to support it with all reasonable means at his command.

He concluded with some powerful thoughts. "When we show disrespect to law officers, we lose some portion of our own self-respect in the process for they are only representing us. When a cop dies, a little of you dies, too!"

He said that although a citizen's responsibility to law runs deep, ours runs far deeper indeed. When an attitude of indifference or disrespect persists, we must determine why. As heads of sheriffs' offices, we must patrol our own ranks more carefully than we patrol our towns, cities and counties. We have a responsibility to keep our ears tuned not only to plaudits but also to complaints of critics. We have a duty, he said, to serve all citizens with equal civility, openness and respect.

I have thought about his words many times over the years. I believe that he may be one of the unsung heroes in the war against corruption in government. I know that when Nixon's presidential tapes were heard, White House special assistant John Ehrlichman answered presidential counsel John Dean's question about what they should do about acting F.B.I. Director L. Patrick Gray with these words: "I think we ought to let him hang there, let him twist slowly, slowly in the wind." It is true that Gray's testimony not only led to the demise of the Nixon administration but to his own career in Washington, D.C. as well. Most recently, I heard that Gray is with a Connecticut firm of attorneys.

Image and Police Integrity

The soaring economy of the 1990s caused the number of law enforcement applications to dwindle. Thus administrators across the country had to pick the best from a small pool of poor applicants. Therefore, many departments hired officers they never would have hired ten or twenty years ago. In fact, some hired the kind of people we used to put in jail according to a friend of mine.

The recent firing of Dallas police chief Terrell Bolton is an example of what has been happening in many departments. Bolton came into office under a cloud. The Dallas Police Department had a policy of selecting the highest test-scoring minorities to fulfill quotas. It was rumored that Bolton was selected for promotion at least once when he had scored below other white officers, a move which always hurts police morale. Later he became the first black police chief in Dallas.

His four years were marked by the highest crime rate among large cities for each of his years. He has been called "slow to react to bad news and too defensive when he has." He was accused of hiring problematic officers and was involved in lawsuits by demoted commanders. In addition, there was a scandal in which officers reportedly planted fake drugs on innocent people. When the mayor announced Bolton's termination, about 50 protesters marched to City Hall August 29, 2003, to demand that the mayor and city manager resign. Since then he has sued the City of Dallas for wrongful termination.

Did Bolton's leadership serve as a role model to his men? Only they can say whether his character inspired them to do well or badly. Character does not change easily. As time goes by, the bad character of a leader affects staff through the usual cynicism and frustration, which soon becomes misconduct and corruption.

Neal Trautman has defined stages in the growth of organizational corruption.

1. First officers perceive that there is administrative indifference toward integrity.

2. Next is the perception that obvious ethical problems are ignored as leaders intentionally look the other way or even cover up misconduct.

3. The third stage is the growth of fear as officers perceive that to survive as a leader, one must abide by the unwritten rules of internal politics. This stage may be accompanied by bitterness, officers rationalizing unethical acts in conversations with each other, and the hopeless conclusion that "everyone else is doing it."

4. The fourth phase is the survival of the fittest as good employees fear the corrupt dishonest ones, and the code of silence prevails as administrators hide misconduct rather than try to resolve it.

Deep within us, we assess the behavior of individuals, agencies, institutions, and societies by the measuring stick of integrity. Law enforcement must have integrity if it is to be acceptable to the people.

Events in the 1990s such as I have described rocked public trust in the integrity of law enforcement agencies. This motivated the National Institute of Justice (NIJ) and the Office of Community Oriented Policing Services (COPS) to create a symposium to examine the issue of integrity.

The National Symposium on Police Integrity was held in July 1996 in Washington, D.C. The 200 participants included police chiefs, sheriffs, police researchers, police officers, professional disciplines, community leaders and members of federal agencies. It attracted international interest and was attended by representatives from the Netherlands, Belarus, Nicaragua, Haiti, El Salvador, Honduras, Sweden and the United Kingdom.

During the 2½ days, there was a clear understanding of the tragic consequences in the profession as well as the country if integrity was seriously eroded. Brainstorming of "healthy" organizations with little or no problem around the issues of integrity took place in small and large group sessions. The attendees felt they could learn at least as much from examining what is right in police organizations as what is wrong in them.

The conclusions were set out in a report submitted to the Attorney General by Joseph E. Brann, then Director of COPS and Jeremy Travis, Director of N.I.J. The recommendations were categorized into short-term and long-term recommendations. Many of them are so important that I have summarized them.

Police leaders were urged to infuse integrity and ethics into curriculums and build it into those in charge of recruits, in-service, and training programs. They also suggested using model media relations programs that have focused successfully on police integrity. Then they suggested a survey of participants to learn which actions were instituted and how they worked out.

Long-term recommendations included assessing entry-level screening and hiring processes to see if they reliably predict ethical behavior, and determine the best predictors. They wanted to do research on whether officers with more education maintain a better track record of professional performance. They wanted to explore alternatives to methods of receiving and responding to citizen complaints about officer performance to avoid adversarial environments.

I was glad to see that they wanted to delve deeper into the issue by these recommendations:

- Identify the kind of training that keeps recruits from becoming cynical and critical of their work early in their careers.

- Research officers with integrity violations and explore why they were not deterred.

- Track incoming recruits and officers during their careers to determine why some commit integrity violations while others don't.

They also made recommendations about how supervisors are being oriented, guided, educated and held accountable for maintaining integrity among officers.

Their recommendations even touched on unions, politicians and the press. They suggested conducting research on trends over the past five years in arbitration rulings for and against police agencies in matters of integrity. Interestingly, they suggested training for politicians about police integrity and police culture so they may help chiefs set realistic expectations and change programs. They recommended a survey of successful marketing strategies used by police agencies with good integrity records and how they could be applied to other agencies.

I've always thought that chiefs and supervisors must be models of integrity for their employees. This must start with attention to hiring. Psychological and background examinations must be connected with proven predictors of good performance and bad performance to select the best applicants. Once hired, carefully selected people must do Academy and field training and ethics training should be included along with other subjects.

I believe that promotions, discipline and terminations must be made fairly, consistently, and objectively, based on performance instead of "good old boy" favoritism. There must be an open policy requiring officers to report each other's serious misconduct and violations of policy standards. It must be clear that the organization will protect those who report misconduct.

Furthermore, I believe that the highest level of administration must visibly support these policies. We must be willing to have ourselves and our agencies open for inspection whenever there is any question about corruption.

Should We Be a Hero or a Headline?

A new friend, Police Chief Steve Krull of the City of Livermore, California sent me one of his published articles, which beautifully illustrates many of the points I have been making in this book. It is even more potent as I already see the images of public service heroism eroding with recent headlines of improper police behavior.

Chief Krull gave me permission to use all or part of his article in this book and I have chosen to use almost all of it. Thank you for these excellent words and thoughts, Chief Krull!

We all remember that on September 11, 2001, the most horrendous act of terrorism in the United States occurred. Images of public safety workers and others performing incredible acts of bravery and heroism were etched, for a while, in our mind's eye.

Entering fatally damaged structures, helping thousands of people, carrying on while covered with dust and grime and fighting back tears and unspoken emotions, heroes emerged. The evil done to America shook us while the images of police officers, public safety workers, civilians and others, working together, made all of America proud. With the nation reeling from this attack, many people would stop police officers and firemen just to say thank you. Soon after, the cooperative efforts of law enforcement and the intelligence community identified those responsible such as Osama bin Laden.

Before September 11th, we were making headlines but often for the wrong reasons. Our headlines were about police scandals and alleged acts of brutality. You could barely go for more than a day without reports about officers engaged in biased policing, better known as "racial profiling" as dubbed by the media. Instead of being seen as heroes, we were seen as headlines, bad headlines alleging acts of corruption, misbehavior and criminal acts. When someone in policing becomes a headline it tarnishes all of us, not just that person. We all get painted with the same broad brush whether it is as a hero or a headline.

We must recognize what the public expects of us. We have the ability to take away one's constitutional rights, personal liberties and even employ lethal force. Our communities trust us to wield this authority wisely, fairly and without bias. They want to know that those they entrust with their very safety and well-being, those they give the awesome authority to preserve the basic rights and freedoms that are America, are equal to the challenge. It is the people of our profession who are to be held accountable.

In policing, we have been, and always will be, engaged in a people business. People call for help, people answer that call, people dispatch others, and those people dispatched arrive to help those people who originally called. It is a circle of trust that cannot be broken.

Technology is a benefit and has enhanced our ability to do our jobs. We should seek out, develop and utilize current technology to our best advantage. But, without the best people, technology simply does not matter. So it begins and ends with our people. They make us what we are, and what we can become: a hero or a headline.

Only the best candidates should be given the opportunity to become part of this special group. This means a selection process that will yield only the most qualified, but also the most acclimated to our profession. Stringent background investigations with zero tolerance for those persons who display traits and characteristics that are incompatible with our profession and would lessen the trust from the communities we serve. In California, as in many other states, validated psychological and medical testing is required.

I would also strongly encourage the use of a polygraph for entry-level candidates. There have been some instances where background investigations would not have uncovered what would be disqualifying information. It came to light by use of the polygraph.

Once we have a candidate that passes such a background check, they are sent off to a basic academy for initial training. Given the selection process, we should already have someone with a strong foundation of core values such as integrity, honesty and others. The basic academy should build on, and strengthen these core values, exposing candidates to what ethical challenges they may face in their careers. But, in my view, it is really after the academy where we need to focus on keeping our officers viewed as heroes, not headlines.

Policing is one of the most complex and challenging professions in the world. With all of the ethical dilemmas and potential erosions of integrity, there is but one answer and that is good leadership. Every executive, manager, supervisor and field training officer, no matter what size department or how it is organized, has the responsibility of setting the example and then holding everyone accountable. Doing the right thing, for the right reasons, at the right time and with the right people should be emphasized and modeled at all levels.

Too many times officers see one of their co-workers going down the wrong path and they do nothing to stop it. Just as officers should be focused on preventing crime and disorder, they should also be focused on preventing another co-worker from getting into trouble. Every member of the policing community must have the ethical courage to confront their co-worker and save them from themselves. Such an action also makes one a hero. By doing what is described, you very possibly could be saving a career life and the reputation of the profession.

We must give recognition to the good work and performance that the vast majority of our people do the vast majority of the time. None of us do enough to recognize and publicly acknowledge the continual high quality of work done by our people. As supervisors, managers and executives, we need to do this better. There is no better way to prevent poor performance or behavior than to publicly support and acknowledge good conduct and exemplary performance.

Even if we do all the things described, there will be police officers that get themselves into trouble. When that occurs, everyone has an obligation to take the right steps to deal with the event in a professional and expedient manner. The right steps may even include a line level officer, who becoming aware of the misbehavior, and having done their best to prevent such an occurrence, now must move it to the supervisory level.

The responsibility to handle such events exists at all levels. There can be absolutely no covering of the facts. If mistakes are made, we must deal with them appropriately. This includes protecting the rights of all persons involved, including the accused employee. It is important to remember that an allegation of misconduct does not connote wrongdoing. It should, however, prompt a fair and impartial investigation to determine the facts of the event. But we must also keep in mind that we have an equal responsibility to the police officer that is the subject of the investigation to get all of the facts.

Once the investigation is concluded and facts determined, an appropriate resolution must be reached. If the complaint is sustained and the allegations prove to be true, we have an obligation to hold the employee accountable. This accountability must be fair and meet the circumstances. Honest mistakes or unintentional violations of policy should be handled as such. Intentional acts of a more serious nature should also be resolved at a level equal to the facts of the event. Fair and compassionate resolution of events underscore that this process is not personal but simply a matter of business.

We need to provide the tools and create the environment that best helps and supports our profession, and most importantly, the people in it, to be successful. Well-written, current policies that are updated regularly give our employees direction and guidance to follow. Expectations of performance, behavior and conduct should also be clear and understood. But no expectation, policy or procedure is worth anything unless they are followed or met.

It is the obligation of all employees to follow policies and procedures and be willing to be held accountable. Supervisors and managers have the additional obligation to carry out this accountability when necessary. A policy that is not followed or is not enforced is no policy at all. As stated before, that accountability must be fair, consistent, and appropriate for the circumstance and professionally administered.

Having said that, policing is among the most complex professions in the world. I believe the answer to retaining heroes is simple enough. Hire the best people, train them well, support and foster integrity, demand ethical courage and establish high but reasonable expectations and standards at all levels of the organization. Then, hold our people accountable at all levels of the organization as well.

Those involved in policing should be role models to our communities and to each other, no matter what position or title we hold. When mistakes are made and we fail to keep one of our own from self-destructing, we acknowledge the mistake. We take corrective or, if appropriate, punitive steps when necessary and do so in a professional manner.

We need to tell the public that when wrongful acts are alleged and factually proven, they are unacceptable to the rest of us and will not be tolerated or condoned. We also need to remind the public that these acts are very few compared to the profession as a whole.

I am proud to be a part of the policing community and one member of a distinguished profession. Most of all we need to remind our people, our most valuable resource, that it is they who have the challenge to be a hero or the choice to be a headline.

Personally, I like being in the company of heroes.

PART V
People

What Makes People Commit Crime?

I think all good cops know what makes people commit crime. In fact, I guess we've all known it for hundreds and even thousands of years.

Some 2,500 years ago, Plato wrote about good and bad behavior. He described Socrates discussing that subject with others in Athens, Greece. He explained that people make decisions based on seeking pleasure and avoiding pain. But he said that some people are overcome by pleasure or the quest for pleasure and do what they know is wrong. To make better decisions and be more virtuous, they must learn more, he said in *Protagoras* and *Meno*.

Plato and Socrates thought that virtue could be learned and better decisions could be made. All those who do therapy with criminals share that philosophy today or they wouldn't be trying to help. The key to living a good and virtuous life, according to Socrates was to "Know thyself."

John Stuart Mill described hedonism in such a way that criminals could easily be called hedonists. He said that hedonism was "the theory that a person always acts in such a way as to seek pleasure and avoid pain." He and his mentor, Jeremy Bentham, reasoned that when making choices about behavior, one should try to obtain the greater good for the greater number of people.

The words and philosophy of the Persian, Omar Khayyam (who died in 1123) were translated by Edward Fitzgerald. Khayyam understood that some people regret their actions, apologize, and wish they could take it all back but it is too late once the act is done.

> "The moving finger writes; and having writ,
> Moves on: nor all your piety nor wit
> Shall lure it back to cancel half a line,
> Nor all your tears wash out a word of it."

William Shakespeare undoubtedly understood why people choose to do criminal acts. He knew that that if we were honest within, we would also be honest with others. In *Hamlet,* he wrote,

> "This above all: To thine ownself be true,
> And it must follow, as the night the day,
> Thou canst not then be false to any man."

Thomas Huxley, like Socrates, thought that learning could overcome crime. "The only medicine for suffering, crime and all the other woes of mankind, is wisdom." But, of course, some people may learn and copy the bad behavior of parents, friends, and role models. If they had new and better models and people to imitate, would they likely make better choices in their behavior?

Sigmund Freud discussed the pleasure principle, and described how people are born with the goal: "I want what I want when I want it!" He called that selfish part of us the "Id." As parents teach children the difference between right and wrong, a child accumulates "learnings" that lead to the development of a conscience. Freud called those "learnings" from parents the "superego." Once children become adults, they make choices about whether to follow their "id" or their "superego." Freud called these choices the "ego," saying that individuals develop "ego strength" to resist temptations.

Moral theoreticians came up with stages that children go through in the development of a conscience. Lawrence Kohlberg and Jane Loevinger and others say that in the beginning, all children are hedonists. Next they learn to do things to avoid punishment and pain from parents and adults, and instead do things that bring love and pleasure. As they begin to interact with other older children, they learn to share, give and take, and follow rules so they can maintain friendships and avoid embarrassment and penalties. Next comes a realization that law and order in their community, school, workplace and society requires that everyone follow rules or they will run into trouble with authorities. Most youth finally accept the social contract to "do unto others as you would have them do unto you."

Eventually, some people may choose to violate the social contract and suffer the consequences for what they think is a higher good. Americans who risked their lives to fight for independence from the British during the American Revolution would fall into this category.

Those who have reached at least the rule-following stage of moral development are less likely to return to their earlier selfish outlook. Those who, for a variety of reasons, do not develop a conscience, tend to be repeat offenders or recidivists. Police have long known that a large proportion of crimes are committed by a small number of criminals. If they are taken out of circulation, the crime rate is reduced.

There are other influences beside morals that persuade people to make criminal choices. Lawrence Cohen and Marcus Felson believe that crime occurs depending on conditions where people are, such as the likelihood of getting caught in a particular area. For example, Ronald Clarke and Derek Cornish (in the textbook *Criminology*) suggest that a would-be burglar examines a house thusly. If the house has a less visible entryway, if there are few who could see the criminal, if there is no visible alarm, if there is no barking dog, he is more likely to run the risk. He therefore chooses to avoid pain and gain pleasure/profit.

Criminals began early to choose how they would spend time, who they would spend it with, what they would do for pleasure, what they would use as excuses, who they would choose as victims, and what they would tolerate in the way of pain or punishment. There are no experts today who think, like some in the days of old, that criminals are born. They are made as F.B.I. profiler John Douglas believes and expresses in books such as *The Anatomy of a Motive, Crime Classification Manual*, and his newest, *Anyone You Want Me to Be*.

In his book *The Anatomy of a Motive*, he writes:

> With the exception of a very few truly insane (and generally delusional) individuals, these men choose to do what they do…. They are not compelled. They choose to do it because it makes them feel good.

Stanton Samenow, Ph.D., author of *Inside the Criminal Mind* and *The Criminal Personality* believes the same thing. He wrote a book to warn parents about children's early behavior called *Before It's Too Late*. Samenow and his colleague Yochelson found in interviewing criminals that they had several "criminal patterns of thinking."

John Douglas found some of the same thinking patterns also. In *The Anatomy of a Motive*, he wrote:

> Most violent offenders, we found after some study, had two factors warring within them. One was a feeling of superiority, grandiosity: social mores were not meant for them; they were too smart or too clever to have to start at the bottom and work their way up, or to live by the normal rules that govern a relationship. The other, equally strong feeling was of inadequacy, of not being able to measure up, of knowing they were losers no matter what they did.

Despite those feelings, Douglas emphasized how criminals make choices about what they are going to do. Just as the criminal considers his options, so do potential victims. People choose where they will go and when (dark is the criminal's friend), whether there are risks in the environment, how much they care to protect their living space such as their house or car, and how prepared they are physically (strength, self-defense training, etc.) and with safety items (pepper spray, cell phone, weapon, siren, etc.) to encounter a criminal.

There are more things that influence a criminal as he decides whether to risk getting caught for the pleasure and profit he might gain. If the community looks disorderly, he may suspect that residents are less vigilant and police presence is less responsive.

James Q. Wilson and George Kelling introduced this "broken window" theory in 1982. Their article suggested that attention must be paid to the little things. For example, a broken window that is not repaired tells the residents and the criminals that nobody is in charge. As residents go inside for fear of an uncontrolled neighborhood, nobody is present to see the criminals. Social order and civility are restored when residents and police care for the neighborhood.

The professional movement in policing brought in components that are still used today: preventive patrol, rapid response and follow-up criminal investigation. In between service calls, patrol officers were to randomly cruise neighborhoods making their presence felt to reassure citizens and deter criminals. Researchers found that for 90% of reported crimes, victims take between 5 and 10 minutes to call the police. With 9-1-1, police response to the scene of a crime is fast enough to sometimes catch the criminal but certainly to assist victims. When the criminal is not caught, officers gather evidence and pursue leads to close and clear cases.

Unfortunately, for crimes like auto theft, the clearance rate is extremely low, an average of 14%, similar to the clearance rate for burglary which is around 13%. However, the clearance rate for larceny is about 20% and about 24% for robbery nationwide. Fortunately, the highest clearance rate is for homicide at about 65% in the United States.

What Do People Care About?

Which do people feel more positive about: the direction of our country or the direction of their own community? Recent surveys show that they feel better about their own communities. That is probably because we can make more of a difference in our own community than we can in our nation. The League of Women Voters conducted a poll in April 1999 and found that less than half of those polled (46%) believe our country is going in the right direction but 72% believe that their own community is going in the right direction.

Researchers believe that what makes the difference is whether people are "engaged" or "disengaged" in their community. If they believe they can make a difference, they are certainly engaged. If they feel helpless and believe that their voice, their vote, their letter makes no difference, they are probably disengaged.

The survey included males and females of all ages and educational backgrounds, various ethnic groups and here are some of the results. More Asian Americans (63%) believe their communities are going the right direction than whites (56%), African Americans (43%) and Hispanics (only 37% thought their community was going the right direction.)

People were asked whether they thought they could make a difference in solving problems in their own community. Among college graduates, 72% thought they could make a difference but women felt they could make less difference than men. However, working women and married mothers (60%) felt they could make more of a difference than women over age 65, where only 32% felt they could make a difference in solving community problems, whether they had a college education or not.

Of those with high school education or less or with an annual income under $20,000, only 42% felt they could make a difference in solving community problems. However, if they had an annual income of over $40,000 or were Internet users, 55% thought they could make a difference. Asian Americans (57%) felt more able to make a difference in solving community problems than did African Americans (43%). Of those not registered to vote, which was of interest to the League of Women Voters, only 45% felt they could make a difference in solving community problems.

People had more confidence that they could make a difference in solving community problems (75%) than in influencing politicians (65%). Only 31% had participated in a political party in the past few years. However, 54% had worked with other people on local or neighborhood problems or attended community or neighborhood meetings.

I don't know how many times I have found that citizens wanted to turn everything over to the police and didn't realize their own responsibilities. I've tried to show them their role many times.

I told people that effective law enforcement is impossible without citizen interest, support and participation. This means more than the familiar "Support your local police" bumper sticker implies. When a citizen asked me the question, "How can I, as a citizen, help you?" I usually said, "Keep on asking that question. Your continual show of interest in the day-to-day operations of our department is as essential to crime reduction as the capture of criminals."

As Edmund Burke, the British political philosopher once said, "The only thing necessary to the triumph of evil is that good men do nothing."

The police officer that conscientiously performs his duties day after day with dedication and integrity expects very little for doing his job well. The fair, impartial and effective manner in which he conducts himself should earn him the respect of the community. We owe him this much. The people's respect for and confidence in officers is part of their support.

Law enforcement executives and officers must listen carefully to the voice of the community and welcome suggestions and ideas. When they are wrong, citizens must correct them by offering counsel and advice; and when they are right, they deserve our support.

One of the most important things a citizen can do is to evaluate police operations in his own mind, discuss them constructively with his friends and neighbors, and then let his voice be heard.

One very important way to express support is to back police or sheriffs when they request whatever additional men and equipment they need to do their job well. Efficient and effective police service is really a bargain. The costs of police service are highest when we pay the price in lives and property lost or destroyed. The cost in the city of Detroit was inestimable when lives and property were destroyed.

Citizens can provide extra sets of eyes and ears. Call whenever you see or hear something that is suspicious. If you have any information that you think the police department should be aware of, call, write or report it so that proper police action can be taken. A citizen can even help by appearing in court as a witness.

When I was the Police Commissioner of Detroit, I had what I called a "Love-In." I was attempting to create a new way for people to look at police work. I had a proclamation printed for the Love-In and here were some of the things it said about this love.

> "It's caring about your neighbor so you report an assault you witness upon him or his home. It's caring about your city so that you don't want to see it suffer. It's doing your thing well within the law and within the bounds of propriety. It's putting your personal desires and politics second to your concern for your city.
>
> "It's helping to professionalize your police rather than policing your police. It's your never getting tired of asking what can we do to help. It's wanting to change things with calm, cool reason and considered judgments, not with destructive 'to hell with it' attitudes. It's having faith in people and police officers and the hope we can all live together in a better Detroit. It's making the policeman 'my man,' not 'the man.'
>
> "It's believing that a miracle can work in this city. The miracle of those silent, uncommitted citizens of our city speaking out and committing themselves. That's what love is. That's what it can be. That's what it must be."

Minorities and Law Enforcement

My objective is to restore American policing to respectability, to see law enforcement as honorable and needed, but also ethical, moral, proper, and wanted by all communities; black, white, brown, yellow, young, old and in-between.

Blacks have achieved great prominence in sports such as basketball, football, baseball and now tennis. In some ways, blacks are superior to whites. Why? Because of hard work, drills, training, conditioning, and dedication. I want to plead for black communities to come forward with visionary leaders to encourage excellence using brains as well as the body. I want to see them encouraging their youth to go into professions that involve more intelligence and education.

Affirmative action has been used because of long-denied opportunities for minorities in various businesses. There should be affirmative action in getting educated. Blacks could put in similar hard work in the classroom, learning the basic skills to achieve prominence and a better quality of life as they make more money and become someone admirable.

New black leaders are needed to emphasize realism, not always racism. Hard work is required to pull oneself up by the bootstraps. In order to have more, one must do more! And as we consider doing more, we mustn't forget the law enforcement profession.

To be a police officer requires good physical qualities (like the athlete) and good mental ability (which should be fostered in minority communities.) It can be developed and should be. It really is more important than athletic proficiency. Above all, a police officer must have good moral qualities and that seems to be poorly lacking, even in today's law enforcement world.

I was so disappointed to learn that the percentage of full-time black sworn personnel increased so little over the last few years. From 1990 to 2000, the average number of full-time police officers in cities larger than 250,000 increased by 17%. Minority representation among local police officers increased from 29.8% in 1990 to 38.1% in 2000. Hispanics recorded the greatest increase, from 9.2% to 14.1%. But black representation only increased from 18.4% in 1990 to 20.1% in 2000. I hoped it would increase much more.

Let's get back to policing, a term I prefer to law enforcement. Good, respected policing is what any community can get behind and support. That requires good officers, assigned to an area of responsibility, knowing and known to the community, as was the old time beat cop of yesteryear. We must change from almost total emphasis on response enforcements, from wild car chases to safe controlled apprehension.

We must favor slow moving protective patrols over an area known to the officer, who is concerned about its environment and its safety. Such an officer will be alert to the best means for the prevention of crime and the removal of environmental hazards. This appears to be a trend that is catching on. Statistics on cities over 250,000 showed a substantial increase in the use of bicycles with 98% of departments using them in 2000 compared to 39% in 1990. On average, departments operated 44 bicycles per 1,000 sworn personnel in 2000 compared to 3 per 1,000 in 1990. Although sheriff's departments do not show this increase, probably because they have few personnel to cover such a wide area, they train volunteers to patrol in cars and on bicycles in small communities.

Slow-moving vehicles and police assigned to a specific beat become familiar with residents and their problems. Often they are considered community police officers. By 2000, 71% of departments of large cities had a formal community policing plan and 29% had an informal plan. Indicators of community policing include meetings with citizen groups to discuss crime-related problems, assignments of responsibility and cases for specific beats or geographic areas, citizen training in mobilization and problem-solving, upgrading technology to support community policing, and taking the time to talk with individuals and proprietors.

Such police and deputies, bringing some of the good qualities of the past, working with modern electronic marvels, can do much to keep America safe in all our communities. In the black and Latino communities, new leaders should emerge. They should be leaders committed to excellence for their followers, setting examples, not harping constantly on racial matters, wrongly or rightly.

An example of harping constantly on racial matters is the Traffic Stops Statistics Act of U.S. Congressman John Conyers, D-Detroit. After some blacks in metropolitan Detroit complained that they were disproportionately pulled over for minor traffic offenses when they drove through white communities, Conyers proposed the Act. There has been a national debate on whether blacks and other minorities are targets of an alleged practice blacks refer to as "Driving While Black."

Except in a minority of police districts, traffic tickets do not include race. Conyers' bill would force police departments to keep detailed records of traffic stops, race, ethnicity, age, whether a search was conducted, how long the stop lasted, etc. The Justice Department would collect these to see if there are patterns of "Driving While Black" in select communities. Police would be required to keep records of every stop, including those that don't result in a ticket or arrest.

Law enforcement officials oppose it saying that it is burdensome and unneeded. The local American Civil Liberties Union responded to the problem by issuing a "Bustcard: Pocket Guidelines on Encounters with the Police." These guidelines of what to do if stopped include common sense warnings such as: Be polite and respectful, never bad-mouth an officer, stay calm and in control, keep your hands where the police can see them, don't tell the police they're wrong or that you're going to file a complaint, etc. They also inform people, "In certain cases, your car can be searched without a warrant as long as the police have probable cause. It is not lawful for police to arrest you simply for refusing to consent to a search."

But what about the *perceptions* that police are harder on blacks. This perception was backed up by a telephone survey of 925 randomly selected American police officers from 121 departments about attitudes toward abuse of authority by police. The National Institute of Justice printed the results in May 2000. Mostly police said they didn't use too much force in arrests and mostly they believed abuse of authority should be reported, even though whistle blowing might lead to bad reactions by fellow officers.

However, when they separated black and white officers reactions to whether police were tougher on blacks, results were striking. Of the sample, more than half (51.3%) of black officers agreed or strongly agreed that whites receive better treatment by police than blacks. Only 11.9% of white officers agreed or strongly agreed with that statement. Although only 5.1% of white officers believe police officers were more likely to use physical force against blacks and other minorities than against whites, 57.1% of blacks thought they were more likely to use physical force against minorities.

Leaders can encourage young people to excel in more than the sports and entertainment arenas. They can encourage youth to excel in the use of the mind. That's the answer for all of us: black, brown, white, yellow, and every mixture of these. We all need to use education of the mind, effective coordination of the body, and development of the spirit (morality).

Yes, it takes work to be a good tennis player. That racquet has to swing thousands of times. Basketballs must shoot through hoops thousands of times. In the area of education, one must to go class, listen to the teacher, learn, work, study and remember thousands of things. But it can be done!

More respect should be given to blacks for their intellect. New leaders must inspire youth to develop a balance in their way of life, fostering excellence in every way, not just the body. New leaders must work with and support good policing. Good men and women should look upon policing as a moral calling, not just a job. That would prevent corruption and conflict such as the Detroit Police Department is in now.

Even black police officers in the telephone survey cited above believed that community-oriented policing would reduce the number and seriousness of incidents of excessive force in arrests. Additionally, some 85% of the entire sample agreed that a police chief's strong position against the abuse of authority could make a big difference in deterring officers from abusing their authority. Almost 90% believed that a good first-line supervisor was an effective role model in preventing officers from abusing their authority. Over three-fourths of the officers thought that training in ethics, interpersonal skills, and cultural sensitivity would help prevent abuse of authority.

The Blackout of 2003

When people need help, the first responders are police and fire. They needed help when the entire northeast region of the United States and parts of Canada had the electrical plug pulled on August 14, 2003. People feared it was a terrorist attack. Memories of the horrors of September 11th (9/11) came rushing back.

Electricity, lights and all that goes with Thomas Edison's discovery (by the way, he grew up in Port Huron, Michigan) have now come back on—But!

Yes. But! Things are not yet quite the same—and perhaps, never will be. Millions and millions of dollars of food lost, restaurants unable to open for a few days, all because of water impurity. While this may be considered first as severe inconveniences, there is more.

All computers went down, including police. Trouble in River City and elsewhere! For example, I returned a book to the Library but I could not pick up a needed book, nor even look any up. Their Internet access was gone, I was told.

There are manifold stories, some funny, some tragic. Operations were cancelled, some were in progress, hospitals were in trouble, senior citizens were in trouble, trains were stuck in tunnels, etc. In addition, the heat with the oppressive humidity was overpowering.

Millions of gallons of raw sewage were discharged into St. Clair and other rivers because pumps and filters were unable to operate. It brought my mind back to the blackout of 1965 in New York. That one did not impact other areas probably because we had no interconnected power grid there at that time.

I was then in command of the motor scooters I had established in New York City, against much opposition such as macho cops, bureaucratic inertia, and jealousies.

However in 1965, during the electrical power failure, at the height of an evening rush hour, with several million persons stalled in transit, the Manhattan police communications assist center was blacked out for eight critical minutes. The radio motor patrol cars could not hear anything or say anything. Police in those cars could do nothing.

The new scooter patrol maintained immediate, direct radio communication with precinct station houses. They had portable transceivers. A portable radio transceiver was substituted for the base transmitter.

One officer on a scooter was sent from Manhattan to Maspeth, Queens, over a blacked-out and jammed Williamsburg Bridge for emergency radio equipment, an impossible task for an auto over a bridge jammed with cars. The scooter officer went and returned promptly.

In 1965, the blackout did not result in insurrections, looting, or damage to business. I was very proud of our successful scooter operations. Later, I was even prouder when the then Police Commissioner Vincent Broderick, changed his entire budget request to include 700 scooters for citywide patrols.

This was his statement: "The scooter is the most effective police patrol technique which has been developed in recent years. It *preserves the concept of the foot patrolman* and yet provides a mobility and responsiveness which the foot patrolman lacks."

Contrast Broderick's words with those of August Vollmer's self-fulfilling prophecy "With the advent of the automobile, foot patrol is obsolete."

Yes, but we have lost so much. Today's police, enclosed and almost incommunicado in glass and steel, impersonal and striking a punitive image, have caused riots in American cities.

As for responding to trouble, there were quite a few instances in the City of New York where the scooter officers responded and arrived ahead of the radio motor patrol cars, which were stuck in heavy traffic. Have you ever driven a car in New York City, particularly in the garment district? If so, you will understand.

The next blackout of 1977 was a much different story. It began when a burst of lightning knocked out Consolidated Edison's power lines in Westchester County. Alternate power sources weren't tapped in time and within a few minutes 8 million people were without electricity. Even though the power outage lasted only 25 hours, there were riots, looting, shooting and damage. More than 3,400 people were arrested and 558 police officers injured trying to restore order. The looting resulted in $1 billion in damage. People looted about 2,000 stores and were seen carrying whatever they could, such as stereos, clothes, even air conditioners and sofas.

Authorities realized many things from that blackout, such as the fact that the police responded too slowly. So even though the 2003 blackout caused fear at first and problems in its aftermath, Police Commissioner Raymond Kelly put the NYPD emergency plan in place. Extra officers were put on the streets, and every member of the 36,000-strong force knew in advance where to report, so no part of the city was understaffed.

Detroit Mayor Kwame Kilpatrick said that in two days since the start of the blackout, there had been 165 felony arrests, lower than usual for a two-day period. Of the 17 felony arrests made in Detroit, only six were breaking and entering offenses linked to the blackout. Police in Toronto and Ottawa reported no unusual crime as a result of the blackout.

The electric power grid connecting so many states is antiquated. The terrorists know this now. The electricity superhighway is in trouble. What can we do to prepare and prevent problems?

In calamities like 9/11 or blackouts, the police officers and fire personnel are the first responders, caught up in "whatever." We can be caught up in a heap of trouble in America. We must improve our infrastructure, our communications and our policing methods. Too much depends upon electricity. Even cell phones had problems.

But let me now remind you of how police sometimes cause riots. The Los Angeles riot after the Rodney King verdict was an example of a riot created because people thought that the officers who beat King were not punished sufficiently. The Los Angeles Police Department still has not recovered from this. Is the fault with the rioters or with the police officers who acted badly and were not punished for it?

Police will get no respect until they harmonize with the citizens they serve. They currently play two roles; either they are a protector or an enforcer. When they protect, they work among the people in slow patrols like scooters or bikes or on foot. In that role, they listen to people, see wrongs, serve as the eyes and ears of police executives and tend to prevent crime from happening. When they are enforcers, they respond quickly in patrol cars to problems that have already occurred and their job is punitive as they arrest lawbreakers. When they play that role, they are not in harmony with the citizens.

When police and citizens work together as a team to protect their communities, they each respect the other. I used to tell citizens that crime prevention "takes a team, you and your police." In Detroit I promoted the concept of Citizen Watch Patrols. Later as Sheriff, in addition to my posse, I had volunteers on scooters and volunteers on Harley Davidson motorcycles.

Uncaring police who simply respond to incidents and are not known by residents cause riots in American cities. This could be avoided if police served as both a protector and enforcer. Police departments could embrace a dual purpose role, and include "dynamic duo police officers," in the words of my wife Sallie.

I propose a dual purpose police department which could do much to prevent crime, alleviate the drug evil, greatly reduce vandalism, and secure a safer and better looking environment.

There is no doubt that the calamity of 9/11 overwhelmed everyone. Fire and police personnel deployed themselves and created problems. Emotional management made people get mad when others they didn't know (often not in uniforms such as FEMA) were telling them what to do. People cannot work around the clock and make good decisions. Relationships had not been built up and it's too late to swap business cards at an incident. People were deployed and not used because there was nobody to save, so they needed support and someone to talk to.

The International Association of Fire Chiefs met in August 2003 in Dallas and concluded that the training put in place after 9/11 prevented chaos during the 2003 blackout. Of course in the blackout people weren't killed in front of our eyes like on 9/11, but the blackout showed that protective officers had prepared the community. In a preventive and proactive role, police and fire personnel had helped buildings appoint floor wardens and have power emergency kits available. They used their dual role as protector to educate, listen, plan, and serve as role models. As a result, people were helped by wardens to find their way out of buildings, there was little looting, traffic soon began to move again and people helped people. If there had been more officers on motor scooters and bicycles to traverse the crowded streets and bridges, communication could have been even better and quicker.

One of the lessons learned from 9/11 was to train police and fire personnel about what to do when they are deprived of communication and direction from the top. By the time of the blackout, they had a protocol about what to do if they couldn't talk to headquarters. Part of the chaos during 9/11 was the lack of communication between services.

Communication is the key in so many ways because many services must work together in emergencies. People must be treated with respect at incidents because we all want the same things. If our people are trained, ready, and have their equipment at 100% readiness, they can help. Young people who don't know what to do can't help you.

I believe that this dynamic duality (protection and enforcement) police officer will help restore the respect of the public for law enforcement agency. But it will take time and cooperation by politicians, press, people, pressure groups and police to eliminate turf battles and promote harmony. In the end, protection of the people should be the common goal of all these groups.

Cop Shows and Technology

Cop shows on television and in the movies sell well. People seem to be fascinated by the life and death thrills involved in law enforcement. They want to see who can get away with crime. They want to see new modern innovations that help cops catch bad guys. They like exciting car chases, confrontations, guts, bravery, and the special closeness that officers have with each other.

Cartoon readers have laughed at Dick Tracy for years, but his wristwatch radio is here. It's costly but the technological problems have been overcome. A flying platform for cops to zoom from one place to another is no longer a sci-fi dream but a reality. The device has problems of range and control, but it's no longer a pipedream. I wouldn't be surprised to see special purpose flying police in the future. Can it be made practicable? If it becomes practical and economical, would it represent a better method of patrol?

In any event, technology is running ahead of policing still, challenging police officials to find ways of using the dramatic new tools that are coming into being, and to avoid the stand pat syndrome.

What happened with the increasing prevalence of the auto? It took the police out of patrol and converted the police function into a response function.

Future-oriented police have to keep their eyes and their minds open to fresh alternatives. In a car versus foot contest, the car will always win on most counts. What about car versus scooter, car versus video camera, or car versus flying plat-form? Or what about an effective combination that uses the right means in the right circumstances to achieve the best results at the lowest cost? If we think that American policing can do its patrolling and policing job right by relying on the car alone, we're barking up the wrong tree.

We've known for a long time that our communities don't have the financial resources to cover themselves with foot patrolmen. Even if they did, is foot patrol all it is cracked to be? We should ask the questions in the light of all the known alternatives, not just the old alternatives and the old environmental concerns.

If all we have is the car, we're never going to be effective in American policing. The car is two men or one, encapsulated in a vehicle of glass and steel, remote, fleeting, out of touch. The capacity for response is excellent, but its preventive capacity has virtually vanished. And we no longer have the foot patrolman on the beat to fall back on, at least in most precincts throughout the nation.

I think most authorities would agree that police departments in the United States today may talk about "patrol," but in actual practice they are oriented to response. This is partially the result of the workload, but also partly the result of the existence of the car itself, and the growing dependence on it as the mainstay vehicles, the governing factor being the car's convenience rather than the police mission.

Internally police themselves argue over the merits of the so-called "generalist" versus the police "specialist." One group looks down on another with a different assignment. Specialization seems to carry an aura of prestige that makes those who consider themselves "specialists" feel superior to the common, ordinary precinct patrolman, and generates rancor in return from those who are not specialists, and who feel their own unappreciated work is more onerous and less rewarding.

The scout car man can feel antagonized by the man on the scooter. Or the men of the Tactical Mobile Unit. Or the officers assigned to precinct support. Or the motorcycle men. Or the detectives.

Perhaps nobody knows who the "generalist" is any more and every cop is a "specialist," jealous of his own "specialty." Meanwhile, who is giving the citizen the general service he wants and needs?

Since the first city police department was organized early in the 19th century, stories about crime and police work have had a popular place in literature. Public interest in the subject continues to be reflected in contemporary plays, movies and TV shows.

As mentioned earlier, heroes of these tales almost universally have been detectives. Good detectives deserve their laurels. However, the glorification of the detective, who is a specialist in one phase of police work, has tended to obscure the importance of the man in the blue uniform, the man who makes up the bulk of any police department, and must perform the basic functions of prevention and protection as well as response.

Why Did People Create Policing?

From the start of written history, there has been a policing function, at least of sorts, part preventive and part reactive. From the time that men first began to organize their living into communities, we've had police using a variety of manners and methods of patrol or movement through an assigned area to guard, watch and protect.

Like *police* itself, the word *patrol* is of more recent origin than the function it describes. *Patrol* was adapted into the English language from the French. Its French antecedents include the noun for *paw* and the verb *to paw about, to paddle*, and *to walk through puddles.*

This was an appropriate enough derivation for a concept that has come to mean providing civilized society with a visible, mobile, police presence, through good weather and bad, either as a means of forestalling the commission of a crime, or deterring further criminal acts by johnny-on-the-spot arrest and punishment.

The means of patrol have included men on foot, men riding on trained animals, men carried in vehicles, from horse-drawn chariots and carts all the way up to modern automobiles. Police have used watercraft propelled by oar, sail, steam and the combustion engine. Many modern police departments have employed scuba-cops. Police have been airborne in planes and helicopters, and it may not be long before they'll be up in the air on jet-propelled platforms and flying pogo sticks.

The instinct of self-preservation taught man the necessity for alertness and watchfulness to protect his life and his immediate possessions against harm. *Patrol* however is a communal act. It developed out of an organized attempt to provide group security over a wider area than that occupied by a single individual or a single family.

The purpose of a professional force of men to provide this protective service as we in the United States know it today is traditionally associated with the organization in Great Britain and the London metropolitan police in 1829.

Guardianship or watchfulness, as an aspect of what we recognize today as the fundamentals of police service, appear throughout human history. Only the degree of mobility of those providing the guardianship service has changed over the centuries.

I suppose you could say the first application of the idea of watchfulness to *police* human conduct appeared in the Book of Genesis, when God put Adam and Eve out of the Garden of Eden, and put cherubim on watch to make sure they stayed out.

Historians can trace formal police institutions back to the code of Hammurabi, the Babylonian ruler, more than 2,000 years before Christ.

The Spartans in ancient Greece had officials called "ephors" who performed some law enforcement functions, but these were more judicial than police operations in the contemporary sense.

Rome under the Emperor Augustus was served by a substantial body of men, numbering in the thousands, called *vigils*, literally *watchful ones* whose job was to keep the peace and look out for fires. A later emperor, Nero, really put them to the test.

After the fall of the Roman Empire, the Dark Ages descended upon Europe. Chaos and disorder prevailed. The Asiatic horsemen known as *Huns* put pressure on the tribes of Central Europe, pressure that spread in waves all the way to the coastal borders of the continent. Some tribes sailed to the British Isles, the Jutes, Angles and Saxons, from what are now Denmark and Germany.

As these people struggled and mingled with the native Britons and began to take primitive steps to provide local security, the earliest traces of our modern police principles, as well as some of our modern police vocabulary, began to appear. Under Alfred the Great, who was of Saxon descent, the beginnings of an army, a navy and a code of law occurred.

Most importantly in connection with policing, the first major phase in the evolution of today's police role had begun. This was the social determination that the maintenance of local *law and order* was the responsibility of the people themselves, not of the ruler. This responsibility included not only the ideas of watchfulness, protection and apprehension of criminals that we associate with police today, but also other aspects of what we today call the *criminal justice system*.

The people served as their own police, deterring through common watchfulness, sharing a common responsibility to pursue and apprehend, acted as judge and jury, and saw to it that any penalties or punishment were exacted.

Following the Norman Conquest of England in 1066, specialists began to appear to handle some of the duties of law enforcement, the most prominent being called *justices of the peace*. Eventually came the establishment of paid professional police to provide protection and assure *law and order*. Paid professionals began to appear gradually in England, beginning as early as the reign of Queen Elizabeth I, but the fully organized, publicly maintained city police force is less than 175 years old.

Looking back in time, a curtain of mystery hangs over nearly 1,000 years of English history, from the Roman occupation to the time of Alfred the Great. Details of the life of the people of that time are as murky as the North Sea mists that cloaked the approach of Viking raiders in their long ships.

Legends and heroic poems and literary fragments in the changing and lost languages of that day open just a glimpse or two of a primitive rural people, frightened of monsters, dreaming of magic swords and Holy Grails, and huddling together for some small measure of collective security.

With the reign of Alfred the Great, written records and an attempt at something beyond rudimentary local government helped to dissolve the curtain of mystery. There were finally enough records for us to discern social organization and the beginnings of our modern police.

We see a country of forests, fields and small hamlets. There were "tuns" in Anglo-Saxon, pronounced "toons," the obvious ancestor of our suffix "-ton" and the word "town." A single family or perhaps several families occupied the "tun."

But there was an additional association, under Anglo-Saxon law. Families were grouped by tens into *tithings;* and *tithings* were grouped into *hundreds.*

Collective security was the principle of defense, not only against external enemies but also against those within the community who committed crimes. Responsibility for crime prevention, for punishment of the criminal, and for making restitution to those harmed began with the family, carried over to the *tithing*, and on to the *hundred.* Each individual was responsible for his neighbor's conduct as well as his own.

When a crime was discovered, it was up to the one who discovered it or the head of the group to sound the alarm and rally every able-bodied man to pursue the criminal. This public pursuit had a specific designation in Anglo-Saxon law. It was called setting up a *hue and cry.* That French phrase came from a pair of almost synonymous verbs meaning *to set up a loud shouting and clamor.* Our present laws governing *hot pursuit* derive from this practice.

The English practice of pursuing a criminal with horn and voice was the duty of any person aggrieved, or discovering a felony, and his neighbors were bound to turn out with him and assist in the discovery of the offender. In the case of a hue and cry, all those joining in the pursuit were justified in arresting the person pursued, even though it turned out that he was innocent. Proof was not required of a culprit's guilt, but merely that he had been taken red-handed by hue and cry. The

Sheriff's Act of 1887 provided that every person in a county must be ready at the command of the sheriff and at the cry of the county to arrest a felon, and if they didn't, they could be fined.

The countryside of Anglo-Saxon Britain was divided up into districts, like counties today. Many *hundreds* might live in one district. The district was given an Anglo-Saxon name, "scir" from which comes "shire." As life within the "shires" and "tuns" became more organized and complex, a petty officialdom developed on a shire-wide or countywide basis. These officials did the work of stewards, involving themselves in such business tasks as directing some aspect of local farming and stock-raising, or collecting rents, occupying minor management roles. The chief official of the whole district was the district steward or "scir-gerefa" in Anglo-Saxon.

From Old Saxon to modern German, "gerefa" comes down to us as "graf," or "count" or a member of nobility with responsibility for governing a county. From Saxon to Middle English, the word became "Reeve." From "shire reeve" to the modern "sheriff" was an easy transition.

Chaucer included a "reeve" among his pilgrims on the way to Canterbury. Eventually the "shire-reeve" assumed from the community the role of judge. He became the authority responsible for raising the *hue and cry* and rallying citizens in pursuit. He did this by authority of the *power of the county,* a legalism contributed by the Romans. In Latin, power of the county comes from the phrase "posse comitatus." It's easy to see where we got our Western "posses" and where the French got their title "comte" for the Count or overseer of a county.

This responsibility was by law, not just by custom. After the Norman Conquest, this was sealed by what was called the "Frankpledge," a freely-given freeman's promise to keep the public peace and be responsible for the good conduct of others. "Frank" was a word of Saxon derivation meaning *free*, and the pledge originated in seventh century France, the land of the "Franks."

What happened when the *hue and cry* turned up a culprit? His friends and neighbors, trusting that God would protect the innocent and unmask the guilty, would give him a little test, maybe a slow stroll over some burning embers, or a total or partial dunking in boiling oil or water. This *trial by ordeal* was subsequently modified into a *trial by combat,* a literary example of which is preserved for us in Sir Walter Scott's *Ivanhoe.*

You or your *champion* took on your opponent, or the *people's champion* took on the accused, as the case might be, in *mortal combat.* No Marquis of Queensbury rules, just "praise the Lord" and mash the opposition.

Oddly enough, there was no provision for capital punishment but after the trials, what was left? If a criminal survived the *trial* and was found guilty, he would probably be branded in some way to indicate the nature of his crime, and restitution would be exacted for the injured party. And if the criminal could not make restitution, his family and the tithing men were responsible. Our present day system of civil law found its origins here.

This system exerted a lot of pressure on members of the tithing to avoid crime, and to prevent it by others, but once it occurred, the system also generated a lot of pressure to conceal the crime. No tithing was particularly anxious to be charged with costly reparations because of a peccadillo by one of its weaker members.

The key point is that this was an era both of local and personal responsibility for the prevention of crime and the apprehension and punishment of the criminal. There was no formal *preventive patrol* as such, because the people themselves provided the omnipresence of the law, serving as police, prosecutor, jury, judge, and corrections system. This era began to change under the influence of William of Normandy, who conquered the Saxons and became ruler of England in 1066.

After the Battle of Hastings, where William earned the title of *The Conqueror*, he imposed on the Anglo-Saxon inhabitants of England their first genuine *national* government, the beginnings of which had been started by Alfred the Great. In the process he preserved the Anglo-Saxon system of local organizations into *tithings* of ten families, and *hundreds* of ten *tithings*, and local responsibility for law and order. But he adapted the existing institutions for his own purpose, which was to enforce obedience to Norman rule.

The *sheriff*, the principal Anglo-Saxon official of the shire or county, was responsible to the king rather than to the people of the shire. He imposed the king's justice, rather than the people's, and exacted the king's retribution for any crimes that were committed, before retribution was granted to the victims. The sheriff also became the king's tax collector. Since his tax-gathering efficiency affected his own income, the sheriff evolved into the kind of villain that was memorialized in literature like the Robin Hood tales.

The office of sheriff in Great Britain today has diminished to the level of a non-paying, honorary and chiefly ceremonial title, but for many years the sheriff was the chief enforcer, judge and royal administrator in each shire or county.

Under the sheriff of the county, the *tithing man* or leading citizen of each Anglo-Saxon group of ten families continued to be responsible for keeping the peace at the lowest level of social organization. Gradually this local official's responsibility was shifted, from local control by his neighbors who elected him, to royal control exercised through the sheriff. He remained responsible for raising the *hue and cry* and for rallying the *posse* for the sheriff, to chase wrongdoers throughout the county.

This frequently involved the provision of horses, so the Normans gave him a new name, "constable," from the Latin *comes stabuli,* or companion of the stable. Today, all uniformed British police officers, whether in London or the rural shires, are known as *constables.*

In the rural groups of ten tithings, known as *hundreds,* the chief official became known as the *head constable.* As towns and cities grew, districts rather than numbers of families became the basis for assigning officials. Constables became the officials of *parishes* and *boroughs.*

As one Norman king followed another after William the Conqueror, new laws were passed and crimes were listed in categories as *felonies* or serious crime against the king, and *misdemeanors* or lesser crimes of bad behavior. The king assumed the responsibility for judging and punishing, so that it no longer devolved upon those injured by the criminal. The judicial function was taken away from the people and the sheriffs, and assigned to specifically chosen *justices of the peace,* some of whom traveled from place to place, hearing cases. A court-sitting was sometimes called an *assize* from *asseyez,* the French word for sit.

Juries appeared to help determine facts in a case by means of an *inquest,* from a Latin word meaning to *search out,* ending trials by ordeal. After completing the inquiries, the jury issued a *vere dictum* or true saying.

Constables dwindled in importance from authorities in their own right to assistants to the courts. As the honor of the office diminished and the burdens became more onerous, citizens sought ways of avoiding taking their turn as elected constables for a year, and began to hire substitutes.

Since those who offered themselves as substitutes tended to be those who had no other work to do, the quality of work performed by the stand-in constables left much to be desired.

At this point, when the responsibility of preserving peace passed from the individual citizen to his representative, and then to a paid *stand-in* for the representative, effective local law enforcement in England began to break down.

The erosion of local responsibility was not the only cause for the failure of law enforcement, but it serves as the benchmark for a period of some 500 to 600 years in England in which rising population and economic and cultural shifts created environmental conditions which encouraged crime and public disorder.

Society became too complex for a simple rural-based system in which everybody was responsible for the conduct of everybody else. In effect, nobody was any longer responsible, and not until the middle 18th century was there even the start of any kind of organized service to assume responsibility for keeping civic peace on a basis acceptable to the citizens.

The laws stressed local and individual freedom, but effective measures for enforcing the laws were resisted out of the fear that they would abrogate freedom.

The Magna Carta was signed to curb abuses of royal power, reinforce the right of local self-government, and apply the *due process of law* to all citizens. At Westminster, the seat of royal government (now one of the major districts of Central London), the king passed a statute instituting some new local security concepts, including a curfew, street patrol and inspection of strangers. The word "sergeant" comes into our vocabulary from a now obsolete French expression meaning "great scrutinizer."

One of the many Charleses who sat on the English throne instituted city street watching, called *Watch* (for night duty) and *Ward* for daytime patrol. The people nicknamed the king's watchmen *Charlies* and then after noting how many were doddering or drunken oldsters, easily chilled in cold weather and frightened by pranksters, began calling them the *Shiver and Shake* watch.

As late as the early 1800s, a few of these old parish watchmen could still be seen on the streets of London, operating out of a small brick sidewalk cubicle, dressed in a long coat, wearing a cumbersome sword, carrying a large lantern, a wooden rattle to sound the alarm, and a *stave* or small wooden club.

Rising British commerce and the wool trade stimulated the conversion of many farms to sheep-raising, driving thousands of poor tenants off the farms and into the cities. The Industrial Revolution capitalized on this supply of labor, but without sharing the new wealth with those who helped produce it. There was tremendous addiction to alcohol as an easy way to forget one's troubles, especially to the new cheap intoxicant introduced in Holland called *gin*, from *genevre*, the French word for juniper berry. Sadistic public executions stirred holiday crowds like ancient Roman circuses.

The British suffered through a civil war in the mid-17th century which sent many to settle in the colonies. When the victorious Oliver Cromwell tried to govern his people by dividing the country into districts controlled by military police, the effort had to be abandoned as too oppressive for a freedom-loving people.

Near the beginnings of the history of our own country, however, the British still had found no satisfactory method of keeping internal peace except for the emergency use of troops. The first light in this dark era was thrown by a man named Henry Fielding, who is probably better known as the father of the English novel *Tom Jones* than as the forefather of modern democratic police.

Fielding was one of a class of gentlemen of learning but not much wealth, who were willing to perform judicial duties in the cities, similar to those of the rural *justices of the peace.* The magistrate made his living from fees and fines, and some magistrates extorted as much as they could, hardly a way of building respect for what little civil law enforcement authority there was.

As a young man, Fielding had made his living in London writing satirical political plays. When they became too radical and too uncomplimentary to local officials, a form of local censorship was imposed which put Fielding out of the playwriting business. He then began to study law and to support himself he began writing some of the first great samples of the English novel, a new literary form.

The non-salaried post of magistrate, with its opportunity for graft, was made available to him through friendly patrons. The former magistrate, who served the *city* of Westminster, had held court in the ground floor rooms of his home in Bow Street, a location that is at present in the theater district in the heart of downtown London. Fielding simply occupied the former magistrate's home and court. There is still a court in Bow Street in London today.

Instead of a venal exploiter, Fielding was a magistrate who was determined to serve the law, not his own pocket. He assessed only legal fines, took pity on the poor, tried to settle cases without fines where possible, and, wonder of wonders, shunned bribes. He generated so little income for himself that the government finally put him on the first salary ever offered a British magistrate.

Cases came before Fielding either because one citizen brought in another on a complaint, constables or military detachments made arrests, or private individuals called *thief-takers* brought in suspects in expectation of an established bounty or reward. The bounty system could be too easily abused, encouraging the unscrupulous to bring in the innocent on fraudulent charges.

The champion exploiter was an unscrupulous individual named Jonathan Wild. Thirty years before Fielding, he established himself as the leading *thief-taker* and *fence* or receiver of stolen goods in London. He got the criminals of London to report the results of their thefts, and then contacted the original owners, who paid to get their goods back. If one of his thieves got out of line, Wild turned the man in to a magistrate. Before he received his comeuppance, Wild had established a London *mafia* that could have served as a model to today's *dons* of organized crime.

The idea of paying a bounty to citizens for arresting their fellow-citizens was hardly a desirable substitute for the lack of professional police.

Fielding had no budget to hire outside help. He sought to correct the situation by taking the best of the constables who had served their year in his jurisdiction, and persuading them to continue under him as professional *thief-takers*. They were still to be paid through the bounty system, but under Fielding's supervision offered a crime-detection service of an efficiency and honesty not previously known. However their function was primarily response following criminal action, not preventive patrol.

Fielding circulated crime news, and in effect *advertised* for business for his Bow Street *runners*, since it would never have occurred to most victims of crime to report to any of the existing authorities.

Fielding's service as a magistrate lasted less than seven years, but before his death in 1754 he wrote one of the first essays on the causes of crime, pointed to the evil effects of environment, poverty and unemployment, lashed out against public executions, and first suggested the crime prevention potential of the right kind of public peace-keeping officials. The word "police" had not yet come into popular use, except as a derivative of a French verb that meant to "civilize" or to "establish policy."

His half-brother, John Fielding, who served 26 more years as Bow Street magistrate, succeeded Henry. John expanded the work started by his elder brother, and established a record made even more remarkable by the fact that he was totally blind.

It was John who finally began to popularize the word "police" in its present meaning, making a careful distinction between the *police of an arbitrary government* and *a police proper for England*. This, he said, "must always be agreeable to the just notion of the liberty of the subject as well as to the laws and constitution."

But even the efforts of men as dedicated as the Fieldings were a drop in the bucket compared to the widespread prevalence of all sorts of crime. This was complicated by the predilection of London mobs to riot when the spirit moved them. There was no effective public response except by the military, and all the soldiers did was aggravate the mobs still more.

No person was too high in rank to be immune. A prime minister was robbed in the streets. An English queen escaped being robbed only because the gang that was set to waylay her was busy with an earlier victim when her entourage passed by. When George II was king, shortly before the American Revolution, a member of parliament named John Wilkes incited riots in his own behalf, and although punished briefly, was returned to Parliament with mob support, and remained there for 16 years, dying respectably at 72.

Some English historians assert that the lack of civil police and the use of soldiers to put down mob disorders in Boston, which radicalized the moderate majority, had more to do with American independence than the Declaration signed at Philadelphia in 1776.

The peculiar tactics used by the British Army at Bunker Hill, Long Island, Philadelphia and other confrontations with inferior and less well-trained colonial forces have also been blamed by English historians for the inability of British troops to win the decisive military victory over the Americans that was so often within their grasp.

The same officers who smashed French armies in Canada and Europe, these historians say, abandoned military principles in favor of civilian crowd-control principles when they faced the American colonists. They used the same riot-control tactics against the colonists that they used against mobs in London, showing enough force to intimidate but always leaving the mob an escape route to disperse.

Be that as it may, life in England before, during and after the American Revolution, in retrospect seems far more turbulent than the events that trouble us in the United States in the last half of the 20th century.

Lacking effective means to enforce the laws that existed, the lawmakers of Great Britain tried to frighten criminals into socially acceptable behavior by increasing the severity of penalties. The crowd could pelt a man in the pillory to blindness or death. A child could be hanged for stealing. By the 19th century, the number of crimes calling for capital punishment had risen to 223, according to one historian. The truth had not yet been learned that the certainty of punishment is more of a deterrent to crime than the severity.

As far as the English people were concerned, they stubbornly continued to resist the idea of a professional force of public law enforcers, fearing that it would be a greater danger to individual liberty than rampant crime and mob rule.

Finally the idealism of the two Fieldings and other concerned students of the *law, order and justice* problem found an outlet in the practical idealism of a skilled politician in the early 19th century. Only then was it brought home to Englishmen, and eventually to Americans, how it was possible to *insure domestic tranquility* and to *secure the blessings of liberty* without repression.

This political idealist was Sir Robert Peel. He was appointed Home Secretary, the member of the British Cabinet in charge of internal affairs including domestic security, in 1822.

The Fieldings, Henry and John, had sought to apply the law humanely, for the benefit of the poor as well as the rich. So did Patrick Colquhoun, another police reformer who served as a magistrate near the close of the 18th century. Colquhoun helped form the Thames River police, a special force that patrolled in boats to protect the docks and shipping that attracted thieves by the thousands. The example of these magistrates and their writings served as the basis of a bill introduced by Peel to reform and improve the policing of London on a metropolitan basis.

Peel's Police Act in 1829 sketched out the concept of a new kind of police force in broad detail. He left it to two well-chosen commissioners to make it work, a 46-year-old former officer in Wellington's army named Charles Rowan, and a 32-year-old lawyer named Richard Mayne.

The new police were given uniforms, so they would be easily recognizable, but great pains were taken to keep the uniforms from looking *military*. Coat and pants were *civilian* blue; white trousers were worn in summer. The hat was an Abe Lincoln-style stovepipe, reinforced with leather, marked with the letter "P." The men carried no arms, only a baton, a lantern and a wooden rattle as a signaling device.

They were put on foot patrol in six divisions, covering most of the city with about 1,000 men, including supervision. Eventually they became known affectionately as *Peelers* or *Bobbies* after Sir Robert. But at first they were detested so much they were called *crushers, raw lobsters,* and *Peel's blood gang,* both by much of the public and the press.

There were many complaints of *police brutality.* Only after a long period of insistence by the commissioners on high standards of police conduct, and the patient endurance of the best of the original constables on the force, did fear and detestations of the police turn into grudging admiration, and finally respect and acceptance.

The basis of this ultimate acceptance can be found in some of the principles established under Peel by Rowan and Mayne, many of them derived from the words of their predecessors. As the following representative samples show, they remain today sound principles for the guidance of modern, professional police in a freedom-loving, democratic society:

> ...the power of the police to fulfill their functions and duties is dependent on public approval of their existence, actions and behavior, and on their ability to secure and maintain public respect.
> ...to secure and maintain the respect and approval of the public means also the securing of the willing cooperation of the public in the task of security observance of the law.

...the extent to which the cooperation of the public can be secured diminishes, proportionately, the necessity of the use of physical force and compulsion for achieving police objectives.

...public favor (is preserved) not by pandering to public opinion, but by constantly demonstrating absolutely impartial service to law, in complete independence of policy, and without regard to the justice or injustice of individual laws; by ready offering of individual service and friendship to all members of the public without respect to their wealth or social standing; by ready exercise of courtesy and good humor; and by ready offering of individual sacrifice in protecting and preserving life.

...physical force may be used only when the exercise of persuasion, advice and warning is found to be insufficient to obtain public cooperation to an extent necessary to restore order; and...only the minimum degree of physical force may be used which is necessary on any particular occasion for achieving a police objective.

...the police are the public and...the public are the police, the police being only members of the public who are paid to give full-time attention to duties which are incumbent on every citizen, in the interests of community welfare and existence.

...the test of police efficiency is the absence of crime and disorder, and not the visible evidence of police action in dealing with them.

Summing it all up was the opening observation in the first *manual* provided for the guidance and instruction of the London Police: "The primary object of an efficient police force is the prevention of crime."

Their method of crime prevention was the first organized mass approach to foot patrol on a systematic, citywide basis.

In the United States, a study of the history of policing suggests that we Americans have been all too patient a people when it came to facing up to the problems of increasing crime.

In fact most major steps to provide or improve police services and establish a system of preventive patrol were finally triggered not so much by crime itself as by serious public disturbances which jeopardized the peace and safety of the entire community.

The public riots in Watts, Newark, Detroit and elsewhere in the mid-1960s helped to stimulate the most massive national study of crime in the nation's history, and also the largest effort on a national scale to provide better police services and do a better job of controlling crime.

But this was by no means a new and unusual sequence. Public disorders on a scale that frightened the citizenry in the 19th century led to reform and the establishment of the first metropolitan police forces, with emphasis on organized foot patrol, in many of our cities.

In the early days of American colonization, the colonists simply brought with them the ideas of local policing that prevailed in the mother country. The English system of county sheriffs and local constables was put to use, and these police titles still survive in our counties and smaller communities. Urban communities provided for part-time "watches," to guard against fire as much as anything else.

Some garrison towns were under martial law rather than civilian police during much of their early existence. Detroit, founded in 1701 as a French trading and military outpost on the narrow strait (d'etroit), which connected the upper and lower Great Lakes, for the first hundred years of its history was policed first by French and then by British military authorities. British rule actually survived for 13 years beyond the signing of the Treaty of Paris in 1783, which recognized the existence of the Thirteen Colonies. This was due to the post's frontier remoteness, and the slowness of the new U.S. authorities to assume control of the vast territories beyond the borders of the thirteen states.

As settlers moved west and formed new communities beyond the original state boundaries, a citizen who could be prevailed upon by his fellows to assume police responsibilities was given the badge and title of "Marshal," under the sanction of the national government.

Just as in England, the earliest police functionaries were expected to take turns serving on a voluntary, part-time basis. When this proved as inadequate in America as it had been in England, citizens began to pay others to handle the police responsibility.

An individual's availability, rather than his ability, as often as not was the only requirement for police employment as watchman, constable, sheriff or territorial marshal.

The *Shiver and Shake* watch of London was duplicated in old New York, which filled its night watch with the indigent elderly, some alcoholics, sleepy workmen who also held daytime jobs and even some criminals who were forced into service as part of their punishment.

Gay young blades of New York found it just as hilarious as their opposite numbers in London to sneak up on a watchman's box and tip it over with him inside, or lasso him as he dozed.

Perhaps the earliest known police official in the English colonies of North America was a man named Josiah Pratt, who in 1634 was chosen to serve as constable in Plymouth, Massachusetts.

A night watch was established in Boston as early as 1636. The Dutch began a rattle watch in "Nieuw Amsterdam" in 1658, which was superseded by the English constable system after the British takeover in 1664, when the city was re-christened "New York." Philadelphia had a night watchman in 1700.

People began paying for this kind of part-time protection service about the start of the 19th century. But it wasn't until after four riots in New York City, riots in Philadelphia, and a fire brigade riot in Boston that the cities began to do something about full-time paid police services.

Philadelphia organized a paid police force in 1833 of 23 men who worked days and 120 who worked nights. A captain appointed by the mayor headed the force. Boston appointed six policemen in 1838, expanding eight years later to a force of 30 men working days, and eight at night.

Meanwhile, in 1833 a delegation from New York City went to London, England, to study the metropolitan police system inaugurated by Sir Robert Peel four years earlier. However, another decade passed before the fruits of this study were translated into action in New York. Finally in 1844 the state legislature took action establishing New York City's first metropolitan police force. The legisla-tive act provided for a force of 800 uniformed men under a chief to patrol the city, operating 24 hours a day, on day and night shifts.

Other cities followed: Chicago in 1851; Cincinnati in 1852; Baltimore and Newark, New Jersey in 1857; and Providence, Rhode Island in 1864. Following what amounted to a race riot, Detroit organized its first metropolitan police force in 1865. After the Civil War, the metropolitan police concept spread to most American cities.

For the past century, policing in general has preserved at least a nominal com-mitment to its dual mission of the prevention and detection of crime, but the pri-ority of the preventive function has become more theoretical than actual. How policing has gone about its dual mission has undergone evolutionary change, influenced by the same factors that have affected the lives of all citizens.

The size and composition of the population, industry, and commerce have shifted the focus of city life from concentration to dispersion. This has influenced architecture, transportation, communication and all these changes impacted poli-tics and public attitudes toward morality and authority. These shifts required new approaches to social relationships and organizational theory and practice.

Change brought new problems and new means of tackling them. More often than not, however, as police struggled to find an adequate response to each change, things shifted and a new struggle had to be launched for a different kind of answer.

The inevitable lag between the appearance of a problem and its solution remains a fact of life in contemporary policing, an irreversible condition that policing shares with all forms of human endeavor and life itself.

A more complex, heterogeneous society has made the work of police agencies more complex but the police mission has remained basically the same. While still giving lip service to prevention, police have been drawn by the attractions of new technology and the frailties of human nature. They have moved away from prevention to effective reaction to crime after the fact. Rising crime statistics indicate that it has turned into a losing rear-guard action. The increasing volume of crime has tended to swamp police response capability, even with the advantages that science and technology have brought to modern detection, pursuit and apprehension methods.

New and special problems led the police into specialization and then over-specialization. This led to organizational complexities, which police theorists have been attempting to deal with for more than 40 years.

The need for a better informed, better trained, better controlled and psychologically more levelheaded type of police officer has stimulated increased attention to better education and higher professional standards. At the same time the need for greater numbers of police officers has created a conflicting objective. Limited budgets, inflation and the economic advantages of other types of available employment, combined with the hazards and stresses of police duty, have made it difficult, and perhaps impossible to recruit quantity as well as quality for today's police departments.

Where quality is achieved, the best men are almost inevitably attracted away from patrol and prevention, and into response and detection or up the organizational ladder into administration.

Ironically, the very technological advances that have made the street patrolman's life on his job physically easier, more protected, and more mobile, and provided him with unparalleled means of "instant" communication and information, have had a major share in gradual erosion of the preventive aspect of his mission.

The man on patrol gained added mobility when the horse also became a police recruit. Mounted elements still have specific utility in certain environments, even in this day of the automobile.

In the 19th century, the horse-drawn "Black Maria" made transportation of prisoners easier, and helped keep the beat-man on his beat.

When the popularity of bicycles created a special kind of "traffic" problem, some police were outfitted with bikes too. Some communities called them "scorcher" cops, because they pursued "scorchers" (bike speeders) who broke the traffic rules of the day.

The application of the gasoline engine to transportation came just about in the nick of time for police, for cities were getting too big to be handily covered by men on foot. Foot patrol continued to prevail initially even as gasoline-powered motorcycles were used for pursuit and the early police cars for response. Also the growing public ownership of autos created a new problem that only similarly equipped officers could "police."

Powerboats gave police a new tool for harbor and waterway protection. More recently airplanes and helicopters have added another dimension to policing for traffic observation and event crime surveillance, command control and some degree of response and rescue work.

The effectiveness of all of these transportation methods has been enhanced by developments in communications. Indeed, without the parallel development of new direct means of communication, the mobility advantages of the new vehicles would have been largely nullified.

The telegraph in the19th century speeded the flow of information from police force to police force, and from station to station. It did not affect the local patrol function, however, and the man on the street still had to signal for help by sounding his rattle, rapping with his nightstick, or blowing his whistle. The only way the sergeant or the captain could find his men was physically to go out and round them up.

The telephone opened the way to call boxes on the beat. However, the radio made instant contact possible. The mobile radio was the addition that really changed things as far as patrol was concerned. With the telephone, the patrolman checked in on a regular schedule, so the boss would know he was faithfully making his rounds, and to receive any new instructions. If the patrolman had anything of an emergency nature to report, he could do so through the nearest call box instead of making a long trip back to his precinct station.

In the first stage of development, the system operated on a one-way basis. Radio-equipped cars could receive immediate orders but still had to use the telephone call box to report. Two-way communication between car and headquarters was the second stage. The third stage has been the development of two-way radios so small that the individual officer can carry them, so that he need not be in a car to be in instant contact with other police.

The availability, mobility and communicability of the radio car so impressed police with its versatility and convenience that it has gradually become the staple element in contemporary police patrol. Yet these same qualities, or virtues, have helped to diminish its value for preventive patrol. As a matter of convenience, a distant car with a radio was called to make a run, even though the beat patrolman might only have been a block away. He was unreachable until he made his next scheduled call box report. Eventually radio cars were being dispatched to all the calls and eventually too many of them were spending all their time responding rather than patrolling.

Today's law enforcement executive is much different than what was envisioned by the people who created policing years ago. For example, the law enforcement executive of today must understand politics, have the ability to deal with the power structure and yet not jeopardize his professionalism, and not compromise with crime and corruptions. He or she must have the highest order of intelligence, capability, judgment and flexibility. At times he must reach decisions within himself or herself that place the job on the line, and require resignation rather than compromising professionalism. A rare combination of courage, integrity and independence must display itself in the law enforcement executive of the future.

One of the most revered and blindly accepted principles in the history of metropolitan policing is the one enunciated in Great Britain nearly 150 years ago, to the effect that the best evidence of effective police work is the *absence* of crime.

Equally hallowed by time and general acceptance is the principle that the greatest deterrent police can provide to the commission of crime is a visible police "presence," especially at times and places that offer potential criminals their greatest opportunity. This presence is provided by patrol.

With crime in the United States escalating faster than the population, obviously current efforts at crime prevention, including police patrol methods, have been inadequate. Many have said that this increase demonstrates that prevention is not the true role of policing. The presence of police in some instances may even trigger certain kinds of crime.

A social scientist named David Bayley (Dean and Professor of the School of Criminal Justice at the State University of New York) wrote *Police For the Future* in 1994. He presented an interesting decision for the public to make: Should the police be responsible for preventing crime? He made the case that police efficiency is measured in terms of response time, number of arrests, but not an outcome like a reduction in the number of crimes committed. It is easier to measure crime reduction, (simply compare before and after statistics) than it is to measure crime prevention. He is an advocate of a form of community policing included in the acronym CAMPS (consultation, adaptation, mobilization, and problem solving). His preferred form of mobilization to achieve these goals is foot patrol.

The surest method of crime prevention is the foot beat, which puts the officer in close contact with the neighborhood he is paid to protect or so thought Robert Peel who created the role of the policeman. But population growth, urban sprawl and municipal economics have so taxed the ability of police departments to provide sufficient foot patrolmen that police agencies have had to try other methods of increasing the range of the individual officer.

Aggressive service patrol officers look for what is right and wrong in the neighborhood. They try to be active servants of the people, guardians and protectors rather than enforcers. If they don't prevent crime, this puts them in the position of being punitive enforcers of the law once the crime is done.

The most popular means of spreading available police personnel over miles of city streets is the police car. As the use of the automobile has increased, the original preventive function of the police officer has gradually shifted to response.

The all-weather comfort, convenience and versatility of the automobile have indeed been assets to quicker response once a crime has been committed. But this has been of small comfort to the thousands of victims of crime who wish they could have been spared the experience in the first place.

Cocooned in their steel and glass vehicles, the response-oriented police officers of today lack personal visibility. They lack the opportunity to know and be known by citizens as personal protectors who can be recognized and trusted. Some of the alienation that has developed between police and some community segments has its basis in this lack of personal contact on a one-to-one basis.

Only in recent years has there been a serious attempt to re-examine patrol methods and to develop innovative practices to correct police thinking that motorization was the answer to effective crime control.

August Vollmer, a great pioneer in the advancement of police professionalism, helped to put police administration on a businesslike basis. Yet his great generalizations of the 1930s, significant innovations in their day, that foot patrol was obsolete and the scout car was the patrolman of the future, were swallowed a little too absolutely by police executives and theorists everywhere.

Obviously, the record indicates that motorization has not been the answer to crime control, if by motorization is meant the total disappearance of police into scout cars.

V. A. Leonard, who wrote *Police Organization and Management* in 1951, presented the case for Vollmer dicta in terms that may help to explain some of the tension that police operations have generated in subsequent years among various elements of the community.

Leonard said,

"Among the innovations which characterized the Vollmer system of police administration as the major contribution of the present century to crime control was complete motorization of the force. He held that the patrolman on foot was obsolete. Motorization amplified enormously the striking power of the force through increased mobility, maneuverability and speed of movement. The implications of this development in terms of combat strength or striking power are important."

Authorities have assumed for too long that the essence of patrol is simply movement, and the greater the mobility, the better the patrol.

But if observation and contact and the gathering of useful intelligence to anticipate and hopefully prevent crime are also characteristics of effective patrol, then emphasis on the mobility aspect at the expense of other essentials is misdirected.

"Shank's mare" or walking may be as obsolete as the old gray mare as far as sheer mobility is concerned, but the community contact and involvement with citizens which foot patrol provided is far from obsolete, as the disappearance of police-citizen rapport and the decline of citizen cooperation with police attests to this fact.

The tribute paid by Leonard to the increased "combat strength or striking power" of motorized police forces solely stresses the response capacity of such police elements. Indeed the very notions of "combat" and "striking power" are conceptually at odds with the Anglo-American institution of a civil police agency, as well as anathema to contemporary police-citizen relationships.

Another revered police pioneer, O. W. Wilson, who served as police executive, author and academician, wisely made a more balanced assessment of the car versus foot case. In his book, *Police Administration*, Wilson writes:

"Foot patrol…has some advantages over all over methods…It provides the best opportunity for observation within range of the senses, and for a close contact with people and things, enabling the patrolman to be of maximum service as an information source and counselor to the public, and as the eyes and ears of the police department…

"Foot patrol…does not enjoy many of the advantages of a patrol car. Lack of mobility and communication contact with headquarters lessens the emergency value of the officer and greatly reduces his ability to provide called-for services. Walking is the least efficient mode of transportation; the limited area that can be covered on foot makes this method of patrol costly."

Mobile foot patrols (scooters) can change all this. Turning this assessment around, the disadvantages of the foot patrol method are the advantages of the car. But few if any have taken equal pains to point out that the advantages of foot patrol are the disadvantages of the automobile. The undeniable advantages of foot patrol simply do not carry over into automobile patrol. Motorization of the police force trades off one type of service, which foot patrol did better, for another type of service, which the scout car does better.

On the basis of movement and economy alone, most police departments over the past 40 years have simply written off the advantages of foot patrol. No one has taken the concept of mobility and visible, protective presence and combined them to use both manpower and technological power to offer something better than total commitment to the automobile.

G. Douglas Gourley and Allen P. Bristow, police authorities 40 years ago, stressed the prohibitive cost of foot patrol, but acknowledged that there might be exceptions, such as crowded downtown areas or high concentrations of people that would justify the additional cost of food patrol. Is there no alternative to limited-range, costly foot patrol or highly mobile automotive operations with their inevitable isolation from neighborhood contact and loss of deterrent police presence?

As we see it today, police patrol has been reduced to cruising in anticipation of a call, instead of the systematic observations, inspection and gleaning of police intelligence, which adds visible "presence" as the preventive element in patrol. The idea of movement, of course, is inherent in the concept of "patrol," but movement alone without contact between the police officer and the people and surroundings that comprise his beat is "patrol" of the most superficial and inadequate kind.

PART VI
My British Police Experience

My British Police Experience

As a professor at John Jay College of New York I have had the privilege and pleasure of being in association with two wonderful English professors, Philip John
Stead, Dean of Academic Studies at the Police College, Bramshill in England and
also Jerry Lamford, Commandant of the Police College.

Both of these gentlemen were also my guests at my home in Farmington Hills,
Michigan and both gave superlative lectures to our students at Mercy College of
Detroit, when I was the Director of the Law Enforcement and Protection program. (Notice that this was in the early 1970s and I used both *law enforcement*
and *protection* in the title of my program.) Now that has become the essence of
this book—the dual purpose policing, so necessary to really provide the best in
community policing.

I have also had the pleasure of luncheons and discussions with several high-
ranking British police officials. Commissioner of Police Sir Robert Mark and Sir
John Waldman of the Metropolitan Police of London, Chief Constable Peter
Matthews of Surrey, the Chief Constable of Kent, and particularly Colonel Sir
Arthur Young, the Inspector-General Royal Ulster Constabulary and Commis-
sioner of the City of London Police (1950–1969). Sir Young invited me, my wife
Elinor, and my young daughter Betty to spend a night at the City of London
Woodstreet Police Station. They had a tower with guest rooms.

When we rolled up to the Woodstreet Station with our bags, the quizzical cab
driver said, "Well, I see Governor you're finally giving yourself up." We all had a
good guffaw at that.

I also was privileged and honored to be invited to a major conference on
Police Community Relations at Ditchley Park, May 29-June 1, 1970. The Conference membership involved a very distinguished and representative group of fifteen British and fifteen from the United States.

By calling together an expert Anglo-American conference on police-community relations, the Ditchley Foundation provided opportunity, in quiet surroundings, for a valuable interchange of experience and opinions between police
officers, criminologists, lawyers, representatives of local authorities and the public
interest, from both sides of the Atlantic.

The conference was convened "To consider the relations between police and the public, and their mutual responsibilities, in Britain and the United States, in the light of present social (including racial) conditions, with special reference to conduct in urban disturbances, to the selection, education and training of police officers, and to systems of control and inspection of police forces, and of complaint and disciplinary procedure, in the context of police-community relations."

There were plenary sessions with much discussion. There are widely divergent backgrounds of conditions in Britain and the United States. In Britain there is relative homogeneity whereas there is great diversity of the American population. Also there is disparity in size and population.

The British and American systems of justice have developed along entirely different historical lines, with far-reaching consequences for the structures and practice of police forces.

The report of Plenary sessions brought out that there was little in common between our two countries at that time. Police in the United States were fragmented into nearly 40,000 separate departments. In Britain (excluding Scotland and Northern Ireland) police forces numbered 47 in all, with centralized inspection and training and uniform pay structures. No such system for the application of common standards existed in the United States.

In regard to politics in Britain, civil service status and tenure are the rule, whereas in the United States often there was political patronage exercised over the appointment of police officers.

It would be unthinkable in Britain to see the police involved in politics, whereas in the United States it appeared to be the exception when they were not.

As to police methods, there was a striking difference between the two countries in their attitude toward the use of firearms. British police officers went unarmed, unlike their American colleagues. (There have been some changes necessitated now in England.)

The Plenary Report contrasted two fundamentally different conceptions of the police in relation to the public at large.

"Whereas in Britain they were primarily ordinary citizens, although in uniform and with special functions as constables to be exercised within the law, in the United States there appeared to be much less emphasis on their common citizenship with the rest of the community than on their executive role under the law as agents of government. This seemed to leave the door much wider open in the United States to friction between the police and the public than in Britain, where the relationship was more intimate and cohesive."

It was against this background of differences that the common aims of the police in the two countries and the best methods of fulfilling them were discussed. A dominating factor was soon seen to be the influence of what was perhaps the outstanding characteristic of the age, the rapidity of social and technological change.

"This placed the police in a particularly difficult, not to say ambiguous, situation. On the one hand, the police must show themselves ready and able to adapt to change, in order to avoid alienation from the rest of society and a major loss of public support; on the other hand, by their very nature as an instrument for upholding law and order, they could not help being guardians of the status quo."

The question of how to resolve this dilemma in its varied facets and in the different national circumstances was the essence of the whole debate. Some of the issues discussed are as follows. Salient points are covered. While this occurred in 1970, it is not surprising that they are not much different from problems of today.

The Effects of Change

A basic point was made that we live today in a doubting society in which authority is questioned and no longer wins automatic respect.

Increases and movements in population, changes in its composition, technological innovations, new outlooks and, above all, a shifting of the basis of power confront the forces intended to maintain order.

Mounting problems ensue which were never contemplated years ago. Growth of civil rights movements, unrest of minority communities, unrest in universities, the Vietnam War and its effects, all add up to challenges to the status quo. The police too often find themselves the middlemen between warring factions; often targets of hostilities.

Tension and conflict undoubtedly are more prominent in the American than the British scene. However pressures were mounting on both sides.

Increases in Crime

Increases in crime are disturbing; especially with regard to the use of violence. Drug use is escalating fast. A most disturbing feature is the upsurge in predatory crime, taking robbery as the yardstick.

Social Offenses

A contentious matter for police and community relations was held to be the enforcement of social laws. "The discretion allowed the police in deciding what action was to be taken in such matters gave rise to anomalies and a constant abrasion of their relations with the public."

Since enforcement of social laws often places an unfair burden upon police, for the sake of good public relations, police should be required to enforce only standards acceptable to contemporary society.

The use of the motorcar and the ensuing multiplicity of traffic regulations were also seen as significant sources of friction. This is an area in which the police can be excessively absorbed, to the detriment not only of their police image, but also of the resources they could devote to the major task of preventing and investigating crime.

Other social misdemeanors that burden the police, while demanding the exercise of their discretion, include drunkenness, prostitution, homosexuality, and gambling. A most serious discussion centered on the crimes committed by addicts in quest of money to buy drugs.

There was a tendency to distinguish between crimes that directly injured others and those in which the offenders and those dependent upon him were the principal victims. In such cases it was felt it might be more productive to think in terms of rehabilitation rather than arrest and sentences to prison.

Demonstrations

On such occasions, police are in the front-line, with their duty to maintain order, while at the same time avoiding the use of excessive force. The police at the conference wholeheartedly endorsed the public's right, within the law, to freedom of speech and freedom of behavior. It was not their business in any way to take sides or to discriminate between one cause or another, whether political, religious or social. The problem police face is how best to carry out their tasks, without forfeiting public confidence. Actions should be avoided which tend to deepen the cleft between the police and the demonstrators; such as using special riot squads or tear gas or barbed wire. In coping with demonstrations, an important factor is communication and a high degree of police organization and training.

Racial Minorities

The most sensitive area which came up was the relations of the police with racial minorities—problems affecting both countries but in different ways.

American Assessment

From American viewpoints it appeared that the picture was somber and that the present state of police and community relations was "terrible and worsening." (That was 1970!) Police were exposed to attacks when called in to deal with confrontations. The report showed a tendency to see issues in extreme terms of right and wrong, of friends and enemies, of battles to be won or lost.

A phrase much used in the United States was the "war on crime," (now it is the "war on drugs") typified by military orientation, which had been taken over into the social sphere. The report continued, "the lack of homogeneity in the United States population gave rise to class-economic and racial conflicts which, although fundamentally problems for government, were handed over to the police to control."

British Viewpoints

To most British eyes, the prospect looked much less bleak. Evidence for the generally good relationship between police and community was the fact that in a population of some 55 million, less than 100,000 police were needed to keep order. Since then British police have found more volatile and racial problems confronting them.

Relations with the Community

The need for vigilance regarding community tensions underlined the importance of good police and community relations, which is not subsidiary but is the essence of the police officer's job.

This requirement was clearly not intended to detract from the general agreement on such basic functions of the police as the preservation of law, order and liberty and the prevention and detection of crime. Its purpose was rather to emphasize the growing significance of the police role in providing a range of social services. "Police forces" would be benefited in their relations with the public by being re-named "police services."

There was, in the view of a British speaker, more room for developments of this kind in the United States where social services were generally less extensive than in Britain. As *law enforcement officers*, the police could not be universally loved; they could only hope to be respected.

A common factor was the need to identify social problems and to assert the impartiality of the police. This could happen only when the police were non-aggressive and kept in mind the precept that force did not deter. It meant creating a climate of understanding among individual police officers for the role they were asked to play, especially with regard to racial groups. It also meant that the police should be seen to be in constant touch with the community.

When I spoke to the group, I deplored the isolation caused by the extensive use of police cars to the detriment of foot patrols. I suggested that more such patrols, more scooters, more talk was required, and fewer screaming sirens on the street.

It was felt that a greater involvement in social services was bound to add to the already extensive duties of the police. One member thought it was too much to expect the police to act as social workers and psychologists unless they received better pay and higher status. (This I agree with.) Many police out there do some social work and psychology.

In the United States it was said that their status was lower than in Britain and many officers were not professional enough because of the fragmentation of police forces.

Recruitment

With the object of improving race relations, the need to recruit more non-white officers on both sides of the Atlantic was generally recognized. However attempts to recruit them ran into serious obstacles in both countries. Most blacks regard the police as "on the other side" and would shun any of their fellows who went in for police work. Many had not reached the educational standards to make them eligible to become recruits and those that had could often find better-paid jobs elsewhere.

The Public Image

Concern was expressed over the public image of the police and what could be done to improve it. Several aspects include the impression that the behavior of the individual officer made on members of the public who had dealings with him. Next, a more general factor was the effectiveness of police methods, and what measures are needed to remove sources of conflict within the community. Social strains and stresses went far beyond the police orbit, into the realm where the duty fell on political leaders and the public itself to insist on thoroughgoing action.

Conclusion

The conference provided a forum for a wide-ranging exchange of views, which, it was agreed, could be fruitfully continued between the two countries. The conference was marked by a notable openness of discussion, an absence of any seeking to excuse failure or to exaggerate success, and a dedicated concern for the upholding of civilized values.

The closing paragraph of the report was this: "If much was asked of the police officer of today the demand came from a deeply-rooted desire to see him playing a full and constructive part in the community. Lastly, for a civilian observer (C.F.O. Clark, Conference Reporter) it was both striking and encouraging to see executives of law enforcement as intent on respecting the rights and liberties of the citizen as those who criticized them for not doing so enough."

Reports of Groups from the British Conference

Report of Group A:

Role of the Police: There was general agreement that the police are only a part of two separate systems. The first was a system of criminal justice embracing the courts, prosecutors, corrections, as well as the police. (As an elected sheriff for 12 years, I have been involved in the entire criminal justice system and was even on both sides of the bars in the system as I describe elsewhere.) Police-community relations are often affected deeply by what other institutions in the system do, as much as what the police do themselves.

Secondly, the police are also part of a system of government rendering social services. Perhaps if some social services are weak or non-existent in some communities, a void is left which police must fill if anyone is to do so. I feel it would be preferable, in terms of relations with the community, to refer to a "police service" rather than a "police force." In "Dual Purpose" policing, the service should be as important as the control function of police.

Now it's important to state that the scooter patrols I've advocated for the prevention of crime (before the fact) and the community protection role is also a function of the automobile response role when it is possible to so engage. Likewise the scooter patrols, while engaged with rendering a variety of social services, are not excluded from responding, where feasible, to incidents of crime.

The preservation of law, order and liberty are functions and responsibilities of Dual Service policing.

Good relations between the police and the community will be furthered by the police taking greater responsibility for helping those who call for police assistance, or who are brought to the attention of the police to receive needed social service. (Scooter patrol officers could best do this. They could be in communication with other social service agencies as needed.)

The group also discussed Recruitment, Selection and Promotion. With respect to good police community relations, there is no doubt that diversity is needed. Future police officers should be recruited from minority groups and also from the ranks of college graduates. However, selection should be made only of high quality types, especially for the scooter type officers, charged with the community's crime prevention and protection.

Today in most departments, an officer can realize a wage increase for 3 or 4 or 5 years. Then he or she is still at that level unless he or she makes sergeant or maybe detective. One must make sergeant to advance higher. There should be opportunities for leadership roles for those remaining in the patrol service for adequate remuneration. (This is sorely needed and lacking today, and so we have the sad experience of the recent Cincinnati police case of a heavy fat guy who died in a struggle with several Cincinnati policemen, who were older, out of shape, and still required to respond to major scenes of conflict.)

Training and Education: The rapidity of social changes, the increasing complexity of society and its problems requires training in human relations, constitutional and political processes, and the kinds of social factors affecting police work and relations with the public.

College and university should be a major source of personnel and a means of adding to the education of existing police personnel.

An important aspect of training and education involves the development of the capacity for making judgments that will result in effective use of the very considerable discretion which is vested in the individual police officer.

Equipment: The increasing use of sophisticated equipment is useful and necessary for effective police work. But also the excessive use of vehicles can isolate the police from the public. Impersonal policing is not satisfactory. The public wants policemen to be visible, and to be in such a relationship with the citizens that the police officer is readily accessible. Consequently, the deployment of police personnel is of very great importance in police relations with the public.

The general conclusion was that there should be the utmost flexibility in the use of personnel and equipment and that it is an area where experimentation with different patterns may be used to develop those that are most satisfactory to both the police and the public.

Lastly concern was expressed over the need for the development of non-lethal alternatives to police weaponry. The issue of firearms focused upon the extent to which the practice of carrying arms served to present a constant source of citizen fear and thus added to police isolation (today we have Tasers.)

Report of Group B:

The British policing system was discussed thoroughly. But there was difficulty in constructing an equally precise picture for the United States, as different states, counties and cities operated different systems.

Both countries have systems of local control but there are great differences. The United States has close to 40,000 police agencies. England and Wales only 47. English police chiefs enjoy long tenures and therefore an independence rarely found among American chiefs. Control over American police departments is to be found concentrated in mayors, committees of City Councils, political leaders, businessmen, newspaper owners, or in the chiefs themselves.

The tenure of American police commissioners and police chiefs is generally short—usually less than two years. Therefore, in my opinion, there is little time for opportunity, for continuity of purpose or programs. Also American police are becoming increasingly politically active. Police federations and unions also diminish whatever control the police chief executive has.

Central and Local Control: Discussions ensued over whether there were features of the British system of control that might with advantage be copied in the United States.

The issue of whether transferring responsibility for law and order to state or possibly federal authorities was discussed. Surprisingly American representatives felt that state control would not be as effective as federal influence.

Certainly as in the United Kingdom, centralization seems inevitable and it was felt that positive gains can be had from the creation of metropolitan units. Consolidation of police units would be encouraged at city levels through federal guidelines and the allocation of grants. My views are somewhat different from this.

There was much discussion over what was bad about the idea of a national force and good about local forces. In some respects, England and Wales had a national police service. The Home Secretary's powers of control were increasing simultaneously with his accountability to Parliament. The process of amalgamation of police forces seems out of step with local government.

Community problems hinge directly on police policy and activity. It was felt that an effective local interest was vital, so that areas of police discretion could constantly be re-examined.

Concern was expressed on both sides as to the dangers of police officers becoming isolated from the rest of the public.

Complaint Procedure: The group agreed that the handling of complaints against the police was a very important aspect in maintaining good relations between the police and the public. They were further agreed that methods of informing complainants of the results of investigations ought to be improved. It was agreed that some complaints arose through misconceptions about police practice and the law.

Much discussion was had about the role and importance of education and the responsibility that police and society at large share for undertaking such education. Education for the young was stressed, but reference was also made to adult education. Here the role of the press was thought important, although there was a sharp difference of opinion on both sides as to how positive or negative the press in fact was in dealing with police matters.

General: It was held that ways and means of improving relations between the police and the public should include:

1.   The provision of as much information as possible as to the functions, difficulties and methods of the police, particularly when dealing with a matter originated by any member of the public such as a complaint.

2.   The continuing provision of information to those professionally concerned with the police on the differences between the systems in the U.S. and the U.K. so that the advantages and disadvantages of each may be more widely appreciated by comparison.

Report of Group C:

I was in this group and I thought we had the best recommendations. This group was concerned with a wide range of issues involving the scope of police responsibilities, methods of policing, and the approach of the mass media in presenting news on police-related problems.

Police Goals, Organization and Policies: There was widespread agreement that the appropriate responsibilities of the police include not only the prevention of crime and apprehension of suspects, but additionally the provision of certain peacekeeping and social services. Such services can be justified where they maintain public order and develop responsible citizenship, and when other organizations cannot provide them equally well, e.g. the "cautioning" of youth offenders, handling of family disputes where they may lead to violence, etc.

These services can be justified because they encourage police officers to develop a broad concept of their professional role (in contrast to a narrow concern with apprehending criminals) and because they provide an opportunity for developing constructive relationships with local communities.

The importance of close contact between police officers and citizens within their divisions or precincts was emphasized.

(Considerable concern was expressed by me regarding the tendency, in large cities, to rely on automobile patrolling combined with technical police forces and other special squads of "faceless" police officers. I brought up what had happened in Detroit and anti-Viet Nam demonstrators breaking windows of stores, etc. I described the argument with my assistant, John Nichols, about whether police should have masks, shields and batons versus sending in the scooter cops. I prevailed and there was peace.)

While some increase in motorization of the police was viewed as inevitable given increasing crime rates and manpower limitations, it was urged that some urban areas be provided with foot patrol officers, available on at least an 8-hour per day basis, to increase personal contact between the police and the public. The Unit Beat Policy systems in Britain and the experimental precinct patrol projects in Detroit illustrated this approach.

Technical and Special Events Squads: There was criticism of the way in which some of these organizations have been set up, trained and deployed. In some American cities, officers in such squads are isolated from the general public and from other members of their own police forces.

When called to assist in crowd control, they sometimes use excessive force and they are at times used to provide a kind of "neighborhood control," stopping and searching members of the local community without (at times) sufficient cause.

There was agreement that special technical squads should be used only with particular care, since their isolation from precinct work and their general style are likely to lead to conflicts with citizens stopped without reasonable cause, and thus create additional problems in police-community relationships for the regular precinct officers who must work daily in that community. The use of such squads may lead to confrontation and overreaction on both sides, which increase the possibility of massive public disturbance.

Street interrogation and search must be used with great care so as not to exacerbate police-community tensions and should be carried out by officers who are well-trained in procedures and respected in the local community, (such as the scooter cops.)

Police Leadership and Approaches to Police Change: There was discussion of the importance of forward looking leadership in handling emerging problems in police-public relationships and in experimenting with ways of improving police organization and policy. Police officers should understand and show a sensitive concern regarding the social problems that underlie much police-public conflict.

The Mass Media: There was considerable concern expressed regarding problems of the press and broadcast coverage of police-related activities. It was noted that the concern of most media organizations with making a profit led them to search for issues and incidents that attract an audience. Examples of violence receive far more coverage than general patterns of harmonious relationships. The result is that the media at times worsens relationships when a more balanced presentation would serve a better public service.

(I must note that in the Buckeye, Arizona prison standoff of 15 days during February 2004, the press did well. They held back coverage so that the hostages were not further endangered.)

At the same time, the press can bring to light important issues that hinder effective police-public relationships. It was agreed that media that adopt a balanced view of complex community problems should be helped by the police as they can.

Lastly it was suggested that a continuing and effective commission on Media Responsibility might be established to evaluate problems in this area and recommend ways of improvement, consistent with maintaining freedom of the press.

Problem of Community Accountability: It was felt that there is no more important or perplexing problem of police-community relations than that between police and those who live in minority neighborhoods (Black, Latino, immigrant, etc.)

The problem has to do with the remoteness of police and their accountability for their actions and conduct to the citizens in whose neighborhoods they serve. (My feeling, of course, is that police cars are remote and do not really serve. They are reactive, not proactive.)

As we have grown larger, more complicated and more bureaucratic, all forms of accountability have drifted from our neighborhoods and communities to remote city halls, state capitals, and federal agencies.

This statement was made: "There will be little relief from the seriously deteriorating state of police-community relations until and unless we are willing to make the police in some way directly accountable to the citizens in whose name we say we serve. The modes of accountability (community control, community review boards, citizens' participation) may vary considerably from community to community. But the need is clear—citizens must feel that they have some say about the decisions and arrangements that affect their lives."

(This is why I believe scooter officers and scooter patrol teams assigned to a neighborhood can relate to, interpret police methods, and provide bridges of understanding in troubled communities.)

Related Considerations: The group conference emphasized that there are other changes needed if the quality of police-public relationship is to be improved significantly. Improvement will be needed in the exposition of justice provided by the courts, and in the effectiveness of rehabilitative efforts, through prisons and partnership with community-based methods.

If the police officer is to have an opportunity to carry out his essential functions with a reasonable degree of effectiveness, it is critically important that government leaders and the general public take vigorous action to solve basic problems that generate urban unrest and violence such as those of unemployment, poor housing and racial discrimination.

Finally, if the proposal for skilled community involvement by the police and other suggestions are to be carried out, it is essential that sufficient police manpower of high quality be provided. Otherwise the police will not be able to meet adequately their important responsibilities in the community.

PART VII
Community Policing

Community Policing

"Community policing is law enforcement's latest new idea. But its promise is elusive." This was a headline in the *U.S. News and World Report*, August 2, 1993.

The article went on to state, "Community policing has become a mantra for police chiefs and mayors in cities big and small across the country. Indeed, community policing is the new orthodoxy of law enforcement."

(To me, the term "law enforcement" and "policing" are almost an oxymoron, and are relatively contradictory. "Policing," or good policing, should include or provide a preventive or protective concept.)

In Community Policing, rather than just reacting after crimes are committed, police should try to create partnerships with communities in advance to solve problems that otherwise lead to crime.

Community Policing came to the fore when President Bill Clinton stated, "We're determined to put more police officers on the street and to expand community policing."

I've been told I'm ahead of my time. Perhaps, but it sometimes comes at a price.

Now the big thing in American law enforcement is called Community Policing. This caught fire in America during the 1990s. England's John Alderson wrote about it in the 1980s. There were attempts at Community Policing in America during the 1970s. But I did it in the 1960s in New York (1964–66) and in Detroit (1968–69).

I even called my patrol method (using motor scooters going out to the community) Community-Oriented Patrol Service (COPS). I had catch phrases such as "It takes a team to prevent crime; you and your police" and "Buck up your police" which was a donation program to give a buck to support police.

About 1993–94, the U.S. Department of Justice established an office called the Office of Community-Oriented Police Services (COPS). How strange and how belated!

In addition to this office, the U.S. Department of Justice has produced a Community Policing Consortium composed of:

- International Association of Chiefs of Police
- National Organization of Black Law Enforcement Executives
- National Sheriffs Association
- Police Executive Research Forum
- Police Foundation

I have been a member or associate of all the above except the one of color.

On February 12, 2004, I called the Office of Community-Oriented Policing Services (COPS) and the Community Policing Consortium in Washington, D.C. to inquire about a publication. At this date, the phone number is 800-833-3085.

I had the most delightful chat with an Arnold Ajello who was very accommodating and he sent me the material on Community Policing I requested.

I discovered he could speak German and that he and his wife, Denise, had spent five years in Germany. Speaking German with him, I found him to be not only a great help to me in finalizing this book, but a wonderful guy. The Department of Justice and America are fortunate to have such a fine man thus employed.

From the information I received, I can give some history of the national COPS program.

Joseph E. Brann, first Director of the Office of Community Oriented Policing Services said about COPS,

> The COPS Program has been the most effective legislation in support of police and America's neighborhoods to come out of Congress in decades. It is working.
> The COPS office, in partnership with local communities and police agencies, has already authorized the hiring and redeployment of more than 43,000 officers for community policing. Eighty-seven percent of the American people live in jurisdictions served by agencies that have received COPS grants.
> There is a word for this record: Success!

The present Director is Carl R. Peed, former Sheriff of Fairfax County, Virginia.

This COPS Office probably started in 1993 or 1994. I was pleased to note that in 1996, a Special Edition of Information Access Guide was printed and used the word "services" rather than "law enforcement."

COPS publishes a bi-monthly newsletter called Community Policing Exchange. It reports on the newest developments in Community Policing Partnerships. It is written exclusively by practitioners and is mailed to more than 60,000 law enforcement, municipal and private organizations. This newsletter showcases the agency's contributions to the advancement of community policing. Its statement of purpose is "to assist law enforcement practitioners by bridging the distance between communities, facilitating the exchange of information, and giving voice to all involved in the implementation of community policing."

I will now address some comments and positions from the Community Policing Exchange Newsletter and I will emphasize certain points in italics. One of the newsletters had this header: "Community Policing Strategies Offer Promise of Improved Public Safety."

> The time is ripe for *change* within policing, within government.
>
> Violent crime rates are soaring. Inner cities continue to deteriorate. Suburbs, once havens from the harsh realities of urban decay, can no longer claim that privilege.
>
> Citizens in many areas of the country are increasingly frustrated and in many cases *alienated* from the police...
>
> In the search for *solutions*, the concept of community policing surfaces with ever more regularity. There have been escalating demands for *change* throughout the criminal justice system. Nowhere within that system has the need for a *new approach* been more apparent *than in law enforcement*.
>
> In addition to calls for better laws and tougher law enforcement have been those for a *different style of policing*, one focused on *prevention* as well as on apprehension.
>
> The clear winner *thus far* has been *community policing*.

In this newsletter, the Community Policing Consortium in its inaugural issue pointed out that "for all the attention given to the concept by academics, the media, politicians, civic leaders—community policing is not a proven panacea."

A survey by the F.B.I. and the National Center for Community Policing at Michigan State University indicated 50% of police officers serving cities with populations of more than 50,000 said they were following this approach in policing; and an additional 20% planned to inaugurate it within a year. "It's reached the point that it's like Mom and apple pie," said John Eck of the Police Executive Research Forum.

And therein lies a problem according to *U.S. News and World Report.* "Despite its allure on paper, turning the theory into practice on the unforgiving streets of urban America is proving complicated. If community policing can't deliver quantifiable results quickly, it could end up on the scrap heap of innovation."

An example is Houston, Texas. Community policing there was called Neighborhood-Oriented Policing. Houston is a cautionary tale. Crime rates soared. Budget cuts had reduced many officers. Neighborhood-Oriented Patrol (NOP) became "Nobody on patrol." Police chief Sam Nuchia shelved most aspects of NOP, preferring old-fashioned "get tough" tactics.

While some police department proponents have made major commitments to community policing, other cities borrow the name but make only cosmetic changes, thus creating a variety of incomplete and superficial programs.

Changes needed and recommendations often cut to the core of a stubborn paramilitary police culture. Recruiting must attract people interested in "service," not just adventure. Training needs to expand beyond arrest procedures.

The *U.S. News and World Report* article goes on to suggest that police departments must find ways to free officers from what's called the "tyranny of 9-1-1:" non-stop calls that send cops bouncing around like pinballs. Dispatchers are forced to screen out non-emergency calls or calls to fake burglary alarms, domestic disputes, neighborhood quarrels, sick cases, past burglaries, etc.

Police experts went on to say, "Many questions remain not only about how the community policing strategy will be implemented on a grand scale, but also about the expected results of such a program."

That is why the Bureau of Justice Assistance (B.J.A.) established the Community Policing Consortium. The Consortium was established to help the nation's police plan and implement community-policing strategies in their communities.

The passage of the 1994 Crime Bill reinforced the federal government's commitment to that change.

The newsletter further states, "Research done on early community policing strategies clearly shows that they made residents feel more secure, increased trust between the police and the citizens, and enhanced citizen perception of police services."

At that time, March 1995, the newsletter also stated that community policing causing "increased contact between the citizens and the police will result in a police force more aware of the criminal activity in a given community and more able to collect and analyze information that will contribute to prevention of crime as well as apprehension of criminals. Although these conclusions do appeal to logic, crime control has yet to be indisputably proven as a benefit of community policing."

Yes! Research goes on! James Q. Wilson, like so many academics, asserted that community policing is based upon the following principles:

- Preventing crime is as important as arresting criminals.

- Preventing disorder is as important as preventing crime.

- Reducing both crime and disorder requires that police work cooperatively with people in neighborhoods to (1) identify their concerns, (2) solicit their help, and (3) solve their problems.

The Community Policing Consortium aim was to lend assistance to the nation's police to incorporate these principles in their operational plans. The newsletter stated that it would not be an easy task.

Most previous programs generally had one common element. The police were supposed to get out of their patrol cars and into their neighborhoods. But the newsletter had this comment: "For decades prior, conventional wisdom had held that omnipresent motor patrol would deter crime. Research in the early 1970s proved that assumption to be false."

I knew that in the 1960s in New York and Detroit the motor patrol car was not a complete answer. The motor scooter, both in New York and in Detroit, and even later in the 1970s in Oakland County where I was sheriff provided a better omnipresence. This could be seen by the *New York Times* article and by peoples' reactions. (See Early Start of Community Policing)

Since the Introduction of Community Policing

Since the introduction of Community Policing in 1993 with the Office of Community-Oriented Police Service in the Department of Justice, there have been articles and reports in the *Police Chief* magazines such as the following:

1. *Distribution of COPS monies well underway*: December 1994.

    In summary, during the fiscal year beginning 1995, $1.3 billion was designated for "Cops on the Beat" by President Clinton. Under "COPS" Phase 1, $200 million in grants were available to 392 police departments to help hire more than 2,600 beat patrol officers. (There had been $150 million Special Supplemental Appropriations made in 1993.)

    On October 17, 1994 at the I.A.C.P.'s 101st conference in Albuquerque, New Mexico, President Clinton indicated he had instructed the Department of Justice (D.O.J.) to speed up the distribution of the $1.1 billion remaining "Cops on the Beat" funds as provided by the new crime law.

    In addition, another $700 million was made available for future COPS programs to procure equipment, technology, or support systems, and result in an increase in the number of officers deployed in community-oriented policing.

    Other grant programs for the "15% remaining money" which could be used for purposes such as:

    * Proactive crime control and prevention

    * Specialized training for skill to work in partnership with members of the community

    * To assist in developing new technologies to assist law enforcement agencies in reorienting the emphasis of their activities from reacting to crime to preventing crime

    * To increase and enhance proactive crime control and prevention programs involving law enforcement officers and young persons in the community

- To facilitate the adoption of community-oriented policing as an organization-wide philosophy.

2. *Integrating COP into selection and promotional system:* March 1995

    Deals with why personnel are frequently very slow to accept the advent of community policing and offers a variety of explanations for community policing. It is vital that the best candidates be identified and the article suggests ways to do so. Training should include role-playing for various candidates and problems a community service officer might encounter.

    (This brings me back to my Police Academy days in the New York City Police Department. Bill McCullough, who I had brought into the Police Academy, and I were both lieutenant instructors. We instituted the idea of bringing lectures into role-playing demonstrations. I was sent to the Southern Police Institute and then taught promotion courses, Bill masterfully continued and the Academy Playhouse was born.)

    (Playlets of all kinds were developed with actors, some from the Recruit Schools, and playlets focused on a different and important subject. There were ever-present threads of super-important themes in all of them like the position of public relations. Bill made a most significant advance in police training in the years 1952 to 1958 so recruits could apply the New York Police Department philosophy and values to their everyday work.)

3. *Community surveys help determine policing strategies:* March 1995

    Response to serious crimes is important but citizens also want police to attend to the minor annoying problems within their neighborhood. Surveys ascertained the community's true feelings about crime and disorder. Problems identified were abandoned cars, poor street lighting, drug houses, vandalism, graffiti, and incidents that caused concern and contributed to the deterioration of the community.

    A key component of community-oriented policing is the physical placement of officers in neighborhoods where they can walk the beats, meet the residents and begin to focus greater attention on creative problem-solving strategies.

4. *Placing community-oriented policing in the broader realm of community cooperation*: April 1995

    Advocates of community-oriented policing described it as a philosophical movement that is changing the way we view law enforcement in a societal context. It is a direct response to an increase in social problems that are affecting the mainstream citizens, and the only viable approach to moderating these problems is community-wide participation and cooperation.

5. *Cooperative policing: Bridging the gap of community policing:* July 1998

Deals with the fact that while public safety services are delivered primarily at the community levels, they rely strongly on services delivered from the county, state and federal levels. Cooperative policing can help address problems that are pushed into a community by outside forces and that need assistance and support. This is an Oregon State Plan for assistance to communities.

6. *Crime prevention—The changing role of the beat officer:* December 1998

This deals with community leadership suggesting that police officers should see themselves as community leaders. During a lecture at the F.B.I. Academy, George Kelling referred to police as "natural leaders" because they are the front line of governmental services and should be catalysts to activate other agencies in the problem-solving process.

Patrol officers must be empowered to face the challenges of battle, including crime prevention techniques and the use of community programming to prevent and solve problems. Achieving the vision of safer communities and a brighter future will require unprecedented leadership.

7. *Community policing in Israel:* December 1998

A former commissioner of police in Israel decided that his major initiative during his term of office would be to bring about a conceptual change within the organization, from a basically reactive form of policing to community-oriented policing. It has not been easy, anti-terrorist and emergency matters related to ensuring public safety have become of paramount importance and emphasis. However, this is an interesting and informative article about the planning, implementation, and organizational change in the development of the community-policing unit, Israeli Police Headquarters, Jerusalem, Israel.

8. *Organizational leadership and change management:* December 1998

This is a quite thorough article about removing systems barriers to community-oriented policing and problem solving. The article points out that police bureaucracies flourished in the 1940s and 1950s (when I was on the job) and that policing, because of anti-corruption and reform movements, redefined its mission as law enforcement and became the most autonomous element of local government.

The result, the adoption of rigid organizational structures known as machine bureaucracies has produced tall hierarchies, closed systems, comparatively narrow jobs with distinct specialization, one-way communication and centralized command and control using an elaborate system of rules, regulations, policies and procedures. Significant flexibility was not required.

Yet community-oriented policing and problem-solving (COPPS) required flexibility and innovation. The article suggests a solution could be found in moving the traditional police organization toward a more organic design while retaining sufficient bureaucratic structure for stability and support.

Teams are suggested and would be used at the operational level to accommodate greater innovation than that typically found in traditional professional bureaucracies.

In the machine bureaucracy performing tasks are controlled by rules, regulations, policies and procedures. In a professional police bureaucracy, officers are highly skilled and perform work relying on their skills and knowledge without undue bureaucratic control.

Restructuring for community-oriented policing does not mean "giving away the store." A bureaucratic structure still is in place and functioning but officers need flexibility to be innovative in developing solutions to community problems. Restrictive bureaucratic rules do not foster innovation; rather, they suppress it. (In New York, I fostered the team approach with a sergeant in charge of eight officers in the 7th precinct and in Detroit also did similarly.)

9.   *Model for community mobilization:* December 1998

This article describes a model that police departments can use to bring together members of the community and take advantage of individual and organizational resources to create sustainable crime prevention efforts.

Crime prevention plans typically focus on particular crime problems, such as youth violence, drugs, property crime and neighborhood deterioration, but actually have as an end goal a healthy, crime-free community.

There is growing interest in multi-disciplinary community-based crime prevention efforts. This community mobilization model is one approach that shows promise in organizing communities to combat crime.

10.   *The changing face of policing in the U.K.:* December 1998

This British article deals with the fact that police needs to respond flexibly to the demands of the criminal environment. On April 1, 1998, two national police organizations (National Criminal Intelligence Service or NCIS and National Crime Squad or NCS) were born and this birth was not an easy one.

"The law enforcement environment is a sophisticated business area, and the planning process was historically focused on community policing." But it became apparent that organized crime posed a significant threat. Its effects were increasingly being felt across the country.

There was broad acceptance that to effectively address the top level of criminality, the former policing model was an inadequate response. N.C.I.S. was designed to gather, develop and disseminate intelligence on the most active criminal elements in the U.K., "to provide leadership and excellence in criminal intelligence." The N.C.S. addressed serious and organized crime, to target criminal groups, accrue evidence and effect their destruction.

11. *Service organizations—Your community policing ally:* December 1999

This is an interesting article on the changing unique values and assistance that service organizations such as the Lions, Rotary, and Kiwanis can bring to community policing.

12. *Transformational leadership and community policing—a road map for change:* December 1999.

This article states, "The movement toward community policing signals a major effort at transformational changes to redefine how a police agency operates...While much has been written about the overall philosophy and general principles of community policing, fewer efforts have been directed to providing leaders with specific information on what they need to focus on to make change happen in their police agency."

The article explains the Michigan Regional Community Policing Institute (R.C.P.I.) commitment to facilitate organizational changes within police agencies, and to the development of community partnerships to instituting community policing and presents a roadmap for making the change to community-policing happen.

This is mainly an academic treatise but it does point out some salient facets. Among them: to restructure the organization, leaders must focus on concepts such as roles and responsibilities of police officers and issues of divisional alignment and work emphasis. Traditional policing models focus on individual officers as specialists within a tightly controlled organizational hierarchy. A community policing perspective requires moves toward the officer as a generalist with realignment of divisions to allow for greater focus on geographical areas of responsibility and a teamwork emphasis. (Of course, I did teamwork with heads of the scooter patrol in New York and Detroit.)

Police leaders must begin by having a firm belief that changing the way the agency is run is critical and as worth the effort. The leader must emphasize that the status quo is not good enough, that business as usual cannot be tolerated, and that the move to community policing as a philosophy of doing business differently might be a strategy worth pursuing.

Transformational change requires a long-term commitment to challenging the status quo. The move to community policing is an attempt to deal with long-standing problems that require creative and innovative solutions.

A key step is for leaders to "model the new way." The article provides a framework for change and is a catalyst to police agencies that are moving towards becoming a community policing organization.

13. *The structure of successful community-oriented police departments:* November 2000.

This article said, "At the beginning of the twentieth century, police departments throughout the nation, during what has been called the reform movement, changed their organizational structure to that of a bureaucracy.

"This structural change occurred to deal with the problems of political patronage and corruption in police departments.

"The result, over time, was the development of municipal police departments into rigid, formalized, centralized structures that were not responsive to the communities they served.

"Police officers became professional crime fighters who sought little community input."

(Yes, and they operated almost entirely in police patrol cars isolating themselves from the good people in the community.)

Some statements of this article were the following:

"If contemporary reformers are correct, the departments that implement the philosophical and pragmatic components of community-oriented policing, without the appropriate structural changes, will lack the infrastructure to support community-orienting policing activities.

"Community-oriented police departments are structured differently from traditional police departments: Their organization is less complex, their decision-making less centralized, their administration less dense."

14. *Community safety—a policing imperative:* December 1998

This is a British contribution regarding community safety.

"Working in partnership with the community to reduce crime, the fear of crime and antisocial behavior is now a feature of police work.

"In the United States, the influence of the partnership approach is seen as the movement away from law enforcement and toward community policing. In the United Kingdom, it is reflected in the requirement that local authorities deliver community safety."

This article discusses partnership arrangements with community groups and changes in styles of policing. Problem-oriented policing solutions depend on partnerships through imaginative social programs.

"The constant challenge for police leaders is to navigate policing through the seas of political influence without foundering on the rocks of hard-bitten police attitudes."

(How true! The politicians and the police continually disagree. Can we ever really "serve and protect" the people?)

The Early Start of Community Policing

What is Community Policing and what will it do for police departments and the communities they serve?

The COPS newsletter answers in this way:

> It is an evolutionary rather than a revolutionary idea. It is a quest to safeguard and revitalize our communities.
>
> Since the late 1970s, it has cropped up as a police strategy in various ways, in various places, under various names, including team policing, problem-oriented policing, and community-oriented policing.

Their time line is wrong.

My Community Oriented Patrol (scooter cops) in Detroit was 1968–69, and in New York City, 1964–66. The *New York Times* article covered my police scooter patrol in 1965. There I was really ahead of my time. My comments then were, "We have got to win the hearts and minds of people, all people in the United States, and we need their assistance in the battle against crime and efforts to keep our communities safe and habitable. We must allow police to return to the people."

In New York I introduced the concept of motorized, two-wheeled scooter patrol, first in parks and then to all 79 police precincts in the city. Despite much bureaucratic opposition and roadblocks, they were successful.

In the city of Detroit, again against much political opposition and after some police opposition, I instituted motorized scooter patrols with great success.

In Detroit in 1968 and 1969, I referred to scooter patrols as "Community-Oriented Patrol Services" or COPS. Now years later, our federal government Department of Justice has an office called COPS and dispenses millions of dollars to police agencies for various types of community services policing (but not scooters.)

Later after Detroit, I was a professor at John Jay College of Criminal Justice in New York City and also at the same time became Director of the Law Enforcement and Protection Program at Mercy College in 1970 until almost 1980. (Note the term Protection. I felt then that Law Enforcement was not enough).

My theme in courses and in this book is that we need both law enforcement and protection. Yes, we must take proper action when crimes are committed. But we must also serve as protectors and preventers of crime, which police in police cars really cannot do well.

As Professor at John Jay College and Director at Mercy College, I met Phillip John Stead who was a visiting professor at John Jay College from England. I also invited Professor Stead to visit in my home and lecture to my students at Mercy College. He gave a great talk and was very well received there in 1971.

In 1973, P. J. Stead along with John Alderson, a well-known Chief Constable in England wrote *The Police We Deserve*. That was something that John Stead and I had often discussed at John Jay College.

Later in 1984, John Alderson who had a distinguished career, probably Britain's most distinguished policeman, retired from the force in 1982 to write his book *Law and Disorder*, published in 1984. (That was the year I retired as Sheriff of Oakland County, Michigan.)

John Alderson in England also advocated community policing against much opposition from those set in their ways such as Sir David McNee, Commissioner of the Metropolitan Police (Scotland Yard) and other chief constables.

In my first book, *American Police Dilemma*, the dilemma was whether we are protectors or enforcers. I will quote a few paragraphs from John Alderson's book, pp. 221-222 under the caption "Keeping the Peace or Enforcing the Law?"

> It is repeatedly proclaimed that the task of the police is to keep the Queen's peace, that state of tranquility in which our daily lives can carry on reasonably free from interference. It is not the same thing as law enforcement. Law enforcement is part of the concept of keeping the peace but by no means is exclusively so.
>
> To put it simply, if in order to enforce laws methods are used which in themselves result in widespread disorder, then the Queen's peace has been disproportionately broken. Thus, in striving to enforce laws police have to do so in a manner which would not be disproportionate in the social damage caused by police law enforcement activity. In practice this can mean achieving objectives by prevention and proactivity rather than solely by reaction; by summons instead of arrest; and by caution instead of prosecution...The issue highlights the difference between police efficiency and police effectiveness.

Response times, the time lapse between a call for police and their attendance, are also a measurement of police efficiency though not necessarily of
effectiveness. By that is meant that effective policing may reduce the need for
some response requests by, for example, better community policing.

A strategically placed foot patrol would prevent street crime and be effective, whereas an efficient, high-powered radio car would react to a victim's
call.

It may be possible to have a police force regarded as efficient…but
regarded by the public with indifference and even hostility. It is generally a
fact that the public prefers human contact with police before conflict to
impersonal mobile police afterwards.

I was quite pleased to read on page 12 of John Alderson's book these lines
written in 1984. "The police have to be seen and to see themselves as *protectors of
liberty* within the law. Freedoms depend on the ability of the police (and the
courts) to protect them equally, not unequally…"

This is the exact expression I first used in 1968 and 1969 when I was Police
Commissioner of Detroit. I had "Protector of Liberty" bumper stickers on all
police cars. It stood for an acronym for the word POLICE: Protector Of Liberty
for the Individual, the Community, and Everyone Equally.

I had taught this to my students at John Jay College in 1970 and 1971 and
explained my concept of POLICE to Professor John Stead and also my Community Oriented Police Scooters (COPS).

John Alderson in his book argued that "We were losing the art of preventive
policing and that much of the crime then plaguing society was preventable but
only if we were to develop new strategies. The concept which I argued for then
and since was the establishment of community policing."

I couldn't agree more. Throughout his book, John Alderson points out the
problems he had and the naysayers he encountered.

Yes, I had problems in putting Community-Oriented Police in both the City
of New York and later in the City of Detroit.

Perhaps my discussions with Professor Stead resulted in some thoughts in his
book *The Police We Deserve* 1973 with John Alderson and then to Alderson's
book *Policing Freedom.*

John Alderson's premise for Community Policing is to get the community
involved and supportive of police efforts. Many parts of the book are devoted to
this concept. This is also what I did in 1968 and 1969 in Detroit with excellent
results.

I certainly agree to combat crime and vandalism the police and the citizens have to get down to business together. The police should not feel they are alone in the fight. They need support and cooperation toward this concept.

In 1969, I was asked to do a speech at the 12th precinct on Valentine's Day. This is what I said. It's called "Love and Crime" and I strongly believe in it. It shows where the community individually and respectively can help.

> The problem of crime is complex and difficult and requires competent, well-trained, acceptable, professional police and sheriff's departments to cope with it. But, if I had to pick one thing that could really do the job and solve the problem, it would be love.
>
> Love! What is it? It can be called a hundred different things, and the young don't have a monopoly on it. We seniors over 30 know about love also, and we are, hopefully, balanced by our experience. Maybe we can teach the younger generation a few things about love and work together for a pleasant and peaceful future.
>
> What is this love that can cut down crime and cancel community tensions? What is this love that can do more about crime than all your law enforcement agencies, vigilantes, guns and tanks? Let's try to define it:
>
> - If it's caring about your neighbor so you report an assault you witness upon him or his home, that's love.
>
> - If it's caring about your community so that you don't want to see it suffer, that's love.
>
> - If you care about your fellow citizens no matter what their hue, that's love.
>
> - If you care enough to willingly serve your country and your community, that's love.
>
> - If you are concerned about the conditions that can tempt man to harm his neighbor, and you want to see them alleviated, that's love.
>
> - If you get concerned about crime and do something constructive about it, that's love.
>
> - If you feel that there are things wrong, injustices, evils in this world, and you earnestly wish to do something about them, that's love.
>
> - If you want to change things that do not seem right to you, calmly, coolly, with considered judgment, rather than with a destructive "to hell with it all" attitude, that's love.

- If you do your thing well, within the law and within the bounds of propriety, that's love.

- If you put your personal desires and politics second to your concern for your community, that's love.

- If you concentrate more on helping to professionalize your police than to complain about or ignore your police, that's love.

- If you can take a negative and help turn it into a positive, that's love.

- If you follow the principles of honesty, truthfulness and fairness, that's love.

- If you use consideration, care, courtesy and compassion in your dealings with all you meet, that's love.

- If you live according to the Golden Rule, the Ten Commandments, or your moral, ethical or religious beliefs, that's love.

- If you consider the feelings of the other person as an individual who is with you on this small spinning speck of dust called earth, that's love.

- If you have faith in people and in your police, that's love.

- If you have hope that we can all live together in a better world, that's love.

- If you offer charity to all your fellow men, that's love.

- If you believe there may be a spot in heaven for all, regardless of their race, color or creed, that's not only love but heaven on earth."

People see police departments and police as distinct from the people.

What really does constitute quality policing? I believe it is a philosophy that engenders police and community cooperation to address problems within the community.

The community, in effect, gets the police they deserve. Likewise, the police, by their actions, get the type of community they deserve.

Good community policing (not just law enforcement) gets good citizens to do their part. We must allow some of our police to deal with the good people.

PART VIII
Mobile Foot Patrols

Mobile Foot Patrols

I know of many reasons why law enforcement officers get little respect, based on my 84 years of life experiences and 44 years in the practice of law enforcement and policing. They don't serve and protect! The police have created a great gulf between themselves and those they are to protect. They've done this to themselves by being macho and riding around in fast cars talking to each other and to dispatchers rather than walking or peddling or scootering around and talking to citizens.

What are the main functions of police departments? They are first and foremost to prevent crime, detect and arrest offenders, preserve peace, enforce laws and ordinances, and protect life and property. There are other functions of police departments; e.g. regulate vehicular and pedestrian traffic, guard the public health, preserve order at elections, assist at fires, make inspections of certain places, preserve order at assemblages, suppress riots and remove nuisances and mendicants.

But, really, does the officer in the automobile do all this? No!

The old-time beat cop, the foot patrol officer, did but foot patrol is a thing of the past.

True, the automobile has many advantages but the worst culprit in the alienation between the police officer and the people is the automobile. Yes, the automobile provides fast response, in most cases, but provides very little of preventive patrol or furtherance of the many other police functions and good community relations.

Professor George Kelling of Harvard University has criticized some of the "Vollmerian" results of emphasis on the automobile. Kelling suggests that we should "put the cops back on beats" and restore close contact with the public. I agree. The officer in an automobile is in a "cocoon of glass and steel." He has lost the ability to stop, talk, and get to know people.

Yes, the officer in the police car responds quickly but to whom? The criminal, the assailant, the aggressor and those in their clutches. No wonder he becomes cynical, hardened and alienated dealing with such people.

No doubt foot patrol was costly but it was very important. People who went shopping or out for entertainment saw the officer. They felt they could trust someone they knew. That old-time trust is missing with the officer in the car. You can't talk with him with windows closed.

In my opinion, police patrols should include some form of the old-time beat patrol, which had citizen respect. I suggest that that the old-time foot cop rapport be restored in three ways by what I call Mobile Foot Patrols:

1.   By bicycle cops. Some police departments have realized their benefits in special areas.

2.   By motor scooters. I have instituted these in New York City and Detroit, and assisted with them in Washington, D.C. and Flint, Michigan with excellent results.

3.   And for business areas, shopping malls, boardwalks, the foot scooter, now modernized with gyroscopes called the Segway. Police officers now could literally again be foot patrol officers but greatly aided by the Segway to cover streets containing business and commercial stores or what we used to call in New York, the "glass posts." They might also be effective in high-rise buildings.

All three methods in the city should be used to recover our true police function, which is the reduction of crime and community tensions. We need to take another direction on the road toward combating crime and violence, a road toward the people.

New York Scooter Experience

In the spring of 1964, I put nine scooters into service on an experimental basis in Central Park in Manhattan, and Prospect Park in Brooklyn. Robbery and other crimes dropped significantly in the two parks during a four-month trial period. The program continued until September 1, 1965, when 50 more scooters were put into service in 17 precincts, still primarily for park patrol. Each of the 17 precinct commanders evaluated the experiment, reported favorably, and requested that the program be continued.

During the visit of Pope Paul VI on October 4, 1965, the scooter patrolmen were invaluable to commanding officers of sectors along a motorcade route lined with over a million persons. The scooter men served as reconnaissance scouts, inter-sector messengers, and as liaison officers when communications were severed or overtaxed.

Beginning October 20, 1965, the program was tested for general street patrol in 15 selected precincts, and again was received favorably. During the electrical power failure on November 9-10, 1965, during the height of an evening rush hour, several million persons stalled in transit. However, the scooter patrol maintained immediate, direct radio communication with precinct station houses. One scooter was sent from Manhattan to Maspeth, Queens, over a jammed Williamsburg Bridge for emergency radio equipment, an impossible task for an auto. The scooter went and returned promptly.

During the paralyzing citywide transit strike January 1-13, 1966, public transportation was nonexistent. Scooters were in constant demand because they could cut through traffic blockages, even riding on sidewalks when necessary. Besides quickly unlocking vehicular congestion, they could survey problem areas and report to precinct commanders. In the vicinity of bridges and tunnels, when traffic lanes were reversed to expedite the flow of vehicles from major roadway approaches, the scooter men were utilized most effectively. They also delivered messages and supplies through otherwise impassable locations.

The Tactical Scooter Unit became a team patrol because they could keep in touch by radio. They operated either as partners or as a group according to the need. From this point on, the use of scooters became an accepted part of New York police operations, some 700 being acquired and put into operation by the time I decided to retire from the Department in 1966.

The new scooter patrolmen operated either as partners (team) or as a group (unit) according to need, and always under the knowledge, direction, and control of the local precinct commander via two-way radio.

The teams were encouraged to develop various patterns of street patrol—to be systematically unsystematic. One such predetermined pattern was worked out for two men to ride parallel avenues. The pattern was to proceed three blocks, turn into a side street, meet, and continue on to exchange avenues; two blocks later the same procedure; then after one block. This resulted in two faces on an avenue rather than one, added interest for the men, increased alertness, and made for an illusion of omnipresence.

The scooter patrolmen improvised on and changed their patterns of street patrol much as baseball or football players adapt set plays to meet rapidly changing conditions. Within a precinct, teams were organized for group operations; precinct units could quickly be wielded into a swift, highly maneuverable and unpredictable crime fighting force.

The advantages of scooters was that they greatly extended patrol coverage, permitted better police observation, could move easily in congested areas, freed radio patrol cars for response to major incidents, were economical, could be quickly mobilized, reduced the fatigue of foot patrol, increased the morale of and stimulated recruitment, provided a visible crime deterrent, established rapport with juveniles, and were well received by the community.

But in the 1950s and 60s as police became more modernized and motorized, crime still increased, community tensions exacerbated, and youth hostility rose. The police officer was set apart in his police car, dealing impersonally with the public and he was less responsive for the enforcement of community standards and neighborhood interactions. No wonder he does not garner the respect of the citizens when it appears as if he wants to avoid dealing or talking with them. We lose respect for our physicians when they don't want to talk with us about our problems but simply write prescriptions and order things that affect our very lives.

The good, trusted police officer of yesterday, the policeman on post has now given way to the "law enforcement officer" which implies a punitive or repressive role. Let's return to some of the values and respect of yesterday. Today's police officer must do many things to return to his role to serve and protect, but let's put him in a position to do so. The bicycle, Segway or scooter can literally bring back the beat or foot patrol officer who interacts with the public. A willingness to interact with citizens is the only way that American law enforcement will regain respect from citizens.

The origins and success of the motor scooters as I developed them in New York City was astounding, even after much derision. "Macho" cops looked with disdain at this small two-wheeled vehicle. They would prefer motorcycles. They did not understand. The motorcycle, which is good for escorts and chasing speeders, is a two-wheeled "pursuit and punitive" machine. The motor scooter is a "protective patrol vehicle."

The physical difference is that a rider straddles a motorcycle like a cowboy on a horse, but a rider sits in a motor scooter and puts his legs in front of his seat as he wheels about the city. While usually classified as mopeds, motor scooters can be electric or gas-powered, can cost from $500 to $5000, can go from 30 to 100 mph depending upon the make and type, can get as much as 100 miles per gallon and can have a 1.5 gallon gas tank. They can be equipped with headlights, strobe lights, and even sirens. If desired, they can come equipped to carry an additional person or to carry up to 50 pounds of equipment. They require a drivers' license and/or a motorcycle license. They are not toys for children.

Police executives come from the rank and file of macho cops and may view motor scooters askance. So departments in the United States followed along with

August Vollmer's dictum regarding how the automobile made foot patrol obsolete. But let us consider statements from two of the most respected New York City Police Commissioners:

"...the rugged and versatile scooter opens new vistas in crime control. As its use grows it is anticipated that the 'scooter patrol' will provide unprecedented control over crime and criminals in all our far-flung recreational areas." Michael J. Murphy, New York City Police Commissioner in 1964.

"The scooter is the most effective police patrol technique which has been developed in recent years. It preserves the concept of the foot patrolman and yet provides a mobility and responsiveness which the foot patrolman lacks." Vincent L. Broderick, New York City Police Commissioner in 1965.

Commissioner Broderick actually changed his budget, which was almost finalized, to include the purchase of 700 scooters for city street coverage after the wonderful results we had in the parks. Inquiries came from many cities in the United States and foreign countries for information and specific operational techniques. The scooter *could and did extend the range of delivery* of available police personnel at minimum expense.

The history and results of scooters in the City of New York, first for parks and then for city street patrols, is documented in the *Journal of the Northwestern University School of Law.*

As a result of the scooter patrol successes in New York City, some police departments are using either the two-wheeled scooters or bicycles to restore the advantages and benefits of the old foot patrol officer system for crime prevention along with neighborhood rapport and respect. Bicycles incorporate many of the advantages of the motorized scooter except for the ability for fast mobilization in team concepts.

Detroit, Washington D.C., Flint and other cities have utilized scooters for various purposes. But the concept of scooter team units with unique unpredictable patterns of patrol coverage remains to be advanced.

One of my regrets was that I could not develop team patrols more because I was promoted by Commissioner Broderick from Deputy Inspector, Liaison with the Department of Parks and the New York World's Fair to Inspector and Command of the Operations Bureau of the New York Police. It took me away from further developing the Tactical Scooter Team Unit, which was so successful in the 7th precinct.

This I believe is the way scooters should be used in cities in a team concept. The team should have sharp step-in scooters, not quite as big as straddle motorcycles, with sharp officers wearing sharp uniforms with a sharp leader. The leader and his scooter team should be responsible for a neighborhood and knowledgeable about crime trends, community conditions, problems, programs, and people in that area.

Scooter patrol officers should operate as partners, each responsible for part of the neighborhood or community or city. Every effort should be made to have minorities and both sexes represented by the scooter teams though each individual works separate streets or areas.

This can result in a snappy tactical team, a flying unit of scooter officers able to act in concert by keeping in constant touch by radio. Such sharp teams will appeal to kids, as well.

New concepts of team patrol can be developed. Various patterns of street patrol can be systematically unsystematic. The scooter team and their leader can improvise and change patterns of street patrol as fast as basketball or football players adopt set plays and then rapidly change them according to conditions.

There were many advantages to scooter patrol, especially in densely populated areas. Visionary police leaders can discern even more with scooter team operations. In fact, I have some suggestions from the School of Hard Knocks for other visionaries.

1.   Police officers selected for scooter team operation should *only* be volunteers. Forcing someone to ride a scooter when he or she wants a car or motorcycle can ruin the program.

2.   Careful training must be given with emphasis that the scooter's function is as a slow-moving *protective* patrol device, although speedy response as a team is available.

3.   There should be no stunt riding or cowboying with scooters. Scooters do not chase cars. (I removed one officer who pursued a wanted car in Central Park even though he made a good arrest.)

4.   Officers for team scooter patrol should be intelligent, educated, sensitive to cultural differences, and adept at good community relations since they are selling good police services that *serve and protect* the public.

5.   Such officers should be considered generalists, knowledgeable in all aspects of good police work, and should be just as important as special-

ists, investigators or detectives, and should have opportunities for promotion and pay advancement within the patrol division.

6. Motor scooter teams should not be deployed after 10 or 11 p.m. and certainly not after midnight. Those hours are for automobile response units when most good people are home in bed. Better hours encourage volunteers for scooters.

7. Scooter patrols, especially in scooter team configurations, have great potential not only for crime reduction and traffic alleviation but can be quickly mobilized as a "task force" when necessary.

With proper leadership and deployment during hours when the "good people" are around, a resurgence of public confidence will take place. The scooter patrol officer can answer today's plaintive cry: "Where is the cop on the beat? Why isn't he around when we need him?"

With the old-time foot patrol in various new forms (bicycle, scooter, Segway, etc.) all working cooperatively with the automobiles; it will truly be a coordinated team. This will bring back to the people truly Community Oriented Police Services to restore the comfort, health, morals, safety and prosperity to America. Then law enforcement will regain respect because they will have earned it as they again serve and protect citizens.

Two Scooter Officers Typify "Involvement"

After serving as the Detroit Police Commissioner, I wrote columns about various issues for *The Detroit News*. These ideas come from one of my columns in 1971.

Ed McQueen, a 32-year old black patrolman and his white partner, Patrolman Steve Maxson, 29, are two scooter officers who work together.

These two officers play a very important part in the neighborhood effort to end racial hang-ups and develop a better cooperative approach to reducing crime, involving both citizens and police in two adjacent neighborhoods in the Livernois-McNichols area.

The problem, so easy to state and so difficult to resolve, is that citizens and police have to help each other in the war on crime. To do so effectively, police have to relate to citizens, and citizens have to respect police.

These two neighborhoods have cooperated in an effort to "Light the Night," using all available outside residential lighting as a deterrent to criminals. One has a "Citizens' Radio Watch" private car patrol, the other is organizing a similar volunteer service.

Both are pledged to a closer relationship with their neighborhood precinct. A special assist from the Detroit Police Department has been the assignment of a scooter patrol team backed up by a one-man scout car, on an experimental basis.

McQueen and Maxson comprise the scooter team. What is the special answer being provided by this police team? Essentially, it is visible presence, in spite of the seasonal handicap of bad weather and snow-filled streets, and rapport with citizens.

Although snow has been keeping them off some of the residential streets, they have made personal calls on the merchants and the schools in the area. When they stop for lunch, they try to eat in a different neighborhood restaurant each day.

Says McQueen, "When I'm walking a block or two, some of the merchants beg me to park my scooter outside their door. They figure it's a safeguard."

Says Maxson, "We've had good visits with the kids in the schools. When you can't ride, you try to get visibility where it counts, inside."

They operate by alternating their approach, staggering territories, patrolling sometimes on parallel streets, sometimes far apart, but always keeping in radio contact.

They perform the basic police function as it ought to be performed, getting to know individuals on their beat, sometimes on a first name basis; making themselves known as individuals; and spending about 80 percent of their time on patrol, instead of in response to calls.

If they happen to be the nearest officers to the location of an emergency call, they will respond, although most calls are normally taken by the two-man scout cars regularly assigned to the Bagley and university districts, or by their one-man "backup" car.

Even when other police officers have handled crime calls in their territory, McQueen and Maxson like to follow up with a personal call on the victims.

"We want to have a closer relationship with our people than a scout car they might not see again for another six months," said Maxson.

"We try to talk to the people, and discuss what happened and how it could have been prevented," says McQueen. "We don't have just a statistical interest in each case. We know we can't do a good job without good public relations, without building a good image of police work."

When I introduced scooters to the Detroit Police Department in 1968 and called this new force the "Community Oriented Patrol," so much attention was focused on the vehicle that, I think, some people missed the point of what I was trying to do with the man who rode the vehicle.

I was trying to develop men with a new sense of dedication to public service and community involvement who could get policing back on the right track.

McQueen and Maxson are examples of the kind of attitude and performance I was trying to achieve.

"Getting involved takes up a lot of your own time," says McQueen. "More policemen should be 'involved.'"

The Happy Riot

The Pittsburgh Pirates won the World Series in 1969. But the subsequent celebration in Pittsburgh turned into ugly street troubles. Some individual citizens of Pittsburgh failed to match the championship caliber of their professional baseball team.

I felt especially sympathetic for the substantial majority of good citizens of Pittsburgh, and for their police, whom I am sure were appalled by the ugly turn the legitimate celebration took, and the national publicity it received.

The same thing could have happened in Detroit in 1968, when the Tigers beat the Cardinals for the world championship. I had been commissioner for only a little more than two months.

We had similar conditions in Detroit that year; an underdog team pulling a big surprise, a whole city looking for something to cheer about after the trauma of the 1967 riot, and everyone out in the streets downtown.

It was almost like a riot, but everyone was laughing. I called it the "Happy Riot."

For about six hours after the final out, Detroit enjoyed itself. After dark, however, a few individuals who hoped to escape attention in the crowds broke some store windows and some pilfering occurred.

The then Superintendent John F. Nichols had all police units deployed for the crowd-control mission. All precautions were taken to exercise restraint, to allow for the normal human exuberance, but to keep alert for those seeking to capitalize on the crowds and merriment to commit crimes.

In addition, with the cooperation of the news media, I was able to present a public appeal to all citizens of Detroit to keep their celebrating within bounds, and live up to the city's proud slogan, "City of Champions."

Finally, Detroit had a new secret weapon in its emergency police preparations. Thanks to the Greater Detroit Chamber of Commerce, which came up with the funds in the nick of time, the first motor scooters for the newly formed community-oriented patrol were delivered less than two weeks before the Series started.

A team of 30 patrolmen and sergeants was quickly organized, and the first big assignment was series crowd control downtown.

When the happy riot was at its height, of course, the streets were jammed, and traffic was at a standstill. Police on foot were virtually limited to stationary observation. The radio scout cars, symbol of modern police department mobility, were immobilized.

At the first signs of unlawful disturbances, the scooter patrolmen were the only police able to move around, and to respond.

As a result, the scooter patrols made most of the arrests, and to my mind, may have made the difference between a celebration that was contained before lawless elements could get out of hand, and something much worse.

As far as I and others in Detroit were concerned, the scooter patrol won its spurs that night.

The *Michigan Chronicle,* (Detroit's Negro newspaper) which is usually very critical of police operations, used a front-page photo of a Detroit scooter officer overcoming a gunman in the street, as an example of effective police service during the World Series aftermath.

The New and the Old

The August 2003 issue of *Community LINKS* featured a thoughtful article by R. Gil Kerlikowske, Chief, Seattle Police Department, on community policing and his strong belief in it.

Chief Kerlikowske wrote of the recent history of policing:

> After WWII, military returnees entered policing. Emphasis was placed on a paramilitary model of policing. That accompanied media portrayal of the stoic and professional officer—*Dragnet*—"just the facts ma'am" and *Adam 12*—impersonal, aloof, removed from the community.
>
> However, this so-called professional era was unprepared to cope with the social changes, upheavals and deep youthful unrest of the 1960s.

He pointed out that forgotten in this professional model was the old-time familiarity that had existed between the citizens and their police. Community support diminished. Professional police officers were now viewed as an occupying army.

I totally agree with Kerlikowske's views and that is the tenor of this book. Law enforcement must change. It really does not *serve* and *protect*. We threw the baby out with the bathwater.

We should remember the bride's little ditty: "Something old, something new, something borrowed, something blue." I used that line as Police Commissioner for the City of Detroit.

I brought in something new: two-wheeled motor scooters (Mobile Foot Patrol) with personally selected officers, volunteers, educated, with community awareness, etc. Putting them on motor scooters brought back something old. In effect, it brought back foot patrol officers on wheels, now able to cover more ground than the old foot police. They could reach out to more and more of the concerned and conscientious citizens of the community. Something borrowed from the admonition of Robert Peel in 1829, that the object to be attained is the prevention of crime, which is better than all the effects after the crime is committed.

And something blue was a new type of police officers in that blue uniform with some special touch like scarves, which captivated the youth of the community. Rides were given on special days, like the day we opened the building for PAYS, which stood for Police And Youth in Sports.

Yes, the major thrust of the scooter police was to improve community relations and work to organize neighborhoods to prevent crime. We also established a volunteer "Neighbors on Patrol" in certain communities as eyes and ears for police.

The scooter officers were encouraged to be proactive, not just reactive, to win friends for the Detroit Police Department. Our "Buck Up Your Police" fund realized $50,000 in single dollar contributions for scooters, police, books and bookshelves in all 13 precincts. It created a bond, a partnership with police, of old, young, black and white.

Chief Kerlikowske laid out the pros and cons of the military model of post WWII policing, then the professional model and now the community-oriented policing model. In his conclusion, he stated, "Let's take the best of what we learned in this business over the last half century and call it policing."

Yes, I agree! Let's call it policing, which would, of course, include law enforcement and also protective (by proactive prevention), in effect Dual Purpose Policing. This policing defines proper roles and responsibilities for each: the law enforcement and response part and the proactive prevention and protection part. It provides for communication and trust for the people of the community.

Why didn't the scooter patrol teams continue in New York and Detroit and in the Sheriffs' Department in Oakland County, Michigan?

To begin with, it was difficult to start in each place. In the New York Police Department, the Motor Transport Maintenance Division gave little cooperation. I had to bring the scooters down in a truck from Central Park to police headquarters in downtown Manhattan to have them repaired. All they usually had were dirty sparkplugs and later we did these ourselves. At first the precinct captains were quizzical and reluctant but later okayed them after they saw their promise and potential.

In the 7th precinct, the response was tremendous. That was when a *New York Times* reporter rode with me in a car and we followed the scooters. We got a call to a school about a black and white student riot and the scooters got there way before the cars did.

I also had to go and request a personal appointment with Police Commissioner Vincent Broderick regarding the scooters because all officers had to go through proper channels. After that meeting, Broderick was convinced of the value of the scooters and ordered 700 more.

Alas, when Broderick left because of new Mayor John Lindsay, Lindsay wanted to put in a police review board. Broderick said that was a "cruel hoax." I tried to talk to the commissioner about a different way of running a review board but he lost out and they brought in a new police commissioner from Philadelphia.

In Detroit when I was Police Commissioner, I had troubles with Common Council and the press. They laughed a lot and made jokes about the scooter cops. And New Detroit? I couldn't get to first base with them.

Even Mayor Cavanagh was very skeptical at first as well as some black leaders like Coleman Young. But others later saw the potential. The reason I got the money for 30 scooters was from the Chamber of Commerce, of all places. They were very successful. But again, like New York, a change of mayors meant a change of police commissioners. Mayor Gribbs won by a few votes, and was a little dubious about me and I about him.

When I was a sheriff, it was vicious partisan politics. I had a talk with Ed Meese, who later became attorney general under President Ronald Reagan. I told him I ran as a Democrat, talked like a Republican and acted like an Independent. It comes at a price to run as a Democrat in a Republican county. The opposition scrutinized my every move and they instigated several investigations during my tenure. The scooters were well received in all the areas where they were used.

In 1982, I was the Sheriff of Oakland County, Michigan and was successfully using scooters in some townships. That year, the U.S. government increased the emissions and safety standards. Vespa and other foreign-made scooters manufacturers bailed out. Now Vespa and other scooter companies are back with improved scooters, fully meeting U.S. standards.

A Different Police Officer-A Different Style

I introduced two-wheeled motorized scooter community police in both the New York City Police Department as Liaison Officer with the Department of Parks and later as Commander of the Operations Bureau. This was very successful among people of the parks and later in the 79 police precincts of New York.

As Police Commissioner of the City of Detroit, I brought motorized two-wheeled scooter patrolling to Detroit's thirteen precincts.

The people of the communities in both New York and Detroit soon perceived a different police officer and a different style of policing. Most of the media that first scoffed turned around and saw the merits of such policing with a different law enforcement philosophy; one enabling officers on scooters to be seen, talked with, understood, and cooperated with.

This philosophy and its implementation with motorized scooter officers, specially selected and trained, strictly volunteers who understood and agreed with its philosophy and goals was quite successful.

Some comments made at that time were these: "I'd like to see more cops in this community on scooters." "It's an entirely different thing for both the police officers and the community than cops in squad cars." "You can't help but smile when you see a cop on a scooter."

My wife said, "And we're all mirrors. When you smile at me, I smile back."

Those years were in the sixties, long before British Police expert John Alderson promoted community policing (at cost to himself). And now the great hope for the future of crime control and law enforcement in the United States is Community Policing.

Much of the answer focuses around police themselves, politics especially, often the media, and self-interest groups. The people, however, did accept and welcome the scooter officers.

In the New York City Police Department, the Detroit Police Department and as Sheriff in Oakland County, I had caring, concerned police officers and deputies on motor scooters that were much appreciated by the people they served.

211

As professor at John Jay College, I espoused the concept of Community-Oriented Policing. As professor and Director of Programs at Mercy College, I called the program Law Enforcement and Protection. This should be the aim in all police organizations nationwide, not only to provide law enforcement with its sanctions of arrest and punishment but also very much protection of people and neighborhoods with prevention, caring of the environment, diminishing community hazards, etc.

Empirically T. A. Critchley writing about the establishment of the London Metropolitan Police in 1829 described the benefits of turning to this style of policing. In a *History of Police in England and Wales,* Critchley writes, "From the start, the police was to be a homogeneous and democratic body, in tune with the people, belonging to the people, and drawing its strength from the people."

Elsewhere in this book, I have written that Sir Robert Peel, in instructing his new force stated, "It should be understood at the outset that the object to be attained is the *prevention* of crime. To this great end every effort of the police is to be directed. The security of person and property and the preservation of a police establishment will thus be *better effected* than by the detection and punishment of the offender *after* he has succeeded in committing crime..."

This is where the concept of community service officers with two-wheeled scooters can handle many calls and foster people-police rapport, and leave the patrol cars ready and available for serious and emergency type runs.

But many police officers feel the community policing philosophy is soft on crime or isn't "real" police work.

Many sergeants and lieutenants have resisted allowing street cops to devise their own solutions for community-unique problems, fearing a loss of control.

This is why I advocate "Scooter Team Policing" with eight scooter officers, preferably four women and four men but led by a sergeant or "Team Leader" that keeps control and builds rapport among the scooter officers so they are not alone out there. In cities of less population, perhaps four or even two officers would suffice under a leader.

Getting Closer to Citizens With Scooters

Since I am the person who developed and expanded the use of two-wheeled scooters for police, I know better than anyone else what their advantages are. Nobody else has had the breadth of experience in using scooter teams that I had as Commanding Officer of the Operations Bureau of the New York Police Department and later as Police Commissioner of Detroit.

I wrote about the advantages of scooters for *The Journal of Criminal Law, Criminology and Police Science* published by Northwestern University in Volume 57, No. 3, p. 349-353. My article was called "The Motor Scooter—An Answer to a Police Problem." Many of my thoughts still seem applicable so I will summarize them here.

Greatly Extended Patrol Coverage

A foot patrolman on a scooter easily covers at least five times the territory he could by walking a beat, and more efficiently. With the same available force, a department can expand protective patrol, particularly in the outlying or residential areas of the city, where it is difficult to provide adequate coverage by ordinary foot patrol.

Better Police Observation

In a car, a patrolman generally must maintain minimum traffic speed. His view is partly obstructed within the car. The scooter patrolman has 360 degrees visibility, and he can proceed on the flank of traffic lanes as slowly as he desires.

Ease of Movement in Congested Areas

Police experience indicates that many emergencies become greater problems because of the inability or delay in getting men and equipment to the scene. The two-wheeled scooter is the ideal patrol vehicle to cut through traffic-clogged streets that block any three or four-wheeled vehicle. It can patrol dead end streets and cul-de-sacs where cars do not enter because of the difficulty of turning around. It is also valuable on marginal streets and parkway areas where patrol cars cannot penetrate.

Freeing of Patrol Cars for Constant Patrol

Since the scooter handles many minor types of calls for assistance such as minor accidents, aided cases, and other routine duties, cars and their on-board computers are freed for a more constant patrol and response to major incidents.

Economy of Operation

A scooter can be purchased for several hundred dollars. Gas mileage is good and maintenance costs are proportionately low.

Capability for Mobilization

With radio communication, a potential for quick mobilization for any contingency can be realized. While scooter operators will not be suited for computers, they carry communication devices appropriate to their mission.

Reduction of Patrol Fatigue

Constant foot patrol is fatiguing at best. Response to a distant emergency on foot leaves a patrolman winded and at a disadvantage. The aid of a motor scooter appreciably reduces this fatigue factor.

Increased Morale and Stimulation of Recruitment

The opportunity to ride as well as walk stimulates and quickens a man's job interest. The assignment of a scooter gives a foot patrolman more work and more responsibility. As a more active police officer, a greater sense of individual contribution to the police effort follows. Scooter patrol also appears to interest young men in the police service, thus increasing and stimulating recruitment.

Preventive and Deterrent Effect

This is felt to be the most salient feature of the scooter patrol. It is believed that a patrolman on foot often goes unseen or at least unnoticed, whereas a scooter, being both audible and visible, creates a comforting awareness of police presence in the public mind. It was thought, at first, that the noise of the scooter might be a source of annoyance. On the contrary, a considered disadvantage has now become a source of comfort and reassurance to the public, day or night, and an "audio-deterrent" to the potential malefactor.

A New Respect by Juveniles

A parked scooter patrolman draws youngsters like a magnet. The attraction has led to a new opportunity for the patrolman to establish rapport with the younger generation, which we hope will grow to adult respect as the youngsters mature, as well as an aid in recruiting. It is also worthwhile to note that the delinquent youngster, as well as the adult criminal, develops a new respect for the law not because of any affection for the man on the scooter, but simply because of his pursuit potential. No youngster can outrun a motor scooter.

Inter-precinct Support

Spread to all areas of a city, precinct team units can provide a citywide operating network of instantly available task forces.

Operational Experience

The two-wheeled scooter can be operated safely if there is proper selection, screening, and training of manpower. That the scooter must be used as a slow moving protective patrol device and not as a high-speed pursuit vehicle must be inculcated in the minds of the patrolmen.

A minimum of training is required. We have found that three days of training suffices. Injuries have all been minor and generally seem to occur, shortly after an initial period of caution, due to over-enthusiasm and overconfidence, which may lead to "cowboying." Our first experience was in the rough and hilly terrain of our city park system. City streets are more compatible with smooth and safe operation. The training program consists of a half-day at the Police Academy for eye and reaction tests and safety instruction followed by three days of operational and field training with an emphasis on conservatism.

Inclement Weather Experience

The oft-mentioned disadvantage of a two-wheeled scooter operation because of inclement weather has been disproved by winter experiences. Little time is lost because of inclement weather. The scooters can operate on wet ground with caution. During heavy rain or snow, the scooters are placed out of service. Nothing is lost, really, for two reasons: crime decreases in the streets in proportion to the inclemency of the weather, and the scooter patrolmen still patrol on foot. Modern warmth without weight type uniforms suitable for both foot and scooter operation enable the scooter patrolman to function in cold weather.

In conclusion, I encountered some resistance to the change of patrol concept involved in the motor scooter program. However, the public helped our success because it perceived better protection and law enforcement at a lower cost. Additionally, the new morale and enthusiasm generated among our patrolmen by their new scooter helped to create a better, more mobile police patrol able to offer more protection for more people in more territory.

For the cost of ten policemen for one year, a city can buy about 300 scooters. The anti-crime value of the 300 scooters weighed against the negligible effect of adding ten patrolmen to a large force tips the scale decidedly in favor of the scooters.

PART IX

Dual Purpose Policing

What Is Dual Purpose Policing?

What is dual purpose policing? It is simply the addition of Mobile Foot Patrols (male and female scooter officers) to supplement our patrol cars. Dual Purpose Policing offers service and protection on the one hand, as well as responding to crimes already committed and enforcing laws. It is the answer to the question I posed in my first book, *American Police Dilemma: Protectors or Enforcers?*

Patrol cars are mostly for response and enforcement. Scooter units are mostly for service and protection. Both must work together in a designated area of patrol responsibility. Cars can do what scooters cannot do and scooters can do what cars cannot do. In essence, both present a teamwork concept of good policing.

The test of a good police officer is not in his record of arrests or citations, but rather the absence of crimes and disturbances in the area he patrols.

The police officer is unique. He can be a dynamic force in the community for better or worse. He speaks to the public for the public with authority, and there is no reason why a police officer should not possess social graces.

Tact is often more important than technique at times. In Dual Policing, we can bring the functions of police into proper perspective.

The police car partner is needed for quick response and necessary action, and the scooter partner for community service, protection and prevention of crime, and to enlist good citizens of the community.

Both types of officers, the enforcer and the protector, work on a team to prevent crime, reduce community tension, and bring peace and order to the community entrusted to their charge.

To achieve Dual Purpose policing:

- We must change our policing methods
- We must diversify our forces
- We must use mobile foot patrols
- We must include more women in policing
- We must use more non-deadly weapons

- We must have educated police who can speak with and relate to the public

What are the benefits?

- A safer America, safer for people on streets, in schools and in homes
- The concept that "It takes a team, you and your police" can bring our community together, community by community, neighborhood by neighborhood, working with and trusting police again.

We must narrow the gap between the police and the people they serve. Dual Purpose Policing can bring the police and communities together to solve mutual problems.

We are in an era of change. Changes are occurring in society, government, military, schools, family relationships, religions and societal institutions.

Law enforcement must change. Policing must change. Since the mid-1950s, there has been much effort to professionalize the police. Have we succeeded? To a degree, but there are still real problems in contemporary law enforcement.

Here is what I believe is the crux of the matter! In our movement toward professionalism, our police occupation has emphasized Law Enforcement. That term is everywhere. We have lost sight of good protective policing.

The change from "traditional" to "professional" police departments has lowered job satisfaction, lowered police morale, increased cynicism, and left people and police suspicious and distrustful of each other. This I feel has given rise to antagonism as well as officious and negative attitudes by some police executives and officers.

The Law Enforcement part is all we really have in American policing today. We put cops in cars, send them out in response to calls for service or help, *mostly after the fact*. This is American Law Enforcement. Certainly we need it! Crime continues—vicious and horrifying crime at times. We need such police officers in police cars to respond as quickly as possible. That is the Law Enforcement part.

But what about the Protective and Preventive part? Better that a crime never occurs in the first place. There is much more needed, however, to support and keep a community peaceful and beautiful.

This is why I believe Community Policing (or Community-Oriented Policing as I termed it in the early and late 1960s, 70s and 80s) is so very important.

The only way to serve and protect as well as enforcing laws is not just by putting police officers in wonderfully equipped electronic cars but by putting them where people can see them, talk to them, get to know them, confide in them, on visible and accessibly simple two-wheeled scooters.

Yes, we need the Enforcers, most certainly. But we also need the Protectors, and Dual Purpose Policing gives us both.

The Wave of the Future

Community-Oriented Police Services (COPS) of the Department of Justice was in recent years called the "Wave of the Future." All the programs currently use police autos and I believe that is wrong. The car, whether in response mode or community-oriented police services is still a police car, loathed and feared in some communities. You have only to watch the TV show *Cops* to note the fear on the faces of citizens and children as the police car zooms up and cops jump out to nab a presumably bad guy.

I believe two-wheel motor scooters improve interaction between citizens and police, the kind of interaction that prevents crime and restores value like the old-time foot patrol. Bikes are okay but are for limited use. This must change. Dual Purpose Police can do that.

I used the term *Community Oriented Patrol Services* way back as Police Commissioner of Detroit 1968–1969 and while there was much scoffing and much political and police opposition, the people liked the scooter cops. They also liked the scooter cops in New York. In spite of the derision by police and media, the people were actually attracted by scooter cops.

The New York City Police Commissioner Vincent Broderick pushed for scooters. But politics, media at the beginning, and many police themselves gave us problems such as macho cops.

Scooter cops are the way to go to really present Community Oriented Services to the community as I did in 1968–69 and 1964–66. This concept really does the *Protect and Serve* that's on police cars. It is the only way to get the respect and admiration of the people. I did it in tough cities in tough times.

Here's an example of the difference of philosophy in a critical incident in Detroit in 1969. That was the year young people all over America were demonstrating against the Vietnam War.

One day, lots of demonstrators were en route to Kennedy Square in Detroit for a rally. On the way, they broke and shattered windows of a music store. John Nichols, my superintendent in Detroit wanted to call out the riot troops using guns, shields, batons, face masks, etc.

I countermanded his orders. Having had success with public acceptance of the scooter patrols, I said this was not the way to handle these young protesters.

I then ordered our scooters to meet the advancing rebellious crowd and it worked like a charm. Not only did the young protesters respect and engage in conversations with the scooter officers, the scooter officers became an escort for them in their march to Kennedy Square. No further incidents. The day was saved. I'm sure it would have been different with riot troops.

Women in Dual Purpose Policing

There is definitely a need for more women in policing. Law enforcement needs a little softening around the edges.

The percentage of women in law enforcement has been small. In 1972 women comprised about two percent of American police officers. Now that has increased to almost 12 percent.

I feel there is a need to increase the recruitment of women. They can be of great importance for good policing. The position of women in policing should be strengthened and appreciated. Women can make very significant contributions to the public safety and welfare. Many departments lack strategies for recruiting and utilizing women properly.

Today many women shun the job. In the past, women faced bias, discrimination, hostility and sexual harassment. However, the law now ensures that women are treated equally.

Where before, women had special functions in policing such as working with children and females, now they ride in partner cars, responding to whatever; street brawls, bar fights, drunks, stick-ups, etc.

My feeling, after many years in police work, is that not all women are equal to men, that is in certain aspects required in the job, and that they are superior to men in some other aspects.

Well, where is the best place to put women in police work? What interests women in law enforcement or policing? Is there a difference between those two?

Women are more interested in the type of work to be performed than in being "macho," but they strive to improve their strength, prowess, and potential.

Women are interested in personal challenges, such as a position in which they can develop their skills and knowledge. The opportunity to help others often ranks high in their assessment of the police job.

However, most women's perception of the law enforcement job is of job danger, working alone, working at night, with little flexibility in work schedules. They sometimes fear that they will be inadequate in backing up an officer or in handling a situation adequately alone, or will lose the acceptance of their peers.

Women, like male officers, rate financial and job security highly, together with a supportive work climate, plus job enrichment characterized by challenging and interesting work, intellectual stimulation and feelings of achievement.

For all police officers, diversity of tasks and skills required and the opportunity for social contribution is important.

The concept of dual purpose policing is the ideal situation for women to make a great contribution to law enforcement, or rather the part emphasizing the *service* and *protection* role.

Dual purpose policing can help women find their proper niche in this law enforcement-policing world. Some of their roles may be in crime prevention, neighborhood protection, environmental betterment, working with families, kids, community, people, and responding to calls for assistance.

Women would be ideal for motorized scooter patrols. I must add here that policewomen should first serve a time, six months or possibly a year, in that phase of patrol called patrol car response to understand and appreciate their very important law enforcement role and to be able to work in harmony and rapport with patrol cars. But women are well suited to the service and protection role such as crime prevention, neighborhood orderliness, reaching out to the good citizens of a community to gain their cooperation and support.

Motorized scooter patrol should not be used on the "graveyard shift." There should be two shifts; e.g. 6 a.m. to 2 p.m., and 2 p.m. to 10 p.m. Scooter officer functions are not to deal with drunks, ne'er-do-wells, and bar fights. That is the job of burly, beefy "macho cops" who are better suited to the response element of law enforcement in fast-moving cars. Sometimes just the sight of such a big muscular male cop motivates the perpetrator to avoid tangling with him.

Scooter officers, male and female, have a most important role. A trained scooter patrol team, male and female on an equal 50-50 basis, led by a dedicated, professional team leader, can help heal the soul of a city. With such opportunities to provide service and protection to a community, I hope that more and more women will choose policing as their profession.

The Philosophy of Dual Purpose Policing

Police in Britain have evolved along certain principles—the concept of local responsibility for law and order. Their philosophy is that the people are the police and the police are the people.

In 1929, a hundred years after the start by Sir Robert Peel with Commissioners Rowan and Mayne, the Royal Commission on the Police reported: "The police of this country have never been recognized either in law or by tradition as a force distinct from the general body of citizens."

Their police system depends for effectiveness on the good will and moral support of the public.

In America, even though our policing came about following England's example, my position is that unfortunately our American police do really not enjoy the good will and moral support of the American people. Why not? We have drifted away from the old beat cop system to a so-called "professionalism" based entirely on the police radio motor patrol car and new technological equipment.

I have said that the American police face a serious dilemma: are they to be protectors or enforcers? We must re-assess first what it is that the police in the United States should do. It is my contention that the police officer's main role today in society is a lose-lose proposition, not a win-win one.

America is a land of liberty but we also operate under law. Police are very necessary but what kind of police. Police, of course, must enforce the laws but also an equal, and perhaps greater responsibility, is to safeguard liberty.

The generally agreed duties of police are to maintain law and order. They do this by preventing crime, detecting crime, protecting life and property, and by enforcing laws and ordinances. This, in essence, is to be a *peace* officer.

Sir Robert Peel in 1829 made it quite clear to his fledgling police force that policing was much more than even just the prevention of crime. He wrote such phrases as, "Every member of the force must remember that it is his duty to help and protect members of the public no less than to bring offenders to justice."

This was a new, unique and necessary approach after the England of Jonathan Wild and the "thief takers," followed by the Fielding brothers and the "Bow Street Runners."

However there are differences of opinion. I remember Lord Patrick Devlin stating in a lecture at the Police College at Bramshill, "We should try to get back to the idea that the police are a body that exists to deal with real crime, that the duties they are given to do in the enforcement of social regulations are foreign to their nature and that the less they have to do with them the better." (This I disagree with!)

Perhaps I should briefly compare the style of policing between the United States and some European countries. In the United States, the responsibilities of police are predominantly local. The police are at villages, townships, city, county and state levels whereas in England the police have both local and national responsibilities. In France, police responsibilities are mostly national. American and French police carry firearms whereas British police do not except for special units.

I used to tell my students at John Jay College in New York and Mercy College, which is now the University of Detroit, Mercy, that if you asked our police to divest themselves of firearms, almost all would quit their departments. In England, most would leave if they had to wear firearms. I think now there is some reflection on this in England. Riots and violence have increased there too.

Overall I feel that a *primarily legal approach* to the function of police is responsible in America for the dislike of police in many corners. They may see police as the cause of riots and demonstrations in some cases, and are reluctant to help or cooperate with police. In addition, the loss of the old time neighborhood foot patrol officer has deprived our communities of much-needed social services.

This illustrates the theme of my recent book, *American Police Dilemma: Protectors or Enforcers?* American police have over time become more and more only enforcers of the law whereas they could do much more as protectors under law.

I feel very strongly that a police officer must be someone who helps good people as well as hurts bad people.

Unfortunately in most American police forces, whether village, township, city or state, police are constrained by conditions of their servitude (the police patrol car) to operate only as expressed by the British Lord Devlin, dealing with *real* crime. But that is not what police in our fast moving, mainly, response cars really do. In reality, *real crime* takes up a very small percent of their daily response runs, less than 10% and probably more like 5%.

What radio motor patrol sector cars do is respond to *whatever* the people, whether in trouble or not, call for. Many of the community calls for service could be handled better by specially trained socially cognizant culturally sensitive men and women, police officers operating with two wheeled motor scooters (dual purpose policing).

This would leave the radio patrol car free to respond mostly to serious crimes, possibly serious crimes, prowlers, etc. The scooter cops would handle many of the other necessary calls for service.

Police work is concerned with human nature and social vicissitudes. These can be complex and require special kinds of people. What could or would a scooter officer on a motorized scooter do that a police car officer could not do? Working with kids at school, patrolling school areas, particularly at dismissal times, assisting in traffic problems, vandalism, noise complaints, family troubles, street lights out, littering, graffiti, environmental hazards, and the list can go on.

Scooter cops, male and female, could provide major social services to make a community better, more livable, and more secure.

Our police really do have two major roles in our American society, a legal and law enforcement role and a social service role. That's *why I advocate Dual Purpose police forces in our communities.*

Police in America do fulfill their legal enforcer role, that law enforcement role. But police should also return to a more social service role, in fact do much more with it. This will reach the hearts and minds of the people of their communities and their neighborhood.

Scooter police could be the catalyst for neighborhood improvement, neighborhood watch, and neighborhood beautification. Scooter police could become the most omnipresent of all social servants. When heads of other city departments or services are too busy or their offices closed, police are available.

This is why I advance the need for two factors in our American police methods. Community-oriented policing (motorized scooter officers in a teamwork concept) for real community policing is a philosophy of people-police partnership. In Detroit, we had the slogan, "It takes a team, you and your police."

However, crime will still be here and we need the quick response to calls for service involving major crimes and accidents. You might call it the "law enforcement" part of policing.

We need both law enforcement together with community-oriented policing, or *dual purpose policing.*

We feel the only way to reach "rapport" with the people is the old-time foot patrol. But we can get the police back and reach the hearts and minds of good people. How? Three ways: foot patrol, sometimes motorized with the "Segway" for business areas, some bicycle patrols in unique locales, and very importantly, motorized scooter patrols working in unique ways with unpredictable patterns to get to the hearts and minds of good people. We need "Mobile Foot Patrol."

Today we place great emphasis on police power and penal severity. Our jails and prisons are bursting. Not the answer! Rather the prevention of crime, prevention of vandalism, and prevention of disorder are the answers.

How? By citizen involvement and support of police. How? By making the police more amenable to this involvement and support. How? By changing our police methods. By adding to our police radio car response units motorized scooter patrol. Prevention and protection units should be there before the fact.

The theme of this book is concerned with those crimes that put fear into people, and that makes our homes and our streets unsafe, dangerous and deadly. Crime and disorder disintegrate a neighborhood, driving down property values and tearing at the very soul of a city or community.

I was President for a term of the American Academy of Professional Law Enforcement. I advocated that American policing must change the term *law enforcement* to *professional policing. Professional policing* must include two types of police roles: the Enforcers and the Protectors. POLICE should stand for The Protector of Liberty for the Individual, the Community, and Everyone Equally.

Let's hope that there are socially cognizant, creatively minded astute police administrators to realize and implement Dual Purpose Policing.

Conclusion

As a man in police work—law enforcement for over 44 years—I write this about police because I served in that profession. I served for over 25 years in the biggest city in America, New York City; later as Police Commissioner in Detroit, a once great city now in shambles; and finally as sheriff of one of the top five wealthiest counties in America, Oakland County, Michigan.

No police officer works alone. He works under impacts, some good, some bad, some ugly. These impacts or factors have all had effects on me.

The main impacts or factors are:

- the police,
- the press and other media who relate what everyone is doing, for better or worse,
- the politicians who appoint and control police, again for better or worse.

In addition, there are the people who are served, for better or worse, and the pressure groups or special interests that work for the common good or for their own special concerns, including lobbyists.

In this book, I have presented some insights into new approaches to policing (or law enforcement) in America for not only police but for the interested and much affected citizen as well.

The subject of law enforcement (or policing) is surrounded by controversy. Crime, law, order and disorder touches all in society including politicians, people, groups, police both individually and in groups and the media who report daily on this human drama.

Notice that I separated the two terms policing and law enforcement deliberately. Two more terms are law and order. Law, the enforcement of it, is laid down by legislators. Order is the keeping of the peace of the community. Police serve both law and order but not equally. The difference between law enforcement and policing is the major thrust of this book.

All police officers have stories to relate, I'm sure, regarding the personal impacts of politicians, people, pressure groups and the press on them. I have felt and lived under these pressures, which are often obstacles or road blocks in the path of good law enforcement and peaceful order.

The police, of course, have major coverage in this book. I discuss why they are in trouble and because of them, why American cities have changed and are in trouble. I can speak of New York and Detroit, and to some degree Washington, D.C., Los Angeles and Chicago.

I can also speak of the police in England from whom American police devolved (Sir Robert Peel's Bobbies 1829.) I have visited England several times for conferences including a major conference on Police/Community Relations involving British and American officials at Ditchley Park, Enstone, Oxford, England.

As a result of all these 44 years in policing, I offer this conclusion. We must change police work as it is today because police, under present organization and practice have been a major reason for riots, insurrections, demonstrations, and community tensions.

What has resulted over the years has been a hodge-podge, a "mell of a hess," an antipathy against police. In fact, I explain why police today "Don't get no respect!"

Why? Police are in cars usually, isolated from the good people, responding primarily to the bad people, becoming cynical, frustrated, and unable to do a good acceptable job, in effect handcuffed by the police system. We must change this!

We must realize that police today are much more enforcers than protectors. Yes, police must enforce the law, but also must be utilized to preserve order, that is to prevent crime and protect life and property, but in the right way.

Today our police are mostly enforcers, responding to calls for service which include many calls about trouble makers and those in their clutches. Sure, that's necessary but it's almost always after-the-fact crime.

That is my considered opinion, after many years, in the study and practice of policing. I used the term policing rather than law enforcement because police must be more than just enforcers of the laws. They must equally be preventers of crime and preservers of the peace and order of a community.

In addition to these 44 years of actual practice in police work, I have since 1985 devoted myself to thinking about police, reading about police and writing about police. This is what I sincerely believe:

We must allow our police to be much more than enforcers who get begrudging respect. We must allow our police to be seen by the citizens they serve as their protectors who deserve respect.

Why do American police get little or no respect? It's in the nature of the constraints imposed on them. Police are strait-jacketed in an imposing vehicle of glass and steel. This makes them impersonal to good citizens, hardly known as humane beings.

In my first book, *American Police Dilemma,* near the conclusion, I bring out the concept of Protectors versus Enforcers. On the cover of the book are the scales of justice, tilted heavily in favor of enforcers. We must right the balance.

I now suggest we change police work. We need a different approach. We must include another type of policing, a preventive and protective role. We need policing effort *before* the fact as well as *after* the fact. I suggest that all over America, police administrators adopt "Dual Purpose Policing." That word is "dual," not "duel." There should be no struggle between contending parties.

In the past, some police departments have experimented with what was termed "Split Force Policing," realizing the distinction between response policing and preventive policing. But the term "split" implies a separation into parts, to divide into groups or factions, to divide, to break apart. This is not good and can cause enmity and dissension.

Dual Purpose Policing could be compared to the word "dual," "duality," or "dualism." The principles of enforcement and protection can be embraced in dualism, and Dual Purpose Police Departments. Duality means Dual Controls, two fold or double character in policing. In philosophy, "dualism" connotes the two parts of a person into mind and body. In police work, we might consider the mind as the thinking about response *before the fact* (prevention.) The body could be considered the response *after the fact* (enforcement.)

Both need to be put together to work smoothly, to work in cooperation, each respecting the other, and contributing to a smooth police department process.

Hopefully there will be a renewed role of the citizen and taxpayer in the fight against crime. Law enforcement executives like sheriffs and police chiefs need the cooperation of the public.

Crime, disorder and vandalism are threats to our American society. Law enforcement is on the wrong path. We must use the concept and value of the old foot patrol officers in a different way. This would reduce costs and allow more visibility and opportunities to make him or her more available to the community—to really "serve and protect."

September 11, 2001, brought home a shocking fact. Three thousand killed, yes, but the real shock was that war came to America's shores. Then soon after, the snipers and hysteria on the Eastern seaboard showed that in all instances, local police and county sheriffs as well as the fire service are the first responders to all kinds of emergencies. So we must understand what is wrong with those systems of law enforcement and why we have so much trouble responding effectively. If we do respond effectively, we will earn the respect of the public. If we don't, we don't deserve respect.

About the Authors

Johannes Spreen, B.S., M.P.A., and Ph.D. (all but dissertation) was in law enforcement and police service from 1941 through 1984, interrupted by service in the U.S. Army Air Corps from 1943–1945 as Lieutenant Bombardier.

He was a career officer with the New York City Police Department, rising through the ranks to Inspector and Command of Operations.

After he retired from the NYPD, he became Police Commissioner of the City of Detroit. Later he was Sheriff of Oakland County, Michigan, for twelve years as the only Democrat at the County level.

Spreen was also Associate Professor at John Jay College in New York, Professor and Director of the Law Enforcement and Protection Program at Mercy College of Detroit. He was a columnist for the *Detroit News* and the *Port Huron Times Herald.*

Johannes Spreen instituted Scooter Patrols in New York City and Detroit and assisted the Washington, D.C. police with their scooter program.

He wrote the book *American Police Dilemma: Protectors or Enforcers* in 2003.

Diane Holloway, Ph.D., was a Dallas psychologist and was appointed the first Drug "Czar" of Dallas by the Mayor. She also helped the Dallas Police Department develop their first police assessment center for upper ranks in 1987–8, and was an associate member of the International Association of Chiefs of Police.

She wrote *Before You Say 'I Quit'; The Mind of Oswald; American History in Song; Analyzing Leaders, Presidents and Terrorists* and edited *Dallas and the Jack Ruby Trial.* She helped Johannes Spreen compile and organize his previous book, *American Police Dilemma: Protectors or Enforcers?* as well as this work.

References

Adler, Freda et al. *Criminology,* 2nd Ed. McGraw-Hill, Inc.: New York, 1995.

Alderson, John *Law and Disorder.* Hamish Hamilton: London, 1984.

Alderson, John (with Philip John Stead, Ed.) *The Police We Deserve*, Wolfe Publishing: London, 1973.

Alderson, John *Policing Freedom*, Macdonald and Evans, 1979.

Bayley, David H. *Police for the Future.* Oxford University Press: New York, 1994.

Devlin, Patrick *The Enforcement of Morals.* Oxford University Press: London, 1965.

Douglas, John et al. *The Anatomy of a Motive*, Scribner: New York, 1999.

Douglas, John *Anyone You Want Me To Be*, Scribner: New York, 2003.

Douglas, John, et al. *Crime Classification Manual,* Lexington Books: New York, 1992.

Megargee, Edwin et al. *Classifying Criminal Offenders*, Sage Publications: Beverly Hills, 1979.

Samenow, Stanton *Inside the Criminal Mind,* Times Books: New York, 1984.

Spreen, Johannes and Holloway, Diane *American Police Dilemma: Enforcers or Protectors?* iUniverse, Inc.: New York, 2003.

Yochelson, Samuel and Samenow, Stanton *The Criminal Personality* (3 volumes) Jason Aronson: New York, 1976.

Index

0-595-31780-4

www.ingramcontent.com/pod-product-compliance
Lightning Source LLC
Chambersburg PA
CBHW061344280526
45784CB00001B/132